Pocket
NEW YORK CITY

TOP SIGHTS • LOCAL LIFE • MADE EASY

Cristian Bonetto

In This Book

QuickStart Guide

Your keys to understanding the city – we help you decide what to do and how to do it

Need to Know
Tips for a smooth trip

Neighborhoods
What's where

Explore New York City

The best things to see and do, neighborhood by neighborhood

Top Sights
Make the most of your visit

Local Life
The insider's city

The Best of New York City

The city's highlights in handy lists to help you plan

Best Walks
See the city on foot

New York City' Best...
The best experiences

Survival Guide

Tips and tricks for a seamless, hassle-free city experience

Getting Around
Travel like a local

Essential Information
Including where to stay

Our selection of the city's best places to eat, drink and experience:

⊙ **Sights**

⊗ **Eating**

⊝ **Drinking**

✪ **Entertainment**

⊙ **Shopping**

These symbols give you the vital information for each listing:

☏	Telephone Numbers	⊕	Family-Friendly
☉	Opening Hours	☻	Pet-Friendly
P	Parking	☐	Bus
☺	Nonsmoking	☻	Ferry
@	Internet Access	M	Metro
☎	Wi-Fi Access	S	Subway
✎	Vegetarian Selection	☐	Tram
☑	English-Language Menu	☐	Train

Find each listing quickly on maps for each neighborhood:

Bar Hemingway

16 ⊖ Map p233, B2

Legend has it that Hemi
self, wielding a machine
rate this timber-pan
ered bar during
showpiece is a
en by Papa an
town. Dress
s.com; Hôtel Rit
⊙6.30pm-2a

Lonely Planet's New York City

Lonely Planet Pocket Guides are designed to get you straight to the heart of the city.

Inside you'll find all the must-see sights, plus tips to make your visit to each one really memorable. We've split the city into easy-to-navigate neighborhoods and provided clear maps so you'll find your way around with ease. Our expert authors have searched out the best of the city: walks, food, nightlife and shopping, to name a few. Because you want to explore, our 'Local Life' pages will take you to some of the most exciting areas to experience the real New York City.

And of course you'll find all the practical tips you need for a smooth trip: itineraries for short visits, how to get around, and how much to tip the guy who serves you a drink at the end of a long day's exploration.

It's your guarantee of a really great experience.

Our Promise

You can trust our travel information because Lonely Planet authors visit the places we write about, each and every edition. We never accept freebies for positive coverage, so you can rely on us to tell it like it is.

QuickStart Guide 7

Explore New York City 21

Worth a Trip:

The Best of New York City 202

New York City's Best Walks

New York City's Best...

Survival Guide 233

QuickStart Guide

Welcome to New York City

When it comes to X-factor, Gotham slams the competition. A restless whirl of deco towers, bright yellow taxis and glittering marquees, this is the place where Warhol meets Frank Lloyd Wright, where Hollywood greats tread Broadway stages, and where unmarked doors lead to dirty martinis and sax. The world may be awash with great cities, but NYC is the juiciest of them all.

Central Park (p178)
PAWEL GAUL/GETTY IMAGES ©

New York City
Top Sights

Central Park (p178)

One of the world's most romanticized green spaces checks in with 843 acres of rolling meadows, boulder-studded outcroppings, elm-lined walkways and manicured European-style gardens. Did we mention the lake and reservoir?

JEAN-PIERRE LESCOURRET/GETTY IMAGES ©

Empire State Building (p130)

This towering ode to Gotham is the New York skyline's queen bee. Don't miss the view from the top – a sea of twinkling lights as the sun sinks over Jersey.

New York Harbor (p24)

Stellar skyline views, a free ferry, a lookout from Lady Liberty's crown, and a moving tribute to America's immigrants at Ellis Island – unmissable is an understatement.

Metropolitan Museum of Art (p158)

Dubbed 'The Met,' this museum of encyclopedic proportions has over two million objects in its permanent collection, and many of its treasures are showcased in no less than 17 acres' worth of galleries.

The High Line (p86)

These refurbished rail tracks have been transformed into grassy catwalks in the sky. It's the paradigm of urban renewal gone right, enjoying its status as one of the city's best-loved public spaces.

Times Square (p128)

Like it or loathe it, Times Square offers the quintessential New York conglomeration of bright lights and oversized billboards that soar above relentless crowds and thick streamers of concrete.

Museum of Modern Art (p132)

This superstar of the art scene contains a veritable who's who of modern masters. It's a thrilling crash course in all that is beautiful and addictive about the world of art and design.

Guggenheim Museum (p162)

A sculpture in its own right, architect Frank Lloyd Wright's swirling white building is a worthy match for the booty of 20th-century art housed inside.

National September 11 Memorial & Museum (p26)

A soaring tower, an evocative museum, and North America's largest manmade waterfalls are as much a symbol of hope and renewal as they are a tribute to the victims of terrorism.

New York City Local Life

Insider tips to help you find the real city

NYC heaves with big-ticket attractions, but it's the hidden rooftops, unexpected art installations and sneaky speakeasies that give the city its incomparable edge. The real New York will gladly welcome you in if you dare to explore.

Shop Local SoHo (p48)

▶ Unique boutiques
▶ Superlative coffee

Stomping ground of cool hunters, SoHo and neighboring Nolita offer a glut of coveted boutiques and hangouts. Look closely, though, and you'll find a string of local shops and pitstops that provide an altogether more genuine downtown encounter.

Chelsea Galleries (p88)

▶ Emerging artists
▶ Tapas bites

Western Chelsea was once an unbecoming district with countless industrial warehouses. Hundreds of these cavernous spaces have been revamped as A-list galleries, touting the hottest names in the art world.

Harlem (p196)

▶ African American history
▶ Trendy eats

New York's gridiron doesn't end at 100th St – there's lots more of the city to explore, starting with Harlem, a bastion of African American culture. It offers soul food, jazz beats and a riveting history captured in the brick and stone of its churches, landmarks and theaters.

South Brooklyn (p198)

▶ Unfurling green space
▶ Vintage shopping

Though the borough of Brooklyn is decidedly on the tourist radar, most visitors seem to opt out of crossing waterways. For those who do, there's rolling spaces of green, hotspot restaurants, and a famous flea market.

Williamsburg (p200)

▶ Designer drinks
▶ Funky boutiques

One stop over the bridge in Brooklyn, Williamsburg is the undeniable poster child of the hipster movement. Its cache of vintage warehouses, themed cocktail lounges, live music hangouts and highbrow eateries is definitely worth checking out – especially on weekends.

Prospect Park, Brooklyn (p199)

Williamsburg (p200)

**Other great places
to experience the
city like a local:**

Lincoln Center (p191)

Koreatown (p143)

Flea Theater (p43)

Chelsea Market (p98)

Union Square
Greenmarket (p124)

New York Road
Runners Club (p167)

Marie's Crisis (p108)

Garment District
(p152)

MICHAEL MARQUAND/GETTY IMA

New York City
Day Planner

Day One

☀ With only one day in the city, it's all about quintessential New York moments. Zip down to Lower Manhattan to hop aboard a ferry right in New York Harbor, which will take you to the **Statue of Liberty** (p25) and **Ellis Island** (p25) to learn about the city's (and nation's) immigrant past.

☀ Make a beeline for the Upper West Side and pack a picnic at **Zabar's** (p186) to enjoy on the verdant hillocks of **Central Park** (p178) – weather permitting, of course. Take in the park's many architectural and landscaped wonders before pausing at the **Loeb Boathouse** (p187) for snacks and a boat or bicycle rental. Then saunter over to the **Museum of Modern Art** (p132) for the very best in contemporary classics.

☽ Bathe in the impossibly bright lights of **Times Square** (p128) after sunset before treating your eyes and ears to an unforgettable Broadway show, such as **Kinky Boots** (p148), **Book of Mormon** (p148) or **Chicago** (p149). Dinner and drinks are on order afterwards – splurge at **Le Bernardin** (p141) or tuck into Korean tapas at **Danji** (p141) – then sling your tipples back at **Don't Tell Mama** (p151). Warning: you will break into song.

Day Two

☀ Start your second day on the Upper East Side's Museum Mile, attacking the colossal **Metropolitan Museum of Art** (p158) first and then – if time permits – tackling the **Guggenheim Museum** (p162). If you prefer Old Masters, ditch the Guggenheim for the **Frick Collection** (p165) instead. If fashion is your passion, window-shop on A-list Madison Avenue.

☀ Head downtown to the **Chelsea Market** (p92) to lunch on fresh artisanal nosh. Grab a gelato to go and climb up to **The High Line** (p86) for a stroll amid green stretching over the gridiron. Spend the latter half of the afternoon wandering among the **Chelsea Galleries** (p88), which sit in lovingly restored factory warehouses. Walk over to the **Empire State Building** (p130) and take in the twinkling metropolitan lights as the sun sets over the city.

☽ After dark, head back to the West Village for crafty libations at **Little Branch** (p101) and celebrated Asian-fusion fare at **RedFarm** (p96). Nourished, hit up **Village Vanguard** (p106) or **Blue Note** (p106) for smooth live jazz, or try the **Upright Citizens Brigade Theatre** (p105) if you're looking for laughs.

Short on time?

We've arranged New York City's must-sees into these day-by-day itineraries to make sure you see the very best of the city in the time you have available.

Day Three

☀ As the local youngsters are crawling back to their shoebox apartments after a raucous night out, make your way to the **Lower East Side Tenement Museum** (p69) to learn about life in the area long before gentrification. Pair your visit with the **New Museum of Contemporary Art** (p68) if you're in search of mind-bending art at the other end of the spectrum.

☀ Head up to the East Village for lunch at one of the area's many street-side cafes, then explore the city's punk rock roots along **St Marks Place** (p68), before swinging through **Union Square** (p115) to catch the flurry of pedestrians and the popular **Union Square Greenmarket** (p124). Snap your camera at the photogenic **Flatiron Building** (p115) further along, then pause at **Birreria** (p122) for craft beers on the rooftop.

☾ After a pre-dinner saunter around romantic Gramercy Park, tuck into locavore Italian at **Maialino** (p118) or Michelin-starred ingenuity at **Eleven Madison Park** (p117). Either way, cap the night with meticulously mixed cocktails at deco-licious **Flatiron Lounge** (p121) or sneaky hideout **Raines Law Room** (p121).

Day Four

☀ Pay your respects to those who perished in the 9/11 tragedy at the **National September 11 Memorial & Museum** (p26), while glimpsing two of the city's latest architectural wonders: the 1776ft-tall 1 World Trade Center tower and Spanish architect Santiago Calatrava's striking WTC Transportation Hub 'Oculus'. Afterwards, get the blood pumping with a walk along the famed **Brooklyn Bridge** (p28), an inspired neo-Gothic gesture bathed in iron.

☀ On the other side of the bridge lies the borough of Brooklyn. Lap up the spectacular views of the Manhattan skyline and dig into perfect pizza at **Juliana's** (p29). Once fed, head back into Manhattan for some solid retail therapy in SoHo and Nolita, where celeb-studded streets are packed with a mix of mainstream labels and up-and-coming designers.

☾ Toast to your revamped wardrobe with bubbles at **Balthazar** (p55) or pints at **Spring Lounge** (p59), then see-and-be-seen at dining hotspot **Saxon + Parole** (p55). If you've maxed out the credit cards, go easy in Chinatown, home to dozens of noodle and dumpling houses, including legendary **Joe's Shanghai** (p58).

Need to Know

For more information,
see Survival Guide (p233)

Currency
US dollar (US$)

Language
English

Visas
The US Visa Waiver program allows nationals of 38 countries to enter the US for up to 90 days without a visa.

Money
ATMs widely available and credit cards accepted at most hotels, stores and restaurants. Farmers markets, food trucks and some smaller eateries are cash-only.

Cell Phones
Most US cell phones, apart from the iPhone, operate on CDMA, not the European standard GSM. Check compatibility with your phone service provider.

Time
Eastern Standard Time (GMT/UTC minus five hours)

Plugs & Adaptors
The US electric current is 110V to 115V, 60Hz AC. Outlets are made for flat two-prong plugs (which often have a third, rounded prong for grounding).

Tipping
Tip restaurant servers 15-20%, barkeeps $1 per beer or $2 per specialty cocktail, taxi drivers 10-15%, and hotel maids $3 to $5 per day.

① Before You Go

Your Daily Budget

Budget less than $100

► Hostel dorm bed $35–$80

► Self-catering supermarkets, cafes and food trucks $5–$25

► Exploring the city on foot

Midrange $100–$300

► Double room $150–$300

► Two-course dinner with a cocktail $40–$70

► Discount Broadway TKTS tickets $80

Top End over $300

► Luxury sleeps or sleek boutique digs $325+

► Tasting menus at celebrity-chef restaurants $150+

► Metropolitan Opera orchestra seats $100-$390

Useful Websites

Lonely Planet (www.lonelyplanet.com/usa/new-york-city) Information, hotel bookings, traveler forum and more.

NYC: the Official Guide (www.nycgo.com) NYC's official tourism portal.

Advance Planning

Two months before Book your hotel – prices increase the closer you get to your arrival date – and snag Broadway tickets.

Three weeks before Score a table at your favorite high-end restaurant.

One week before Surf the interwebs for the newest and coolest in the city and join email news blasts.

② Arriving in New York City

With its three bustling airports, two train stations and a monolithic bus terminal, New York City rolls out the welcome mat for the more than 52 million visitors who come to take a bite out of the Big Apple each year.

✈ From John F Kennedy International Airport (JFK)

Destination	Best Transport
Brooklyn	Subway A line
Lower Manhattan	Subway A line
Midtown	Subway E line
Greenwich Village	Subway A line
Upper West Side	Subway A line
Upper East Side	Subway E then 4/5/6 lines
Harlem	Subway E then B or C lines

✈ From LaGuardia Airport (LGA)

Destination	Best Transport
Harlem	Bus M60
Upper East Side	Bus M60 & Subway 4/5/6 line
Midtown	Taxi
Union Square	Taxi
Greenwich Village	Taxi
Brooklyn	Taxi

✈ From Newark International Airport (EWR)

Take the AirTrain to Newark Airport rail station, and board any train bound for New York's Penn Station. Shared shuttles and buses are also available. From Midtown, you can hop on a subway to reach your final destination.

③ Getting Around

Once you've arrived in NYC, getting around is fairly easy. The extensive subway system is cheap and (reasonably) efficient. The sidewalks of New York, however, are the real stars in the transportation scheme – this city is made for walking.

S Subway

The subway system is iconic, inexpensive and open around the clock, though it can be confusing to the uninitiated. Check out www. mta.info for public transportation information. If you have a smartphone, download the useful NextStop app, with map, alerts of service outages and countdowns of train arrival times. Subway travel is particularly useful when traveling large distances uptown or downtown, or venturing over to Brooklyn.

🚌 Bus

Buses are convenient during off-peak hours and are a good choice when trying to travel 'crosstown' – there are buses that ply the east–west/west–east route on most two-way streets in Manhattan. Buses are also handy for travel along First and Tenth Aves.

🚕 Taxi

Taxi travel is the most convenient means of transportation, especially outside of rush hour. Taxis are handy if your trajectory is a zigzag through Manhattan as subway and bus lines follow the city's linear avenues and major streets. It can be very difficult to grab a taxi in inclement weather.

⛴ Ferry

There are hop-on-hop-off services and free rides to Staten Island. Check out East River Ferry (www.eastriverferry.com) and New York Water Taxi (☎212-742-1969; www. nywatertaxi.com; hop-on-hop-off service 1-day $26).

New York City
Neighborhoods

Upper West Side & Central Park (p176)
Home to Lincoln Center and Central Park – the city's antidote to the endless stretches of concrete.

◉ Top Sights
Central Park

Greenwich Village, Chelsea & the Meatpacking District (p84)
Quaint streets and well-preserved brick townhouses lead to neighborhood cafes mixed with trendy nightlife options.

◉ Top Sights
The High Line

SoHo & Chinatown (p46)
Hidden temples and steaming dumpling houses dot Chinatown. Next door are SoHo's streamlined streets and retail storefronts.

Lower Manhattan & the Financial District (p22)
Home to the National September 11 Memorial & Museum, the Brooklyn Bridge and the Statue of Liberty.

◉ Top Sights
New York Harbor

National September 11 Memorial & Museum

Brooklyn Bridge

Museum of Modern Art

Times Square

Empire State Building

The High Line

National September 11 Memorial & Museum

Brooklyn Bridge

New York Harbor

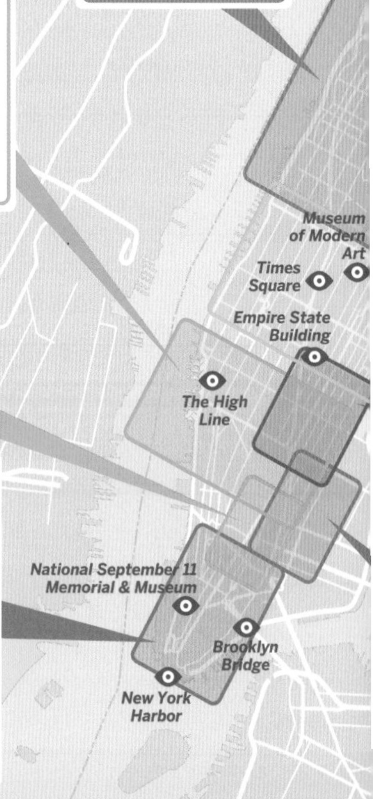

Upper East Side (p156)
High-end boutiques and sophisticated mansions culminate in an architectural flourish called Museum Mile.

◉ Top Sights

Metropolitan Museum of Art

Guggenheim Museum

Central Park

◉ ◉ Guggenheim Museum

◉ Metropolitan Museum of Art

Midtown (p126)
This is the NYC found on postcards: Times Sq, Broadway theaters, canyons of skyscrapers and bustling crowds.

◉ Top Sights

Times Square

Empire State Building

Museum of Modern Art

Union Square, Flatiron District & Gramercy (p112)
The tie that binds the colorful menagerie of surrounding areas. It's short on sights but big on buzz-worthy restaurants.

East Village & Lower East Side (p64)
Old meets new on every block of this downtown duo – two of the city's hottest 'hoods for nightlife and cheap eats.

Explore
New York City

Worth a Trip

The Empire State Building (p130) framed by the
Manhattan Bridge
KENNETH C. ZIRKEL/GETTY IMAGES ©

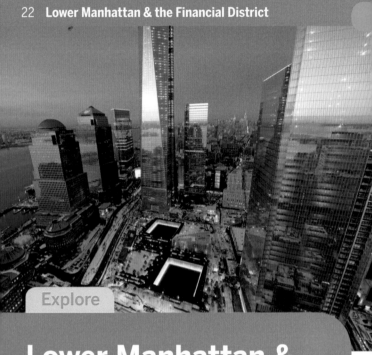

Explore

Lower Manhattan & the Financial District

Home to icons like Wall Street, the National September 11 Memorial & Museum and the Statue of Liberty, Manhattan's southern end is the city's historical heart. While Tribeca has a well-established reputation for hotspot restaurants, bars and shops, the somewhat staid Financial District is slowly catching up as the World Trade Center redevelopment injects new vibrancy and optimism into the area.

The Sights in a Day

☀ Beat the crowds and catch the New York Harbor ferry when it opens to tour the **Statue of Liberty** (p25) and **Ellis Island** (p25). Those with smaller wallets can hop on the **Staten Island Ferry** (p32) for a free ride in the harbor, which offers postcard-worthy photo ops of the southern portion of Manhattan.

☼ Head back to Manhattan for lunch at Anthony Bourdain's **Les Halles** (p39). Refueled, pay your respects to the fallen at the **National September 11 Memorial & Museum** (p26). Afterwards, lighten the mood with some retail therapy at bargain-mecca **Century 21** (p43) or head over to the **Brooklyn Bridge** (p28) for a wander along the cantilevered Gothic wonder.

☾ Do dinner and a show in Tribeca, stopping first at brasserie-style **Locanda Verde** (p38), then hitting up the **Flea Theater** (p43), one of the best respected off-off-Broadway institutions in town. End the night at **Brandy Library** (p41), where you can choose from a veritable encyclopedia of spirits.

Top Sights

New York Harbor (p24)

National September 11 Memorial & Museum (p26)

Brooklyn Bridge (p28)

♥ Best of New York City

Eating
Locanda Verde (p38)

Les Halles (p39)

Drinking
Weather Up (p41)

Dead Rabbit (p40)

Brandy Library (p41)

Shopping
Century 21 (p43)

Shinola (p43)

Getting There

Ⓢ **Subway** Fulton St is the area's main interchange station, servicing the A/C, J/M/Z, 2/3 and 4/5 lines. The 1 train terminates at South Ferry, from where the Staten Island Ferry departs.

⚓ **Boat** The Staten Island Ferry docks at the southern end of Whitehall St. Services to Liberty and Ellis Islands depart from Battery Park.

Top Sights
New York Harbor

Since its unveiling in 1886, Lady Liberty has welcomed millions of immigrants sailing into New York Harbor in the hope of a better life. She now welcomes millions of tourists, many of whom head up to her crown for one of New York City's finest skyline and water views. Close by lies Ellis Island, the American gateway for over 12 million new arrivals between 1892 and 1954. These days it's home to one of the city's most moving museums, paying tribute to these immigrants and their indelible courage.

⊙ Map p30, B8

☑ 212-363-3200, Statue Cruises 877-523-9849

www.statuecruises.com

ferry adult/child incl Liberty & Ellis Islands $17/9, incl Statue of Liberty crown & Ellis Island $20/12

⊙ 9am-5pm, ferries every 20min 8:30am-6pm Jun-Aug

Ⓢ 1 to South Ferry, 4/5 to Bowling Green

Statue of Liberty

Don't Miss

Statue of Liberty

Folks who reserve their tickets to the **statue** (☎877-523-9849; www.nps.gov/stli; Liberty Island; adult/child incl Ellis Island $17/9, incl crown & Ellis Island $20/12; ☉9.30am-5.30pm, check website for seasonal changes; ⓢ1 to South Ferry, 4/5 to Bowling Green) in advance are able to climb the 354 steps to Lady Liberty's crown, where the city and harbor are breathtaking. That said, crown access is extremely limited, and the only way in is to reserve your spot in advance – and the further in advance you can do it, the better, as a six-month lead time is allowed. Each customer may only reserve a maximum of four crown tickets, and children must be at least four-feet tall to access the crown. If you miss out on crown tickets, you may have better luck booking tickets to the pedestal, which also offers commanding views.

Ellis Island's Immigration Museum

Ellis Island's three-level **Immigration Museum** is a poignant tribute to the immigrant experience. It is estimated that 40% of Americans today have at least one ancestor who was processed at Ellis Island, confirming the major role this tiny harbor island has played in the making of modern America. The museum's self-guided audio tour features narratives from a number of sources, including historians, architects and the immigrants themselves, bringing to life the centre's hefty collection of personal objects, official documents, photographs and film footage. It's an evocative experience to relive personal memories – both good and bad – in the very halls and corridors in which they occurred. If you're very short on time, focus on the outstanding Through America's Gate and Peak Immigration Years exhibitions on the second floor.

☑ Top Tips

▶ The ferry ride from Battery Park in Lower Manhattan lasts only 15 minutes, but a trip to both the Statue of Liberty and Ellis Island is an all-day affair, and only those setting out on the ferry by 1pm will be allowed to visit both sites.

▶ Reservations to visit the Statue of Liberty are strongly recommended, as they give you a specific visit time and a guarantee that you'll get in. You can also buy a Flex Ticket, which lets you enter any time within a three-day period. The Flex Ticket is only available at the ferry ticket booth.

✗ Take a Break

Skip the cafeteria fare at Lady Liberty and pack a picnic lunch. Alternatively, visit early and return to Lower Manhattan for lunch at Andrew Carmellini's Locanda Verde (p38) or Anthony Bourdain's Les Halles (p39) – book ahead!

Top Sights
National September 11 Memorial & Museum

Plagued by design controversies, budget blowouts and construction delays, the core parts of the World Trade Center (WTC) redevelopment – the National September 11 Museum and Memorial – are finally open. Titled *Reflecting Absence,* the Memorial's two massive reflecting pools are as much a symbol of hope and renewal as they are a tribute to the thousands who lost their lives to terrorism. The state-of-the-art Memorial Museum is a striking, solemn space documenting the events and consequences of that fateful fall day in 2001.

👁 Map p30, B5

www.911memorial.org

cnr Greenwich & Albany Sts

admission $24

🕐 museum 9am-8pm summer, to 7pm winter; memorial 8:30am-8:30pm year-round

🚇 A/C/E to Chambers St, R to Rector St, 2/3 to Park Pl

Don't Miss

Reflecting Pools

Surrounded by a plaza planted with 400 swamp white oak trees, the 9/11 Memorial's reflecting pools occupy the very footprints of the ill-fated twin towers. From their rim, a steady cascade of water pours 30ft down toward a central void. Bronze panels frame the pools, inscribed with the names of those who died in the terrorist attacks of September 11, 2001, and in the World Trade Center truck bombing on February 26, 1993.

Memorial Museum

Between the reflective pools stands the entrance to the National September 11 Memorial Museum, its subterranean multimedia galleries documenting the terrorist attacks of September 11, 2001 and February 26, 1993. Among the relics is the 'survivors staircase', used by hundreds of workers to flee the WTC site. You'll also find the last steel column removed from the clean-up, adorned with the messages and mementos of recovery workers, responders and loved ones of the victims.

A limited number of walk-in tickets are available at the museum box office, but visitors are generally required to book tickets and a time slot in advance on the museum website to guarantee entry.

One World Trade Center

At the northwest corner of the WTC site is architect David M Childs' *One World Trade Center* (1 WTC). Not only the loftiest building in America, this tapered, 1776ft-tall giant is currently the tallest building in the Western Hemisphere and the fourth tallest in the world by pinnacle height. Its observation decks, which span floors 100 to 102, are scheduled to open in 2015.

☑ **Top Tips**

▶ In the museum, look out for the so-called 'Angel of 9/11', the eerie outline of a woman's anguished face on a twisted girder believed to originate from the point where American Airlines Flight 11 slammed into the North Tower.

▶ Take time to appreciate the design of the new WTC Transportation Hub, rising beside the museum. Conceived by Spanish starchictect Santiago Calatrava, it was inspired by the image of a child releasing a dove.

✗ **Take a Break**

Escape the swarm of restaurants serving the lunching Wall St crowd and head to Tribeca for a variety of in-demand eats, like Locanda Verde (p38), North End Grill (p39) or Shake Shack (p40).

Top Sights
Brooklyn Bridge

A New York icon, the Brooklyn Bridge was the world's first steel suspension bridge. When it opened in 1883, the 1596ft span between its two support towers was the longest in history. Although its construction was fraught with disaster, the bridge became a magnificent example of urban design, inspiring poets, writers and painters. Today, the Brooklyn Bridge continues to dazzle – many regard it as the most beautiful bridge in the world.

Map p30, E4

S 4/5/6 to Brooklyn Bridge-City Hall, J to Chambers St

Don't Miss

Crossing the Bridge

For many visitors to NYC, crossing the Brooklyn Bridge is a rite of passage. The Neo-Gothic wonder was designed by Prussian-born engineer John Roebling, who died of tetanus poisoning before construction even began. His son, Washington Roebling, supervised construction of the bridge, which lasted 14 years and managed to survive budget overruns and the deaths of 20 workers. The younger Roebling himself suffered from the bends while helping to excavate the riverbed for the bridge's western tower and remained bedridden for much of the project. When the bridge opened in June 1883, a shout from the crowd that the bridge was collapsing caused mayhem and the trampling death of 12 pedestrians.

Brooklyn Bridge Park

Across the bridge in Brooklyn is one of the borough's most celebrated new assets, the 85-acre **Brooklyn Bridge Park** (☎718-222-9939; www.brooklynbridgeparknyc.org; East River Waterfront, btwn Atlantic Ave & Adams St; admission free; ⊙6am-1am; ♿; ⑤A/C to High St, 2/3 to Clark St, F to York St). Stretching 1.3 miles from Jay St in Dumbo to the west end of Atlantic Ave in Cobble Hill, the park's highlights include the Empire Fulton Ferry, a state park featuring a grassy lawn with skyline views and the lovingly restored 1922-vintage **Jane's Carousel** (www.janescarousel.com; Brooklyn Bridge Park, Empire Fulton Ferry, Dumbo; tickets $2; ⊙11am-7pm Wed-Mon, to 6pm Nov-Apr; ♿; ⑤F to York St), set inside a glass pavilion designed by Pritzker Prize–winning architect Jean Nouvel. Just south of Empire Fulton Ferry is Pier 1; a 9-acre space complete with playground, walkways, and artist Mark di Suvero's 30ft kinetic sculpture *Yoga* (1991).

☑ Top Tips

▶ When walking across the bridge, stay on the side of the walkway marked for pedestrians. One half is designated for cyclists, who use it en masse for both commuting and pleasure rides.

▶ To beat the crowds, come early morning, when you'll have those views largely to yourself.

▶ From July through August, free outdoor films are screened on Brooklyn Bridge Park's Pier 1, against the stunning Manhattan skyline. Other free open-air events take place throughout the summer. Check the park's website for details.

✕ Take a Break

From May to October, Brooklyn Bridge Park features a few seasonal concessions, including wood-fired pizza, beer and Italian treats at **Fornino** (www.fornino.com; Pier 6, Brooklyn Bridge Park). Year-round classic and creative pizzas are available at nearby **Juliana's** (19 Old Fulton St, btwn Water & Front Sts; pizza $16-30; ⊙11:30am-11pm; ⑤A/C to High St).

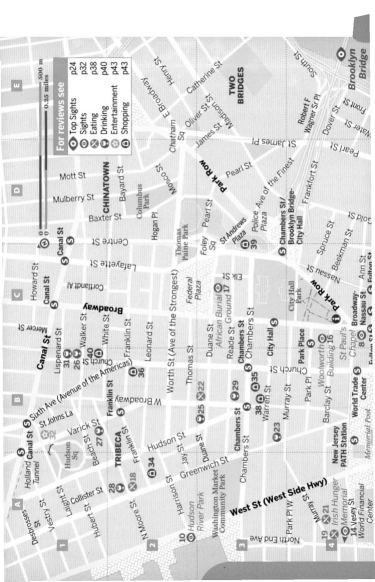

500 m
0.25 miles

CHINATOWN

Mott St
Mulberry St
Bayard St
Baxter St
Columbus Park
Hogan Pl
Centre St
Canal St
Howard St
Canal St
Mercer St
Broadway

TRIBECA

Lispenard St
Walker St
White St
Franklin St
Leonard St
Worth St (Ave of the Strongest)
Thomas St
Duane St
Reade St
Chambers St
Warren St
Murray St
Park Pl
Barclay St
Vesey St

Sixth Ave (Avenue of the Americas)
St Johns La
Varick St
Beach St
Hudson St
Jay St
Hudson St
Greenwich St
Chambers St

Holland Canal St Tunnel

Hudson Sq

Desbrosses St
Vestry St
Laight St
Collister St
Hubert St
N Moore St
Harrison St
Franklin St

West St (West Side Hwy)

Hudson River Park
Washington Market Community Park

North End Ave

New Jersey PATH Station

World Trade Center

World Financial Center

Memorial Pool

Memorial

Irish Hunger Memorial

St Paul's Chapel
Woolworth Building 16

Park Place
City Hall
Park Row
City Hall Park

Broadway-Nassau St

St Andrews Plaza
Foley Sq
Pearl St
Thomas Paine Park
Federal Plaza

African Burial Ground 17

Elk St

Police Plaza
Ave of the Finest

Chambers St/Brooklyn Bridge-City Hall

Moscow St
Park Row
Pearl St
Chatham Sq
Catherine St
Madison St
Oliver St
Henry St
E Broadway
St James Pl
James St

TWO BRIDGES

Robert F Wagner Sr Pl
Dover St
Water St
Front St
South St

Brooklyn Bridge

Pearl St
Frankfort St
Gold St
Spruce St
Beekman St
Nassau St
Ann St
Fulton St

39
17
22
25
26
31
40
36
29
35
38
23
34
18
28
10
19
21
14
8
16

Lafayette St
Cortlandt Al
Franklin St
Church St
Centre St
Hogan Pl

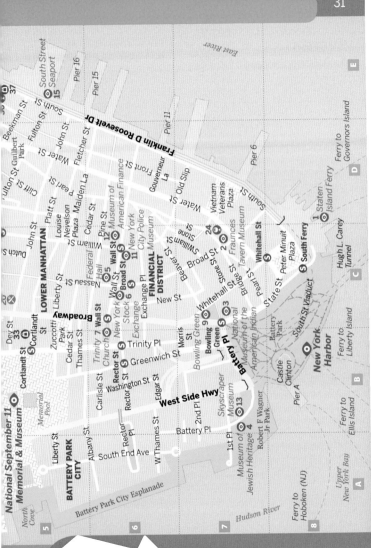

National September 11 Memorial & Museum

LOWER MANHATTAN

FINANCIAL DISTRICT

BATTERY PARK CITY

Broadway

West Side Hwy

Franklin D Roosevelt Dr

East River

New York Harbor

Hudson River

Upper New York Bay

Battery Park City Esplanade

North Cove

Memorial Pool

Dey St
Cortlandt St
Liberty St
Cedar St
Thames St
Carlisle St
Albany St
South End Ave
Liberty St

Cortlandt St
Church St
Zuccotti Park
Trinity Church
Trinity Pl
Rector St
Greenwich St
Washington St
Edgar St
2nd Pl
1st Pl
W Thames St
Rector Pl
Battery Pl

Dutch St
John St
Platt St
Cedar St
Federal Hall
Nassau St
Liberty St
New York Stock Exchange
Exchange Pl
Broad St
New St
Morris St
Beaver St
Bowling Green
Whitehall St
Stone St
State St

Cliff St
Beekman St
Fulton St
Gilbert Park
John St
Fulton St
Guilbert Park
Cliff St
Pearl St
William St
Louise Nevelson Plaza
Maiden La
Pine St
Museum of American Finance
Wall St
New York City Police Museum
William St
Stone St
Beaver St
Whitehall St
Fraunces Tavern Museum
Pearl St
Broad St
Gouverneur La
Old Slip
Water St
Front St
Fletcher St
John St
Water St
South St
Peter Minuit Plaza
Whitehall St
State St
South St Viaduct
Hugh L. Carey Tunnel

South Street Seaport

Pier 16
Pier 15
Pier 11
Pier 6

South Ferry
Staten Island Ferry
Vietnam Veterans Plaza

Ferry to Governors Island
Ferry to Liberty Island
Ferry to Ellis Island
Ferry to Hoboken (NJ)

Castle Clinton
Battery Park
Robert F Wagner Jr Park
Pier A

National Museum of the American Indian
Bowling Green
Museum of Jewish Heritage
Skyscraper Museum

1 South Ferry
2 Fraunces Tavern Museum
3 National Museum of the American Indian
4 Museum of Jewish Heritage
5 Broad St
6 Broad St
7 Wall St
9 Bowling Green
11 New York City Police Museum
12 Museum of American Finance
13 Skyscraper Museum
15 South Street Seaport
24
33 Cortlandt St
37

E
D
C
B
A
5
6
7
8

Sights

Staten Island Ferry
FERRY

1 Map p30, D8

Staten Islanders know these hulking, dirty-orange ferryboats as commuter vehicles, while Manhattanites like to think of them as their secret, romantic vessels for a spring-day escape. Yet many a tourist is clued into the charms of the Staten Island Ferry, whose 5.2-mile journey between Lower Manhattan and the Staten Island neighborhood of St George is one of NYC's finest free adventures. (www.siferry.com; Whitehall Terminal at Whitehall & South Sts; admission free; ◷24hr; **S**1 to South Ferry)

Fraunces Tavern Museum
MUSEUM

2 Map p30, C7

Combining five early-18th-century structures, this unique museum/restaurant/bar combo is an homage to the nation-shaping events of 1783, when the British relinquished control of New York at the end of the Revolutionary War and General George Washington gave a farewell speech to the officers of the Continental Army in the 2nd-floor dining room on December 4. (www.frauncestavernmuseum.org; 54 Pearl St btwn Broad St & Coenties Slip; adult/child $7/free; ◷noon-5pm; **S**J/Z to Broad St, 4/5 to Bowling Green)

National Museum of the American Indian
MUSEUM

3 Map p30, C7

An affiliate of the Smithsonian Institution, this elegant museum of Native American culture is set in Cass Gilbert's spectacular 1907 Custom House, one of NYC's finest beaux arts buildings. Beyond a vast elliptical rotunda, sleek galleries play host to changing exhibitions documenting Native American culture, life and beliefs. The museum's permanent collection includes stunning decorative arts, textiles and ceremonial objects. (www.nmai.si.edu; 1 Bowling Green; admission free; ◷10am-5pm Fri-Wed, to 8pm Thu; **S**4/5 to Bowling Green, R to Whitehall St)

Museum of Jewish Heritage
MUSEUM

4 Map p30, B7

This waterfront memorial museum explores all aspects of modern Jewish identity, with often poignant personal artifacts, photographs and documentary films. Its outdoor Garden of Stones – created by artist Andy Goldsworthy (and his first permanent exhibition in NYC) – is dedicated to those who lost loved ones in the Holocaust. It holds 18 boulders that form a narrow pathway for contemplating the fragility of life. (www.mjhnyc.org; 36 Battery Pl; adult/child $12/free, 4-8pm Wed free; ◷10am-5:45pm Sun-Tue & Thu, to 8pm Wed, to 5pm Fri Apr-Sep, to 3pm Fri Oct-Mar; **S**4/5 to Bowling Green)

Understand
Clues to the Past

Manhattan's Financial District is more than just gleaming towers, stock markets and a lust for profit. It's New York City's cradle and the setting for many important historical tales. Wall St once marked the northern boundary of the fledgling Dutch settlement of New Amsterdam. On it, Federal Hall is the very site on which George Washington became America's first president. Yet beneath these famous facts lie some lesser-known historical anecdotes.

What's in a Name?

Wall St is one of many streets harboring clues to the past. Originally known as Mother-of-Pearl St for the bounty of iridescent shells found in the vicinity, crooked Pearl St traces the foot of a long-gone hill. The leveling of hills became a common practice in the 18th century as Manhattan's population grew and demand for land increased. Dug up and dumped into the East River, the soil created space for the aptly named Water St. By the end of the 18th century, the shore had been pushed back even further to create Front St. Home to the New York Stock Exchange, Broad St was once a canal, crossed by a bridge at... Bridge St.

Blast from the Past

Buildings too can tell a tale. Take the former headquarters of JP Morgan Bank on the southeast corner of Wall and Broad Sts. The pockmarks on the building's Wall St facade are the remnants of the so-called Morgan Bank bombing – America's deadliest terrorist attack until the Oklahoma City bombing of 1995. At exactly 12.01pm on September 16, 1920, 500 pounds of lead sash weights and 100 pounds of dynamite exploded from a horse-drawn carriage. Thirty-eight people were killed and around 400 injured. Among the latter was John F Kennedy's father, Joseph P Kennedy. The bomb's detonation outside America's most influential financial institution at the time led many to blame anticapitalist groups, from Italian anarchists to stock-standard Bolsheviks. The crime has never been solved; the decision to reopen both the bank and New York Stock Exchange the following day led to a swift clean-up of both debris and any crucial clues.

Federal Hall

MUSEUM

5 ⊙ Map p30, C6

A Greek Revival masterpiece, Federal Hall houses a museum dedicated to postcolonial New York. Exhibition themes include George Washington's inauguration, Alexander Hamilton's relationship with the city and the struggles of John Peter Zenger, who was jailed, tried and acquitted of libel here for exposing government corruption in his newspaper. There's also a visitor information hall which covers downtown cultural happenings. (www.nps.gov/feha; 26 Wall St, entrance on Pine St; admission free; ⊙9am-5pm Mon-Fri; Ⓢ J/Z to Broad St, 2/3, 4/5 to Wall St)

New York Stock Exchange

NOTABLE BUILDING

6 ⊙ Map p30, C6

Home to the world's best-known stock exchange (the NYSE), 11 Wall St is an iconic symbol of US capitalism. About one billion shares change hands daily behind the portentous Romanesque facade, a sight no longer accessible to the public due to security concerns. Feel free to gawk outside the building, protected by barricades and the hawk-eyed New York Police Department (NYPD). The online shop has souvenirs like a hooded NYSE sweatshirt, as if you'd actually been inside. (www.nyse.com; 11 Wall St; ⊙closed to the public; Ⓢ J/Z to Broad St, 2/3, 4/5 to Wall St)

Understand
Building Lady Liberty

One of America's most powerful symbols of kinship and freedom, 'Liberty Enlightening the World' was a joint effort between America and France to commemorate the centennial of the Declaration of Independence. It was created by commissioned sculptor Frédéric-Auguste Bartholdi. The artist spent most of 20 years turning his dream – to create the hollow monument and mount it in the New York Harbor – into reality. Bartholdi's work on the statue was delayed by structural challenges – a problem resolved by the metal framework mastery of railway engineer Gustave Eiffel (of, yes, the famous tower). The work of art was finally completed in France in 1884. It was shipped to NYC as 350 pieces packed into 214 crates, reassembled over a span of four months and placed on a US-made granite pedestal. Its spectacular October 1886 dedication included New York's first ticker-tape parade and a flotilla of almost 300 vessels. The monument made it onto the UN's list of World Heritage Sites in 1984.

Museum of Jewish Heritage (p32)

Trinity Church

CHURCH

7 ⊙ Map p30, B6

New York City's tallest building upon completion in 1846, Trinity Church features a 280ft-high bell tower, a stained glass window over the altar and a small museum of historical artifacts. Famous residents of its serene cemetery include Founding Father Alexander Hamilton, while its music series includes Concerts at One (1pm Thursdays) and choir concerts, such as an annual rendition of Handel's *Messiah*. (www.trinitywallstreet. org; Broadway at Wall St; ⊙church 7am-6pm Mon-Fri, 8am-4pm Sat, 7am-4pm Sun, churchyard 7am-4pm Mon-Fri, 8am-3pm Sat, 7am-3pm Sun; **S** R to Rector St; 2/3, 4/5 to Wall St)

St Paul's Chapel

CHURCH

8 ⊙ Map p30, C4

Despite George Washington worshiping here after his inauguration in 1789, this classic revival brownstone chapel found new fame in the aftermath of September 11. With the World Trade Center destruction occurring just a block away, the mighty structure became a spiritual support and volunteer center, movingly documented in its exhibition *Unwavering Spirit: Hope & Healing at Ground Zero*. (www. trinitywallstreet.org; Broadway at Fulton St; ⊙10am-6pm Mon-Fri, to 4pm Sat, 8am-4pm Sun; **S** A/C, J/Z, 2/3, 4/5 to Fulton St)

Bowling Green
PARK

9 ⊙ Map p30, C7

New York's oldest – and possibly tiniest – public park is purportedly the spot where Dutch settler Peter Minuit paid Native Americans the equivalent of $24 to purchase Manhattan Island. At its northern edge stands Arturo Di Modica's 7000lb bronze *Charging Bull*, placed here permanently after it mysteriously appeared in front of the New York Stock Exchange in 1989, two years after a market crash. (cnr Broadway & State St; $4/5 to Bowling Green)

Understand
Buying Manhattan

In 1624, the Dutch West India Company sent 110 settlers to begin a trading post in present-day New York City. They settled in Lower Manhattan and called their colony New Amsterdam, touching off bloody battles with the unshakable Lenape tribe. It all came to a head in 1626, when the colony's first governor, Peter Minuit, became the city's first – but certainly not the last – unscrupulous real estate agent by purchasing Manhattan's 14,000 acres from the Lenape for 60 guilders ($24) and some glass beads.

Hudson River Park
PARK

10 ⊙ Map p30, A2

Stretching from Battery Park to Hell's Kitchen, the 5-mile, 550-acre Hudson River Park runs along the lower western side of Manhattan. Diversions include a bike/run/skate path snaking along its entire length, community gardens, playgrounds and renovated piers reinvented as riverfront esplanades, miniature golf courses, and alfresco summertime movie theaters and concert venues. Visit the website for a detailed map. (www.hudsonriverpark. org; Manhattan's west side from Battery Park to 59th St; $1 to Franklin St, 1 to Canal St)

New York City Police Museum
MUSEUM

11 ⊙ Map p30, C6

Until its Hurricane Sandy–damaged landmark location at 100 Old Slip reopens sometime in 2015, this tribute to 'New York's Finest' will remain on Wall St. Exhibitions span both past and present aspects of city crime fighting, from the mug shots and weapons of notorious New York mobsters, to historic NYPD uniforms, to rare photographic images documenting the September 11 terrorist attacks. Check the website for updates on the museum's move back to its permanent address. (www.nycpolicemuseum.org; 45 Wall St at William St; admission $5; ⊙10am-5pm Mon-Sat, noon-5pm Sun; ♿; $J/Z to Broad St; 2/3, 4/5 to Wall St)

Hudson River Park

Museum of American Finance

MUSEUM

12 ◉ Map p30, C6

Money makes this museum go round, with exhibits focusing on historic moments in American financial history. Permanent collections include rare 18th-century documents, stock and bond certificates from the Gilded Age, the oldest known photograph of Wall St, and a stock ticker from around 1875. Once the headquarters for the Bank of New York, the building itself is a lavish spectacle, with 30ft ceilings, glass chandeliers, and murals depicting historic scenes of banking and commerce. (www.moaf.org; 48 Wall St btwn Pearl & William Sts; adult/child $8/free; ⊙10am-4pm Tue-Sat; S 2/3, 4/5 to Wall St)

Skyscraper Museum

MUSEUM

13 ◉ Map p30, B7

Fans of phallic architecture will appreciate this high-gloss gallery, examining skyscrapers as objects of design, engineering and urban renewal. Temporary exhibitions dominate the space, with one recent exhibition exploring New York's new generation of super-slim residential towers. Permanent fixtures include information on the design and construction of the Empire State Building and World Trade Center. (www.skyscraper.org; 39 Battery Pl; admission $5; ⊙noon-6pm Wed-Sun; S 4/5 to Bowling Green)

Irish Hunger Memorial   MEMORIAL

14 Map p30, A4

Artist Brian Tolle's compact labyrinth of low limestone walls and patches of grass pays tribute to the Great Irish Famine and Migration (1845–52), which prompted hundreds of thousands of immigrants to leave Ireland for better opportunities in the New World. Representing abandoned cottages, stone walls and potato fields, the work was created with stones from each of Ireland's 32 counties. (290 Vesey St at North End Ave; admission free; ⑤ 2/3 to Park Place)

South Street Seaport   NEIGHBORHOOD

15 Map p30, E5

This 11-block enclave of cobbled streets, maritime warehouses and shops combines the best and worst in historic preservation. It's not on the radar for most New Yorkers, but tourists are drawn to the nautical air, the frequent street performers and the mobbed restaurants. (www.southstreetseaport.com; ⑤ A/C, J/Z, 2/3, 4/5 to Fulton St)

Woolworth Building   NOTABLE BUILDING

16 Map p30, C4

The world's tallest building upon completion in 1913, Cass Gilbert's 792ft-tall Woolworth Building is a neo-Gothic marvel, clad in masonry and terracotta, its landmarked lobby a spectacle of dazzling Byzantine-like mosaics. The lobby is only accessible on prebooked guided tours, which also offer insight into the building's more curious original features, among them a subway entrance and a secret swimming pool. (http://woolworthtours.com; 233 Broadway at Park Pl; 30/90min tours $15/45; ⑤ R to City Hall, 4/5/6 to Brooklyn Bridge-City Hall)

African Burial Ground   MEMORIAL

17 Map p30, C3

In 1991, construction workers here uncovered over 400 stacked wooden caskets, just 16ft to 28ft below street level. The boxes contained the remains of enslaved Africans (nearby Trinity Church graveyard had banned the burial of Africans at the time). Today, a memorial and visitors center honors an estimated 15,000 Africans buried here during the 17th and 18th centuries. (www.nps.gov/afbg; 290 Broadway btwn Duane & Elk Sts; admission free; ⊙ memorial 9am-5pm daily, visitor center 10am-4pm Tue-Sat; ⑤ 4/5 to Wall St)

Eating

Locanda Verde   ITALIAN $$$

18 Map p30, A2

Step through the velvet curtains and into a sexy, buzzing scene of loosened Brown Brothers' shirts, black dresses and slick barmen behind a long, crowded bar. Part of the Greenwich Hotel, this sprawling, brasserie-style hot spot is owned by celebrity chef Andrew Carmellini, whose contem-

Understand
Long Before New York

Long before the days of European conquest, the swath that would eventually become NYC belonged to Native Americans known as the Lenape – 'original people' – who resided in a series of seasonal campsites. They lived up and down the eastern seaboard, along the signature shoreline, and on hills and in valleys sculpted by glaciers after the Ice Age left New York with glacial debris now called Hamilton Heights and Bay Ridge. Glaciers scoured off soft rock, leaving behind Manhattan's stark rock foundations of gneiss and schist. Around 11,000 years before the first Europeans sailed through the Narrows, the Lenape people foraged, hunted and fished the regional bounty here. Spear points, arrowheads, bone heaps and shell mounds testify to their presence. Some of their pathways still lie beneath streets such as Broadway. In the Lenape language of Munsee, the term Manhattan may have translated as 'hilly island.' Others trace the meaning to a more colorful phrase: 'place of general inebriation.'

porary Italian grub is seasonal, savvy and insanely flavorful. (☎212-925-3797; www.locandaverdenyc.com; 377 Greenwich St at Moore St; lunch $19-29, dinner mains $28-34; ◷7am-11pm Mon-Fri, from 8am Sat & Sun; ⑤A/C/E to Canal St, 1 to Franklin St)

North End Grill
AMERICAN $$

19 ✕ Map p30, A4

Handsome, smart and friendly, this is celeb chef Danny Meyer's take on the American grill. Top-tier produce (including stuff from the restaurant's own rooftop garden) forms the basis for modern takes on comfort grub, happily devoured by suited money-makers and a scattering of more casual passersby. Dishes are given a kiss of smoke, either in the charcoal-fired oven or on the smokier wood-fired grill, with standouts including clam pizza with chili flakes, and the feel-good roasted chicken for two. (☎646-747-1600; www.northendgrillnyc.com; 104 North End Ave at Murray St; 3-course lunch $39, dinner mains $17-34; ◷11:30am-2pm & 5:30-10pm Mon-Thu, to 10:30pm Fri, 11am-2pm & 5:30-10:30pm Sat, 11am-2:30pm & 5:30-9pm Sun; ⑤1/2/3, A/C to Chambers St, E to World Trade Center)

Les Halles
FRENCH $$

20 ✕ Map p30, C5

Vegetarians need not apply at this packed brasserie, owned by celebrity chef Anthony Bourdain. Among the elegant light-fixture balls, dark wood paneling and white tablecloths you'll find a buttoned-up, meat-lovin' crowd who've come for rich favorites like

cote de boeuf and *steak au poivre*.
(212-285-8585; www.leshalles.net; 15 John St btwn Broadway & Nassau St; mains $14.50-32; 7am-midnight; A/C, J/Z, 2/3, 4/5 to Fulton St)

Shake Shack
BURGERS $

21 Map p30, A4

Danny Meyer's cult burger chain is fast food at its finest: cotton-soft burgers made with prime, freshly ground mince; Chicago-style hot dogs in poppy-seed potato buns; and seriously good cheesy fries. Leave room for the legendary frozen custard and drink local with a beer from Brooklyn brewery Sixpoint. (www.shakeshack.com; 215 Murray St btwn West St & North End Ave; burgers from $3.60; 11am-11pm; A/C, 1/2/3 to Chambers St)

Tiny's & the Bar Upstairs
AMERICAN $$$

22 Map p30, B3

Snug and adorable (book ahead!), Tiny's comes with a crackling fire in the back room and an intimate bar upstairs. Served on vintage porcelain, dishes are soulful, subtly retweaked delights; think burrata with date puree, lemon honey glaze and pistachios, or pan-seared scallops getting zesty with grapefruit and Thai chili-ginger coconut sauce. (212-374-1135; 135 W Broadway btwn Duane & Thomas Sts; mains $22-36; 11:30am-11pm Mon-Thu, to midnight Fri, 10:30am-midnight Sat, 10:30am-11pm Sun; A/C, 1/2/3 to Chambers St)

Drinking

Kaffe 1668
CAFE

23 Map p30, B3

A coffee-geek mecca, with espresso machine, Steampunk, coffee urns and dual Synessos pumping out single-origin magic. There's a large communal table speckled with suits and laptop-tapping creatives, and more seating downstairs. For a hair-raising thrill, order a triple ristretto. (www.kaffe1668.com; 275 Greenwich St btwn Warren & Murray Sts; 6:30am-10pm Mon-Fri, 7am-9pm Sat & Sun; A/C, 1/2/3 to Chambers St)

Dead Rabbit
COCKTAIL BAR

24 Map p30, C7

Far from dead, this new kid on the cocktail block has wasted no time swagging awards, among them World's Best New Cocktail Bar, Best Cocktail Menu and International Bartender of the Year at the 2013 Tales of the Cocktail Festival.

During the day, hit the sawdust-sprinkled taproom for specialty beers, historic punches and pop-inns (lightly hopped ale spiked with different flavors). Come evening, scurry upstairs to the cozy Parlour for 72 meticulously researched cocktails. (www.deadrabbitnyc.com; 30 Water St; 11am-4am; R to Whitehall St, 1 to South Ferry)

Shake Shack

Weather Up
COCKTAIL BAR

25 Map p30, B3

Softly lit subway tiles, amiable barkeeps and seductive cocktails make a bewitching trio at Weather Up. Sweet talk the staff over a Whizz Bang (scotch whisky, dry vermouth, house-made grenadine, orange bitters and absinthe). Failing that, comfort yourself with some seriously fine snacks, including spectacular oysters slapped with gin-martini granita. (www.weatherupnyc.com; 159 Duane St btwn Hudson St & W Broadway; ⏰5pm-2am; ⑤1/2/3 to Chambers St)

Macao
COCKTAIL BAR

26 Map p30, B1

Though we love the '40s-style 'gambling parlor' bar/restaurant, it's the downstairs 'opium den' (open Thursday to Saturday) that gets our hearts racing. A Chinese-Portuguese fusion of grub and liquor, both floors are a solid spot for late-night sipping and snacking, especially if you've got a soft spot for sizzle-on-the-tongue libations. (☎212-431-8750; www.macaonyc.com; 311 Church St btwn Lispenard & Walker Sts; ⏰bar 4pm-5am; ⑤A/C/E to Canal St)

Brandy Library
BAR

27 Map p30, B1

When sipping means serious business, settle in at this uber-luxe 'library', its handsome club chairs facing floor-to-ceiling, bottle-lined shelves. Go for top-shelf cognac, malt scotch or vintage brandies (prices range from $9 to $235), expertly paired with nibbles such as the house specialty Gougeres (Gruyere cheese puffs). Reservations are recommended. (www.brandylibrary.com; 25 N Moore St at Varick St; ☺5pm-1am Sun-Wed, 4pm-2am Thu, 4pm-4am Fri & Sat; S1 to Franklin St)

Smith & Mills COCKTAIL BAR

28 Map p30, A2

Petite Smith & Mills ticks all the cool boxes: unmarked exterior, kooky industrial interior and expertly crafted cocktails – the 'Carriage House' is a nod to the space's previous incarnation. Space is limited so head in early if you fancy kicking back on a plush banquette. A seasonal menu spans light snacks to a particularly notable burger. (www.smithandmills.com; 71 N Moore St btwn Hudson & Greenwich Sts; ☺11am-2am Mon-Wed, to 3am Thu-Sat, to 1am Sun; S1 to Franklin St)

Top Tip

Downtown TKTS

If you're after cut-price tickets to Broadway shows, ditch the main TKTS Booth in Times Sq for the TKTS branch at **South Street Seaport** (Map p30, D5; www.tdf.org/tkts; cnr Front & John Sts; ☺11am-6pm Mon-Sat, to 4pm Sun; SA/C to Broadway-Nassau; 2/3, 4/5, J/Z to Fulton St). Queues usually move a little faster and you can also purchase tickets for next-day matinees (something you can't do at the Times Sq outlet). Smartphone users can download the free TKTS app, which offers real-time listings of what's on sale.

Ward III COCKTAIL BAR

29 Map p30, B3

Dark and bustling, Ward III channels old-school jauntiness with its elegant libations, vintage vibe (including old Singer sewing tables behind the bar), and gentlemanly house rules (No 2: 'Don't be creepy'). Reminisce over a Moroccan martini, or line the stomach first with top-notch bar grub, available every day till close. (www.ward3tribeca.com; 111 Reade St btwn Church St & W Broadway; ☺4pm-4am Mon-Fri, 5pm-4am Sat & Sun; SA/C, 1/2/3 to Chambers St)

Keg No 229 BEER HALL

30 Map p30, E5

If you know that a Flying Dog Raging Bitch is a craft beer – not a nickname for your ex – this curated beer bar is for you. From Mother's Milk Stout to Abita Purple Haze, its battalion of drafts, bottles and cans are a who's who of boutique American brews. Across the street at number 220, sibling **Bin No 220** is its vinophile sibling. (www.kegno229.com; 229 Front St btwn Beekman St & Peck Slip; ☺noon-midnight Sun-Wed, to 2am Thu-Sat; SA/C, J/Z, 1/2, 4/5 to Fulton St)

La Colombe CAFE

31 Map p30, B1

Coffee and a few baked treats are all you'll get at this roaster but, man, are they good. The espresso is dark and intense, brewed by hipster baristas and swilled by an endless stream of eye-candy creatives and clued-in continentals. Don't leave without a bottle of 'Pure Black Coffee,' steeped in oxygen-free stainless steel wine tanks for 16 hours. (www.lacolombe.com; 319 Church St at Lispenard St; ⏰7:30am-6:30pm Mon-Fri, from 8:30am Sat & Sun; ⒮A/C/E to Canal St)

Entertainment

Tribeca Cinemas
CINEMA

32 Map p30, B1

This is the physical home of the **Tribeca Film Festival**, founded in 2003 by Robert De Niro and Jane Rosenthal, and held in late April or early May. Throughout the year, the space hosts a range of screenings and educational panels, including festivals dedicated to themes like architecture and design. See the website for details. (www.tribecacinemas.com; 54 Varick St at Laight St; ⒮A/C/E, N/Q/R, J/Z, 6 to Canal St)

Shopping

Century 21
FASHION

33 Map p30, B5

For penny-pinching fashionistas, this cut-price department store is dangerously addictive. Raid the racks for designer duds at up to 70% off. Not everything is a knockout or a bargain, but persistence pays off. You'll also find accessories, shoes, cosmetics, homewares and toys. (www.c21stores.com;

Flea Theater

One of NYC's top off-Broadway companies, the **Flea Theater** (Map p30, B2; www.theflea.org; 41 White St btwn Church St & Broadway; ⒮1 to Franklin St, A/C/E, N/Q/R, J/Z, 6 to Canal St) is famous for performing innovative, timely new works in its two performance spaces. Luminaries including Sigourney Weaver and John Lithgow have trodden the boards here, and the year-round program also includes music and dance performances.

22 Cortlandt St btwn Church St & Broadway; ⏰7:45am-9pm Mon-Wed, to 9:30pm Thu & Fri, 10am-9pm Sat, 11am-8pm Sun; ⒮A/C, J/Z, 2/3, 4/5 to Fulton St, N/R to Cortlandt St)

Shinola
ACCESSORIES

34 Map p30, A2

Well known for its coveted wrist watches, Detroit-based Shinola branches out with a super-cool selection of Made-in-USA life props. Bag anything from leather iPad and journal covers, to limited-edition bicycles with customized bags, or even jewelry made with metal from torn-down buildings in Detroit. There's an inhouse espresso bar too. (www.shinola.com; 177 Franklin St btwn Greenwich & Hudson Sts; ⏰11am-7pm Mon-Sat, noon-6pm Sun; ⒮1 to Franklin St)

Staten Island Ferry (p32)

Philip Williams Posters VINTAGE

35 Map p30, B3

You'll find over half a million posters in this cavernous treasure trove, from oversized French advertisements for perfume and cognac to Soviet film posters and retro-fab promos for TWA. Prices range from $15 to a few thousand bucks, and most of the stock is original. There is a second entrance at 52 Warren St. (www.postermuseum.com; 122 Chambers St btwn Church St & W Broadway; ⊙11am-7pm Mon-Sat; S A/C, 1/2/3 to Chambers St)

Steven Alan FASHION

36 Map p30, B2

New York designer Steven Alan mixes his hip, heritage-inspired threads for men and women with a beautiful edit of clothes from indie-chic labels like Scandinavia's Hope, Our Legacy and Won Hundred. Accessories include hard-to-find fragrances, bags, jewelry and a selection of shoes by cognoscenti brands such as Common Projects and No. 6. (www.stevenalan.com; 103 Franklin St btwn Church St & W Broadway; ⊙11:30am-7pm Mon-Wed, Fri & Sat, 11:30am-8pm Thu, noon-6pm Sun; S A/C/E to Canal St, 1 to Franklin St)

Pasanella & Son WINE

37 Map p30, E5

Oenophiles adore this savvy wine peddler, with its 400-plus drops both inspired and affordable. The focus is on small producers, with a number of biodynamic and organic winemakers in the mix. There's an impressive choice of American whiskeys, free wine tastings of the week's new arrivals on Sundays, and themed wine and cheese tastings throughout the year. (www.pasanellaandson.com; 115 South St btwn Peck Slip & Beekman St; ⊙10am-9pm Mon-Sat, noon-7pm Sun; S A/C, J/Z, 2/3, 4/5 to Fulton St)

Mysterious Bookshop BOOKS

38 Map p30, B3

With more crime per square inch than any other corner of the city, this mystery-themed book shop peddles everything from classic espionage and thrillers to contemporary Nordic crime fiction and literary criticism. You'll find both new and second-hand titles, including rare first editions, signed copies, obscure magazines, and picture books for budding sleuths. Check the website for in-store events. (www.mysteriousbookshop.com; 58 Warren St at W Broadway; ⊙11am-7pm Mon-Sat; S 1/2/3, A/C to Chambers St)

Citystore SOUVENIRS

39 Map p30, C3

Score all manner of New York memorabilia, including authentic taxi medallions, manhole coasters, Brooklyn Bridge posters, NYPD baseball caps, and actual streets signs ('No Parking,' 'Don't Feed the Pigeons'). There's also a great collection of city-themed books. (www.nyc.gov/citystore; Municipal Bldg, North Plaza, 1 Centre St; ⊙10am-5pm Mon-Fri; S J/Z to Chambers St, 4/5/6 to Brooklyn Bridge-City Hall)

Best Made Company ACCESSORIES, FASHION

40 Map p30, B1

Give your next camping trip a Manhattan makeover at this store/design-studio hybrid. Pick up cool, handcrafted axes, rucksacks, sunglasses, even designer dartboards and first-aid kits. A small, smart edit of threads for men includes designer graphic t-shirts, sweatshirts, flannel pullovers, and rugged knitwear from Portland's Dehen Knitting Mills. (www.bestmadeco.com; 36 White St at Church St; ⊙noon-7pm Mon-Sat, to 6pm Sun; S A/C/E to Canal St, 1 to Franklin St)

Explore

SoHo & Chinatown

Like a colorful quilt of subneighborhoods sewn together in mismatched patches, the areas orbiting SoHo (or SOuth of HOuston) feel like a string of mini republics. Italo-Americans channel Napoli in ever-shrinking Little Italy, style mavens boutique-hop in booming Nolita (NOrth of LIttle ITAly), and extended Chinese families gossip over *xiao long bao* (dumplings) in hyperactive Chinatown.

The Sights in a Day

☀ Start your day with the rush and color of Chinatown. Kneel before the giant gilded Buddha at the **Mahayana Temple** (p54), sharpen your mah-jongg skills in **Columbus Park** (p54) and explore the Chinese American experience at the **Museum of Chinese in America** (p52). Swap continents on Mulberry St, the heart of Little Italy, and find solace inside historic **St Patrick's Old Cathedral** (p53).

☀ In SoHo, nothing beats lunch at **Dutch** (p55) or brunch at **Balthazar** (p55), followed by a round of serious shopping. Wield your plastic at the blockbuster stores along Broadway before hitting side-street wonders like **Kiosk** (p61), **3x1** (p49), and **Rag & Bone** (p60). If shopping is not your schtick, go time traveling at the **Merchant's House Museum** (p52) – the best-preserved Federalist mansion in all of New York.

☽ Come evening, it's time to nosh at hotspot restaurants **Saxon + Parole** (p55) or **Public** (p55). While both have brilliant in-house bars, cap the evening with late-night cocktails at Burmese-inspired **Pegu Club** (p59), home to award-winning mixologist Kenta Goto.

For a local's day in SoHo, see p48.

◌ Local Life
Shop Local SoHo (p48)

♥ Best of New York City

Shopping

Rag & Bone (p60)

MoMA Design Store (p60)

MiN New York (p49)

Museums

Merchant's House Museum (p52)

New York City Fire Museum (p53)

Eating

Dutch (p55)

Saxon + Parole (p55)

Getting There

S Subway The subway lines dump off along various points of Canal St (J/Z, N/Q/R and 6). Once you arrive, it's best to explore on foot. Other useful stops are Brooklyn Bridge–City Hall (4/5/6) and Chambers St (J/Z) for southern access (with a bit of walking).

🚕 Taxi Avoid taking cabs – especially in Chinatown – as the traffic is full-on.

Local Life
Shop Local SoHo

Shopaholics across the world drool for SoHo and its sharp, trendy whirlwind of flagship stores, coveted labels and strutting fashionistas. Look beyond the giant global brands, however, and you'll discover a completely different retail scene, one where talented artisans and independent, one-off enterprises keep things local, unique and utterly inspiring. Welcome to SoHo at its homegrown best.

....

1 Nicaraguan Joe
Charge up with a cup of single-origin coffee from **Café Integral** (www.cafeintegral.com; 135 Grand St, btwn Crosby & Lafayette Sts; ⊙8am-6pm Mon-Fri, 10am-6pm Sat, noon-5pm Sun; SN/Q/R, J, 6 to Canal St), a teeny-tiny espresso bar inside kooky shop-cum-gallery American Two Shot. Twenty-something owner César Martin Vega is obsessed with Nicaraguan coffee beans.

❷ Perfect Jeans

3x1 (www.3x1.us; 15 Mercer St, btwn Howard & Grand Sts; ◷11am-7pm Mon-Sat, noon-6pm Sun; ⓢN/Q/R, J, 6 to Canal St) lets you design your perfect pair of jeans. Choose buttons and hems for ready-to-wear pairs (women's from $195, men's from $285), customize fabric and detailing on existing cuts ($525 to $750), or create a pair from scratch ($1200).

❸ Designer Kicks

Local craftsmanship also defines the footwear of emerging star **Alejandro Ingelmo** (www.alejandroingelmo.com; 51 Wooster St, btwn Broome & Grand Sts; ◷11am-7pm Mon-Fri, from noon Sat & Sun; ⓢ1, A/C/E to Canal St), his imaginative kicks spanning sparkly basketball-style boots to butterfly-inspired stilettos. Sneakers retail for around $600.

❹ Curbside Culture

The sidewalk engraving on the northwest corner of Prince St and Broadway is the work of Japanese-born sculptor Ken Hiratsuka, who has carved almost 40 sidewalks in NYC. This particular engraving took two years to complete (1983–84), police frequently disrupting Hiratsuka's illegal nighttime chiseling.

❺ Gourmet Refuel

NYC loves its luxe grocers and **Dean & DeLuca** (☑212-226-6800; www.deanand deluca.com; 560 Broadway, at Prince St; ◷7am-8pm Mon-Fri, 8am-8pm Sat & Sun; ⓢN/R to Prince St, 6 to Spring St) is one of the biggest names around town. If

you're feeling peckish, ready-to-eat delectables include sugar-dusted almond croissants.

❻ Fragrance Flight

Drop into library-like apothecary **MiN New York** (www.minnewyork.com; 117 Crosby St, btwn Jersey & Prince Sts; ◷11am-7pm Mon-Sat, noon-6pm Sun; ⓢB/D/F/M to Broadway-Lafayette St, N/R to Prince St) and request a free 'fragrance flight,' a guided exploration of the store's extraordinary collection of rare, exclusive perfumes and grooming products. Look out for homegrown fragrances like Brooklyn's MCMC and Detroit's Kerosene, as well as MiN's own coveted hair products.

❼ An Intellectual Pitstop

End at bustling indie bookshop **McNally Jackson** (☑212-274-1160; www.mcnallyjackson.com; 52 Prince St, btwn Lafayette & Mulberry Sts; ◷10am-10pm Mon-Sat, to 9pm Sun; ⓢN/R to Prince St; 6 to Spring St), stocked with an excellent selection of magazines and books covering contemporary fiction, food writing, architecture and design, art and history. Grab a tome on NYC style and kick back in the cafe. If you're lucky, you might even catch one of the regular in-store readings and book signings.

EAST VILLAGE

Forsyth St

Sara D Roosevelt Park

Chrystie St

Rivington St

Second Ave

Stanton St

E 4th St

E 3rd St

E 2nd St

E 1st St

Lower East Side-2nd Ave Ⓢ

Bowery

21 Ⓓ
Ⓧ 12

Ⓧ 33

Ⓧ 13

E Houston St

14 Ⓧ

Elizabeth St

17 Ⓧ

Mott St

5 Ⓓ

St Patrick's Old Cathedral

Prince St

NOLITA

Ⓓ 36

Ⓧ 15

23 Ⓢ

Ⓓ Fourth Ave

Ⓘ 1

NOHO

Merchant's House Museum

Great Jones St

Bond St

Bleecker St

Mulberry St

Jersey St

24 Ⓧ

Lafayette St

Ⓢ

31 Ⓓ

Bleecker St

Broadway

Broadway-Lafayette St Ⓢ

Crosby St

25 Ⓓ Ⓢ Spring St

11 Ⓧ

Spring St

New York University

W 4th St

W 3rd St

Mercer St

Ⓢ

Prince St

28 Ⓓ

26 Ⓓ

37 Ⓓ

Bleecker St

W Houston St

29 Ⓓ

20 Ⓧ

New York Earth Room

8 Ⓓ Ⓢ

Prince St

32 Ⓓ

W Broadway

SOHO

Spring St

LaGuardia Pl

Thompson St

Ⓧ 10

Sullivan St

Ⓓ 4

GREENWICH VILLAGE

Washington Sq Park

For reviews see	
Ⓢ Sights	p52
Ⓧ Eating	p55
Ⓧ Drinking	p59
Ⓓ Shopping	p60

200 m
0.1 miles

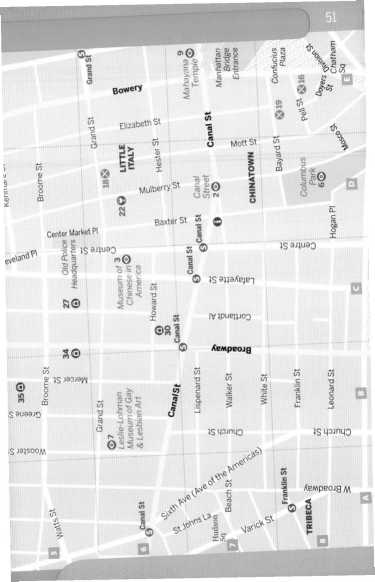

Sights

Merchant's House Museum

MUSEUM

1 Map p50, D1

Walking through the doors of this perfectly preserved mansion is like stepping into a time machine and being transported 150 years into the past. Everything in the house, from the polished floors to the servant call bells, is as it was during the bygone era. The facade is also intact. The gorgeous red-brick house was once the home of merchant magnate Seabury Tredwell and his family, and it remains to this day the most authentic Federal-style house (of which there are about 300) in NYC. (📞212-777-1089; www.merchantshouse.org; 29 E 4th St, btwn Lafayette St & Bowery; adult/child $10/free; ⊙noon-5pm Thu-Mon, guided tours 2pm; Ⓢ6 to Bleecker St)

Canal Street

STREET

2 Map p50, D7

Walking down Canal St is like a game of Frogger played on the streets of Shanghai. This is Chinatown's aorta, where you'll dodge oncoming human traffic as you scurry into back alleys to scout treasures from the Far East. You'll pass mysterious herb shops displaying a witch's cauldron's worth of roots and potions; restaurants with whole roasted ducks and pigs hanging by their skinny necks in the windows; and street vendors selling every iteration of knock-off, from Gucci sunglasses to Prada bags. (ⓈJ/Z, N/Q/R, 6 to Canal St)

Museum of Chinese in America

MUSEUM

3 Map p50, C6

Housed in a 12,350-sq-ft space designed by architect Maya Lin (who created the famed Vietnam Memorial in Washington DC), the Museum of Chinese in America is a multifaceted space with galleries, a bookstore and a visitors lounge. It serves as a national center of information about Chinese American life. Browse through interactive multimedia exhibits, maps, timelines, photos, letters, films and artifacts. (📞212-619-4785; www.mocanyc.org;

Local Life
Merchant's House Ghosts

Perhaps just as well known as its antiques are the Merchant's House Museum's clan of ghosts and ghouls. It is popularly believed that many of the former residents haunt the old mansion, making cameo appearances late in the evenings and sometimes at public events. In fact, at a Valentine's Day concert several years back many attendees spotted the shadow of a woman sitting in the parlor chairs – it was commonly believed to be the ghost of Gertrude Tredwell, the last inhabitant of the brownstone. Each year during the last couple of weeks of October, the museum offers special ghost tours after dark.

Mahayana Temple (p54)

211-215 Centre St, btwn Grand & Howard Sts; adult/child $10/free, Thu free; ⏱11am-6pm Tue, Wed & Fri-Sun, to 9pm Thu; 🚇N/Q/R, J/Z, 6 to Canal St)

New York City Fire Museum
MUSEUM

4 ⊙ Map p50, A4

In a grand old firehouse dating from 1904, this ode to fire fighters includes a fantastic collection of historic equipment, from gold, horse-drawn fire-fighting carriages to early rescue gear like stovepipe firefighter hats. Exhibits trace the development of the NYC fire-fighting system, which began with the 'bucket brigades.' The New York Fire Department (FDNY) lost half of its members in the collapse of the World

Trade Center, and memorials and exhibits have become a permanent part of the collection. (📞212-219-1222; www.nycfiremuseum.org; 278 Spring St, btwn Varick & Hudson Sts; adult/child $5/5; ⏱10am-5pm; ♿; 🚇C/E to Spring St)

St Patrick's Old Cathedral
CHURCH

5 ⊙ Map p50, D3

St Patrick's Cathedral is now famously located on Fifth Ave in Midtown, but its first congregation was housed here, on the northern edge of Little Italy, in this 1809–15 Gothic Revival church designed by Joseph-François Mangin. In its heyday, the church was the seat of religious life for the archdiocese of New York, and an important community center for new, mainly Irish, immigrants. Its ancient cemetery out the back is a beautiful respite in the midst of city chaos. (www.oldsaintpatricks.com; 263 Mulberry St, entrance on Mott St; ☺8am-6pm; ⑤N/R to Prince St)

Columbus Park   PARK

6 ◉ Map p50, D8

Mah-jongg meisters, slow-motion tai chi practitioners and old aunties gossiping over homemade dumplings: it might feel like Shanghai, but this leafy oasis is core to NYC history. In the 19th century, this was part of the infamous Five Points neighborhood, the city's first tenement slums and the inspiration for Martin Scorsese's *Gangs of New York*. (Mulberry & Bayard Sts; ⑤J/Z, N/Q/R, 6 to Canal St)

Leslie-Lohman Museum of Gay & Lesbian Art   MUSEUM

7 ◉ Map p50, B6

The world's first museum dedicated to LGBT themes stages six to eight annual exhibitions of both homegrown and international art. To date, offerings have included solo-artist retrospectives and themed shows exploring the likes of art and sex along the New York waterfront. Much of the work on display is from the museum's own collection, which consists of over 50,000 works. The space also hosts queer-centric lectures, readings, film screenings and performances. (✆212-431-2609; www.leslielohman.org; 26 Wooster

St, btwn Grand & Canal Sts; admission free; ☺noon-6pm Tue-Sat; ⑤A/C/E to Canal St)

New York Earth Room   GALLERY

8 ◉ Map p50, B3

Since 1980 the oddity of the New York Earth Room, the work of artist Walter De Maria, has been wooing the curious with something not easily found in the city: dirt (250cu yd, or 280,000lb, of it, to be exact). Walking into the small space is a heady experience, as the scent will make you feel like you've entered a wet forest; the sight of such beautiful, pure earth in the midst of this crazy city is surprisingly moving. (www.earthroom. org; 141 Wooster St, btwn Prince & W Houston Sts; admission free; ☺noon-6pm Wed-Sun, closed 3-3:30pm mid-Jun–mid-Sep; ⑤N/R to Prince St)

Mahayana Temple   TEMPLE

9 ◉ Map p50, E7

The Mahayana Buddhist Temple holds one golden 16ft-high Buddha, sitting on a lotus and edged with offerings of fresh oranges, apples and flowers. Mahayana is the largest Buddhist temple in Chinatown, and its facade, right near the frenzied vehicle entrance to the Manhattan Bridge, features two giant golden lions for protection. (133 Canal St, at Manhattan Bridge Plaza; ☺8am-6pm; ⑤B/D to Grand St, J/Z, 6 to Canal St)

Eating

Dutch
MODERN AMERICAN **$$$**

10 🍴 Map p50, A3

Whether perched at the front bar or tucked snugly in the back room, you can always expect smart, farm-to-table soul grub at this see-and-be-seen stalwart. Slurp on silky Maine oysters, warm up with the juicy dry-aged burger, or keep it light with the likes of pillow-soft sea scallops spiked with arbol and chile salsa. Reservations are recommended. (📞212-677-6200; www.thedutchnyc.com; 131 Sullivan St, btwn Prince & Houston Sts; mains $19-52; ⏱11:30am-3pm & 5:30pm-late Mon-Fri, from 10am Sat & Sun; 🚇C/E to Spring St, N/R to Prince St, 1 to Houston St)

Balthazar
FRENCH **$$$**

11 🍴 Map p50, C4

Still the king of bistros, bustling Balthazar is never short of a discerning mob. That's all thanks to three winning details: its location in SoHo's shopping-spree heartland; the uplifting Paris-meets-NYC ambience; and, of course, the something-for-everyone menu.

The kitchen stays open till 1am Friday and Saturday, and weekend brunch here is a very crowded (and delicious) production. For a decadent treat to go, grab a pastry from the Balthazar bakery next door. (📞212-965-1414; www.balthazarny.com; 80 Spring St, btwn Broadway & Crosby St; mains $17-45; ⏱7:30am-late Mon-Fri, from 8am Sat & Sun; 🚇6 to Spring St; N/R to Prince St)

Saxon + Parole
MODERN AMERICAN **$$$**

12 🍴 Map p50, D2

A fun, fashionable bistro-bar named in honor of two 19th-century racing horses, Saxon + Parole (pronounced 'pearl') leads the charge with competent twists on comfort surf and turf. You might tuck into tuna tartare paired with yuzu, avocado wasabi and root chips, or an extraordinary Long Island duck, smoked to bacon-sweet perfection.

Belly full, trot through the secret door and kick on at cocktail den Madam Geneva (p59). (📞212-254-0350; www.saxonandparole.com; 316 Bowery, at Bleecker St; lunch $8-17, dinner mains $18-37; ⏱5-11pm Mon-Thu, noon-midnight Fri, 10:30am-midnight Sat, 10:30am-10pm Sun; 🚇6 to Bleecker St, B/D/F/M to Broadway-Lafayette St)

Public
MODERN AMERICAN **$$$**

13 🍴 Map p50, D4

What was once a muffin factory is now a svelte foodie hot spot, complete with sultry bar, industrial touches, and masterfully textured dishes deserving of their Michelin star. Global twists surprise and delight, whether it's kangaroo paired with coriander falafel and lemon tahini, or New Zealand venison loin matched with Cabrales cheese dumplings. (📞212-343-7011; www.public-nyc.com; 210 Elizabeth St, btwn Prince & Spring Sts; mains $21-34; ⏱6pm-late Mon-Fri, 10:30am-3:30pm & 6pm-late Sat & Sun; 🚇6 to Spring St, N/R to Prince St)

Understand

Tales of Two Neighborhoods

While the re-branding of New York City neighborhoods might be a favorite pastime of realtors and developers, some corners of Gotham have roots that burrow deep into the city's psyche. Chinatown and Little Italy are two such areas, their myriad tales an indelible part of New York City lore.

Five Points

Beneath the verdant appeal of Chinatown's Columbus Park lurks a dark and dirty history. In the 19th century, the site formed part of America's most wretched slum, Five Points. A diseased, unregulated jumble of slaughterhouses, tanneries, taverns and brothels, its ill-repute drew a steady stream of high-end New Yorkers on voyeuristic 'slumming tours'. Among the foreign visitors was English scribe Charles Dickens, who later mused: 'Debauchery has made the very houses prematurely old'.

From Bust to Boom

The history of Chinese immigrants in New York City is long and tumultuous. The first Chinese people to arrive in America worked on the Central Pacific Railroad, while others hit the west coast in search of gold. When prospects dried up, many moved to NYC to work in factory assembly lines and laundry houses. Escalating racism led to the Chinese Exclusion Act (1882–1943), which made naturalization an impossibility and largely squashed the opportunity for mainland Chinese to find work in the US. With the introduction of the fairer Immigration and Nationality Act of 1965, Chinese migration boomed, and today over 150,000 citizens fill the tenement-like structures orbiting Mott St.

Crooners & Mobsters

Unlike Chinatown, neighboring Little Italy has been steadily shrinking over the last 50 years. Despite the changes, history looms large: Mulberry Street Bar at 176½ Mulberry St was a favorite haunt of the late Frank Sinatra, and alcohol was openly traded on the corner of Mulberry and Kenmare Sts during Prohibition (leading to its nickname, the 'Curb Exchange'), while 247 Mulberry St was once a hangout for infamous mobsters Lucky Luciano and John Gotti.

Cannoli, Little Italy

Tacombi MEXICAN $

14 Map p50, D3

Festively strung lights, foldaway chairs and Mexican men flipping tacos in an old VW Kombie: if you can't make it to the Yucatan shore, here's your Plan B. Casual and convivial, Tacombi serves up fine, fresh tacos, including breakfast numbers like *huevos con chorizo* (eggs with chorizo). Wash down the goodness with a pitcher of sangria and start plotting that south-of-the-border getaway. (www.tacombi.com; 267 Elizabeth St, btwn E Houston & Prince Sts; tacos from $4; ⏰11am-late Mon-Fri, from 9am Sat & Sun; **S** B/D/F/M to Broadway-Lafayette St, 6 to Bleecker St)

Rubirosa PIZZERIA $$

15 Map p50, D4

Rubirosa's infallible family recipe for the perfect, whisper-thin pie crust lures a steady stream of patrons from every corner of the city. Shovel slices from the bar stools or grab a table amid cozy surrounds and make room for savory appetizers and antipasti. Gluten-free diners have their own dedicated menu. (✆212-965-0500; www.rubirosanyc.com; 235 Mulberry St, btwn Spring & Prince Sts; pizzas $16-26, mains $12-28; ⏰11:30am-late; **S** N/R to Prince St, B/D/F/M to Broadway-Lafayette St, 6 to Spring St)

Top Tip

Family-Style Dining

Chinatown has the best dining deals around and locals love to head downtown to satisfy their hankering for hole-in-the-wall fare. Experience the area's bustling dining dens with a handful friends by eating 'family style' (order a ton of dishes and sample spoonfuls of each). You'll be sure the waiter left a zero off the bill.

Joe's Shanghai
CHINESE $

16 Map p50, E8

Gather a gaggle of friends and descend upon this Flushing transplant en masse to spin the plastic lazy Susans and gobble down some of the juiciest *xiao long bao* (soup dumplings) in town. Dumplings aside, charge your chopsticks at budget-friendly thrills like spicy buffalo carp fish belly or jalapeno-sauteed pork and squid with dry bean curd. Cash only. (📞212-233-8888; www.joeshanghairestaurants.com; 9 Pell St btwn Bowery & Doyers St; mains $5-26; ⏰11am-11pm; 🚇N/Q/R, J/Z, 6 to Canal St, B/D to Grand St)

Café Gitane
MEDITERRANEAN $$

17 Map p50, D3

Clear the Gauloise smoke from your eyes and blink twice if you think you're in Paris: bistro-esque Gitane has that kind of louche vibe, *mon amour*. This is a classic see-and-be-seen haunt, popular with salad-picking models and the odd Hollywood regular. Join the beautiful and their *mignons* for a fashionable nibble on the likes of blueberry and almond friands or Moroccan couscous with organic chicken. (📞212-334-9552; www.cafegitanenyc.com; 242 Mott St, at Prince St; mains $14-16; ⏰8:30am-midnight Sun-Thu, to 12:30am Fri & Sat; 🚇N/R to Prince St, 6 to Spring St)

Nyonya
MALAYSIAN $$

18 Map p50, D6

Take your palate to steamy Melaka at this bustling, cash-only temple to Chinese-Malay *nyonya* cuisine. Savor the sweet, the sour, and the spicy in classics like pungent *kangkung belacan* (sautéed water spinach spiked with spicy Malaysian shrimp paste); rich beef randang, and refreshing *rojak* (savory fruit salad tossed in a piquant tamarind dressing). Vegetarians should go warned: there's not much on the menu for you. (📞212-334-3669; 199 Grand St, btwn Mott & Mulberry Sts; mains $7-24; ⏰11am-late; 🚇N/Q/R, J/Z, 6 to Canal Street, B/D to Grand St)

Original Chinatown Ice Cream Factory
ICE CREAM $

19 Map p50, E8

Chinatown's favorite ice-cream peddler keeps it local with flavors like green tea, ginger, durian and lychee sorbet. If you're feeling reckless, try the zen butter (creamy peanut butter ice cream laced with toasted sesame seeds). The Factory also sells ridiculously cute trademark T-shirts with an ice cream-slurping happy dragon on them. (☎212-608-4170; www.chinatownicecreamfactory.com; 65 Bayard St; scoop $4; ⊙11am-10pm; ; Ⓢ N/Q/R, J/Z, 6 to Canal St)

Drinking

Pegu Club COCKTAIL BAR

20 Map p50, B3

Elegant Pegu Club (named after a legendary gentleman's club in colonial-era Rangoon) is an obligatory stop for cocktail connoisseurs. Sink into a velvet lounge and savor seamless libations from award-winning bartender Kenta Goto – we especially love the silky smooth Earl Grey MarTEAni (tea-infused gin, lemon juice and raw egg white). Grazing options are suitably Asian-esque. (www.peguclub.com; 77 W Houston St, btwn W Broadway & Wooster St; ⊙5pm-2am Sun-Wed, to 4am Thu-Sat; Ⓢ B/D/F/M to Broadway-Lafayette St, C/E to Spring St)

Madam Geneva COCKTAIL BAR

21 Map p50, D2

Hanging lanterns, leather couches and flouncy wallpaper echo colonial Nanyang at this dark and sultry cocktail den. Gin-based cocktails dominate, meticulously crafted and suitably paired with Asian-inspired bites like duck steamed buns, prawn dumplings and chicken wings with tamarind. Next door lies hotspot sibling restaurant Saxon + Parole (p55). (www.madamgeneva-nyc.com; 4 Bleecker St,

at Bowery; ⊙6pm-2am; Ⓢ6 to Bleecker St, B/D/F/M to Broadway-Lafayette St)

Mulberry Project COCKTAIL BAR

22 Map p50, D6

Lurking behind an unmarked door is this intimate, cavernous cocktail den, its festive, 'garden-party' backyard one of the best spots to chill in the 'hood. Made-to-order cocktails are the specialty, so disclose your preferences and let the barkeep do the rest. If you're peckish, choose from a competent list of bites that might include watermelon salad with goat's cheese or bacon-wrapped dates. (☎646-448-4536; www.mulberryproject.com; 149 Mulberry St, btwn Hester & Grand Sts; ⊙6pm-1am Sun-Thu, to 4am Fri & Sat; Ⓢ N/Q/R, J/Z, 6 to Canal St)

Spring Lounge DIVE BAR

23 Map p50, D4

This neon-red rebel has never let anything get in the way of a good time. In Prohibition days, it peddled buckets of beer. In the '60s its basement was a gambling den. These days, it's best known for its kooky stuffed sharks, early-start regulars, and come-one-come-all late-night revelry.

Fuelling the fun are cheap drinks and free grub (hot dogs on Wednesdays from 5pm, bagels on Sundays from noon, while they last). Bottoms up, baby! (www.thespringlounge.com; 48 Spring St, at Mulberry St; ⊙8am-4am Mon-Sat, from noon Sun; Ⓢ6 to Spring St, N/R to Prince St)

La Colombe

CAFE

24 Map p50, C3

Spent SoHo shoppers reboot at this pocket-sized espresso bar. The brews are strong, full-bodied and worthy of any bar in Italy (note the cool Rome wall mural). If you're feeling nibbly, a small selection of edibles includes cookies and croissants. (www.lacolombe. com; 270 Lafayette St, btwn Prince & Jersey Sts; ⊙7:30am-6:30pm Mon-Fri, from 8:30am Sat & Sun; ⑤N/R to Prince St, 6 to Spring St)

Shopping

MoMA Design Store

HOMEWARES, GIFTS

25 🔒 Map p50, C4

The Museum of Modern Art's downtown retail space carries a huge collection of sleek, smart and clever objects for the home, office and wardrobe. You'll find modernist alarm clocks,

✓ Top Tip

Fashion Insiders

Serious shopaholics should consult the city's in-the-know websites, fashion bloggers and Twitterlebrities before hitting the streets of SoHo and beyond. Among the best are **Racked** (www. ny.racked.com), **Bill Cunningham** (www.nytimes.com/video/on-the-street), **Andre Leon Talley** (twitter.com/OfficialAL), and **Women's Wear Daily** (twitter.com/womensweardaily).

wildly shaped vases, designer kitchenware and surreal lamps, plus brainy games, hand puppets, fanciful scarves, coffee-table books and lots of other great gift ideas. (☑646-613-1367; www. momastore.org; 81 Spring St, at Crosby St; ⊙10am-8pm Mon-Sat, 11am-7pm Sun; ⑤N/R to Prince St, 6 to Spring St)

Rag & Bone

FASHION

26 🔒 Map p50, B4

Downtown label Rag & Bone is a hit with many of New York's coolest, sharpest dressers, both men and women. Detail-orientated pieces range from clean-cut shirts and blazers, to graphic tees, feather-light strappy dresses, leathergoods and Rag & Bone's highly prized jeans. (www.rag-bone.com; 119 Mercer St, btwn Prince & Spring Sts; ⊙11am-8pm Mon-Sat, noon-7pm Sat; ⑤N/R to Prince St)

Saturdays

FASHION, ACCESSORIES

27 🔒 Map p50, C5

SoHo's version of a surf shop sees boards, wax and wetsuits paired up with designer grooming products, graphic art and surf tomes, and Saturdays' own line of high-quality, fashion-literate threads for dudes. Styled-up, grab a coffee from the in-house espresso bar, hang in the back garden and fish for some crazy, shark-dodging tales. There's a second branch in the West Village, see the website for details. (www.saturdaysnyc.com; 31 Crosby St, btwn Broome & Grand Sts; ⊙8:30am-7pm Mon-Fri, from 10am Sat & Sun; ⑤N/Q/R, J/Z, 6 to Canal St)

ANGUS OSBORN/GETTY IMAGES ©

Chinatown

Kiosk

GIFTS

28 🔒 Map p50, C4

Kiosk's owners scour the planet for the most interesting and unusual items (from books and lampshades, to toothpaste), which they bring back to SoHo and proudly vend with museum-worthy acumen. Shopping adventures have brought back designer curiosities from the likes of Japan, Iceland, Sweden and Hong Kong. (📞212-226-8601; www.kioskkiosk.com; 2nd fl, 95 Spring St, btwn Mercer St & Broadway; ⏰noon-7pm Mon-Sat; Ⓢ N/R to Prince St, B/D/F/M to Broadway-Lafayette St)

Adidas Originals

SHOES, FASHION

29 🔒 Map p50, B3

Iconic triple-striped sneakers, many referencing Adidas' halycon days from the '60s to the '80s, is what you get here. You can even custom-design your own. Kicks aside, pimp your look with hoodies, track wear, T-shirts and accessories including eyewear, watches and retro-funky bags. DJs occasionally work the decks. (📞212-673-0398; 136 Wooster St, btwn Prince & W Houston Sts; ⏰11am-7pm Mon-Sat, noon-6pm Sun; Ⓢ N/R to Prince St)

Local Life

Bunya Citispa

Ex-models and fatigued shoppers retreat to chic, Asian-inspired **Bunya Citispa** (Map p50, A3; 📞212-388-1288; www.bunyacitispa.com; 474 W Broadway, btwn Prince & W Houston Sts; ⏱10am-10pm Mon-Sat, to 9pm Sun; 🚇N/R to Prince St; C/E to Spring St) for a little Eastern pampering. Tension-soothing solutions include reflexology, head massage with green tea hair treatment, hot stone massage, and the popular 'Oriental herbal compress' Thai massage.

Opening Ceremony
FASHION

30 🔒 Map p50, C6

Opening Ceremony is famed for its never-boring edit of indie labels. The place showcases a changing roster of names from across the globe, complimented by Opening Ceremony's own creations. No matter who is hanging on the racks, you can always expect show-stopping, 'where-did-you-get-that?!' threads that are street-smart, bold and refreshingly avant-garde. (📞212-219-2688; www.openingceremony. us; 35 Howard St, btwn Broadway & Lafayette St; ⏱11am-8pm Mon-Sat, noon-7pm Sun; 🚇N/Q/R, J/Z, 6 to Canal St)

Screaming Mimi's
VINTAGE

31 🔒 Map p50, C1

If you dig vintage threads, you may just scream too. This funtastic shop carries an excellent selection of yesteryear pieces – organized, ingeniously, by decade, from the '50s to the '90s (ask to see the small, stashed-away collection of clothing from the '20s, '30s and '40s). A selection of accessories and jewelry completes any back-to-the-future look. (📞212-677-6464; 382 Lafayette St, btwn E 4th & Great Jones Sts; ⏱noon-8pm Mon-Sat, 1-7pm Sun; 🚇6 to Bleecker St, B/D/F/M to Broadway-Lafayette St)

Piperlime
FASHION, SHOES

32 🔒 Map p50, B4

Piperlime peddles cool, contemporary womenswear at midrange prices. Known for giving newer designers exposure, the store's stock is organized by categories such as 'Shortcut to Chic', 'Girl on a Budget' and 'Guest Editor's Picks', the latter handpicked by the likes of stylist Rachel Zoe and actor/model Jessica Alba. Oh, and did we mention the fab range of shoes? (www.piperlime.com; 121 Wooster St, btwn Prince & Spring Sts; ⏱10am-8pm Mon-Sat, 11am-7pm Sun; 🚇N/R to Prince St, C/E to Spring St)

INA Men
VINTAGE

33 🔒 Map p50, D3

Male style-meisters love INA for pre-loved, luxury clothes, shoes and accessories. Edits are high quality across the board, with sought-after items including the likes of Rag & Bone jeans, Alexander McQueen wool pants, Burberry shirts and Church's brogues.

Next-door is the women's store. There are other branches in NoHo and Chelsea – check the website for details (www.inanyc.com; 19 Prince St, at Elizabeth St; ⊙noon-8pm Mon-Sat, to 7pm Sun; ⑤6 to Spring St, N/R to Prince St)

Scoop   FASHION
34 🔒 Map p50, C5

Scoop up contemporary threads from the likes of Theory, Diane Von Furstenberg, Michael Kors and J Brand at this handy one-stop shop. While there's nothing particularly edgy about the selections, there's a lot on offer (over 100 designers covering both men's and women's), and you can often score good deals at season-end sales. Scoop has several stores in the city. (☎212-925-3539; www.scoopnyc.com; 473 Broadway, btwn Broome & Grand Sts; ⊙11am-8pm Mon-Sat, to 7pm Sun; ⑤N/Q/R to Canal St, 6 to Spring St)

Joe's Jeans   FASHION
35 🔒 Map p50, B5

Sex-up your pins with a pair of jeans from this cult LA label. Options include vintage reserve denim, as well as skinny jeans designed to flatter more forms than just 'Amazonian supermodel'. Mix and match with super comfy shirts, hoodies, sweaters and the odd to-die-for leather jacket.

(☎212-925-5727; www.joesjeans.com; 77 Mercer St, btwn Spring & Broome Sts; ⊙11am-7pm Mon-Sat, noon-6pm Sun; ⑤N/R to Prince St, 6 to Spring St)

Resurrection   VINTAGE
36 🔒 Map p50, D4

Boudoir-red Resurrection gives new life to cutting-edge designs from past decades. Striking, mint-condition pieces cover the eras of mod, glam-rock and new-wave design, and design deities like Marc Jacobs have dropped by for inspiration. Top picks include Halston dresses and Cour-règes coats and jackets. (☎212-625-1374; www.resurrectionvintage.com; 217 Mott St, btwn Prince & Spring Sts; ⊙11am-7pm Mon-Sat, noon-7pm Sun; ⑤6 to Spring St; N/R to Prince St)

American Apparel   FASHION
37 🔒 Map p50, B4

Pick up good-quality, American-made basics produced with a conscience: no sweatshop labor goes into the making of these threads. Stock up on sweats, hoodies, shirts, underwear, swimwear and other everyday staples in a delicious range of colors. (☎212-226-4880; www.americanapparel.net; 121 Spring St at Greene St; ⊙10am-10pm Mon-Sat, to 9pm Sun; ⑤N/R to Prince Street)

Explore

East Village & Lower East Side

If you've been dreaming of those quintessential New York City moments – graffiti on crimson brick, skyscrapers rising overhead, punks and grannies walking side by side, and cute cafes with rickety tables spilling out onto the sidewalks – then the East Village and the Lower East Side are your Holy Grail.

The Sights in a Day

☼ Have a wander around the Lower East Side as its youngsters are stumbling home from a raucous night out on town. Stop at the **Lower East Side Tenement Museum** (p69) to learn about the area's immigrant past. Then warp time with a trip into the future at the **New Museum** (p68) to check out the latest iterations of mind-bending modern art.

☼ Tackle a tagine at East Village favorite **Cafe Mogador** (p73) then slurp down a cappuccino at **Abraço** (p76). If you're still feeling peckish, wander down **St Marks Place** (p68) with a dessert from **ChiKaLicious Dessert Club** (p75), stopping for punk rock wares (and wears) at **Trash & Vaudeville** (p83). Burn off the calories with a Frisbee toss in **Tompkins Square Park** (p69) during warmer weather.

☾ Capitalize on the area's cheap-eats vibe for dinner with a slurp-worthy bowl of noodles at **Ippudo NY** (p74) or **Minca** (p75), or reserve a table at foodie-lauded **Hearth** (p71). Either way, continue with a drink at old-school **McSorley's Old Ale House** (p78) before hitting southern belle **Wayland** (p76), retro **Golden Cadillac** (p76), or cheeky classic **Eastern Bloc** (p78).

♥ Best of New York City

Eating

Hearth (p71)

Freemans (p71)

Tacos Morelos (p72)

Drinking

Death + Co (p76)

Angel's Share (p76)

Golden Cadillac (p76)

Shopping

Obscura Antiques (p81)

Museums

Lower East Side Tenement Museum (p69)

Getting There

S Subway Trains don't reach most East Village locations, but it's a quick walk from the 6 at Astor Pl or the L at First Ave. The F line will let you off in the thick of the Lower East Side.

🚌 Bus If you're traveling from the west side, take the M14 as it will take you further into the East Village.

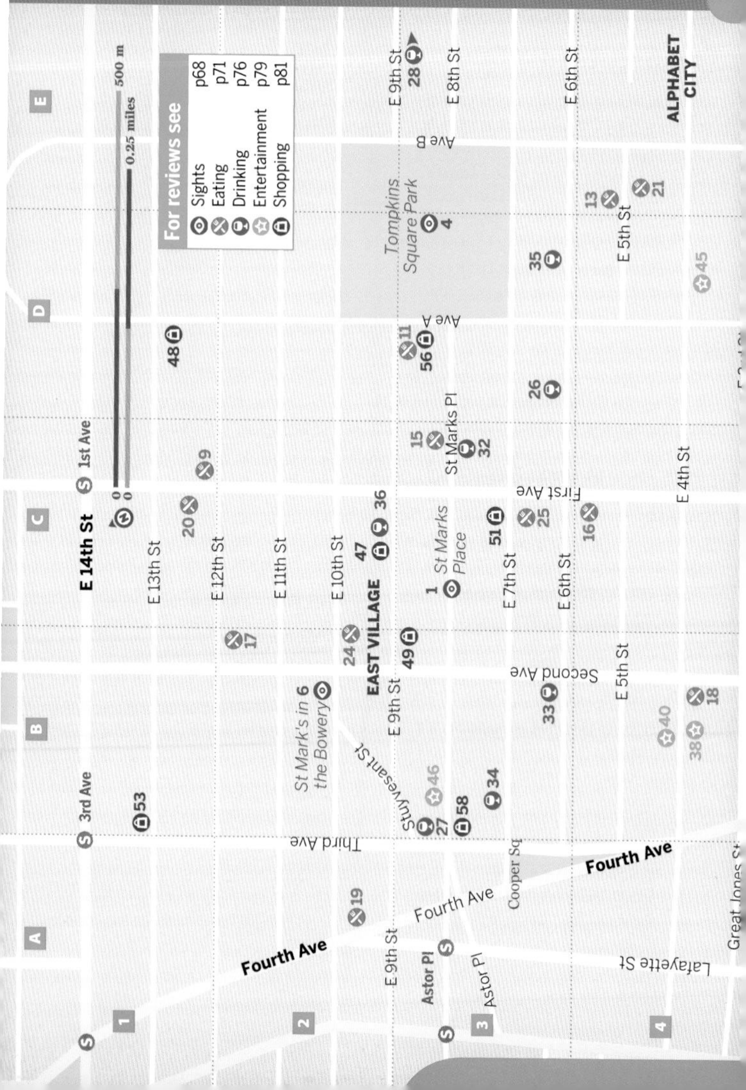

ALPHABET CITY

Tompkins Square Park 4

For reviews see

◎	Sights	p68
✕	Eating	p71
◍	Drinking	p76
◑	Entertainment	p79
◙	Shopping	p81

EAST VILLAGE

St Marks Place 1

St Mark's in the Bowery 6

0.25 miles

500 m

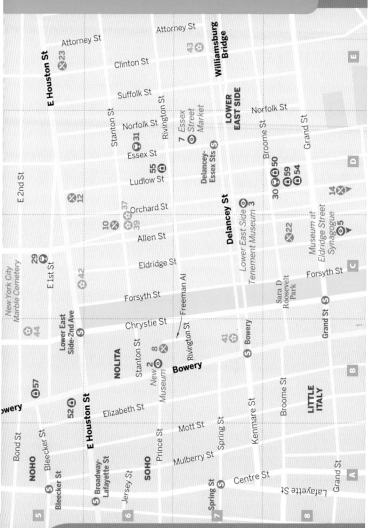

Sights

St Marks Place

STREET

1 (◉) Map p66, C3

One of the most magical things about New York is that every street tells a story, from the action unfurling before your eyes to the history hidden behind colorful facades. St Marks Pl is one of the best strips of pavement in the city for story telling, as almost every building on these blocks is rife with tales from a time when the East Village embodied a far more lawless spirit.

In April 1966, Andy Warhol rented the building at number 19 to 25, refurbishing the interiors and using it for a month-long party he perplexingly dubbed the Exploding Plastic Inevitable. (St Marks Pl, Ave A to Third Ave; ⓢ N/R/W to 8th St-NYU, 6 to Astor Pl)

New Museum

MUSEUM

2 (◉) Map p66, B6

Any modern-day museum worth its salt has to have a structure that makes as much of a statement as the artwork inside. The New Museum's Lower East Side avatar accomplishes just that and more with its inspired design by noted Japanese architecture firm SANAA. The museum's mission statement is simple: 'New art, new ideas', and as the city's sole museum dedicated to contemporary art, it has brought a steady menu of edgy works in new forms.

On the first Saturday of the month, the New Museum hosts special events for budding artists, with hands-on crafts and activities for kids aged 4 to 15. Free museum admission is included for adults (it's always free for kids).

Understand
SANAA's Vision

While exhibits rotate through the New Museum, regularly changing the character of the space within, the shell – an inspired architectural gesture – remains a constant. It acts as a unique structural element in the diverse cityscape, while still fading into the background when necessary to allow the exhibits to shine.

The building's structure is the brainchild of the hot Japanese firm SANAA – a partnership between two great minds, Sejima Kazuyo and Nishizawa Ryue. In 2010, SANAA won the much-coveted Pritzker Prize for its contributions to the world of design (think the Oscars of architecture). Its trademark vanishing facades are known worldwide for abiding by a strict adherence to a form-follows-function design aesthetic, sometimes taking the land plot's footprint into the overall shape of the structure. The box-atop-box scheme provides a striking counterpoint to the clusters of crimson brick and iron fire escapes outside, while alluding to the geometric exhibition chasms within.

Tompkins Square Park

(☎212-219-1222; www.newmuseum.org; 235 Bowery, btwn Stanton & Rivington Sts; adult/ child $16/free, 7-9pm Thu free; ⊙11am-6pm Wed & Fri-Sun, to 9pm Thu; Ⓢ N/R to Prince St, F to 2nd Ave, J/Z to Bowery, 6 to Spring St)

Lower East Side Tenement Museum
MUSEUM

3 ◉ Map p66, D7

No other museum humanizes NYC's colorful past quite like the Lower East Side Tenement Museum, which puts the neighborhood's heartbreaking but inspiring heritage on full display in several recreations of turn-of-the-20th-century tenements, including the 1870s home of the German-Jewish Gumpertz family, and the dwelling of the Italian-Catholic Baldizzi family

who lived through the Great Depression of 1929. The museum runs a variety of tours beyond the museum's walls, and several evenings a month it also hosts talks, often relating to the present immigrant experience in America. (☎212-982-8420; www.tenement. org; 103 Orchard St, btwn Broome & Delancey Sts; admission $22; ⊙10am-6pm; Ⓢ B/D to Grand St, J/M/Z to Essex St, F to Delancey St)

Tompkins Square Park
PARK

4 ◉ Map p66, D3

The 10.5-acre Tompkins Square Park honors Daniel Tompkins, who served as governor of New York from 1807 to 1817 (and as the nation's vice president after that, under James Monroe). It's like a friendly town square for locals,

Local Life
St Marks Addresses

St Marks Place (p68) is jam-packed with historical tidbits that would delight any trivia buff. A cast of colorful characters has left its mark at 4 St Marks Pl. Alexander Hamilton's son built the structure, James Fenimore Cooper lived here in the 1830s and Yoko Ono's Fluxus artists descended upon the building in the 1960s. And don't miss the buildings at 96 and 98 St Marks Pl, which are immortalized on the cover of Led Zeppelin's *Physical Graffiti* album.

who gather for chess at concrete tables, picnics on the lawn on warm days and spontaneous guitar or drum jams on various grassy knolls. The annual Howl! Festival of East Village Arts brings Allen Ginsberg–inspired theater, music, film, dance and spoken-word events to the park and various neighborhood venues each September. (www.nycgovparks.org; E 7th & 10th Sts, btwn Aves A & B; ⊙6am-midnight; S 6 to Astor Pl)

Museum at Eldridge Street Synagogue   MUSEUM

5 ⊙ Map p66, C8

This landmarked house of worship, built in 1887, was once the center of Jewish life, before falling into squalor in the 1920s. Left to rot, it's only recently been reclaimed, and now shines with original splendor. The onsite

museum gives tours every half hour (included in the admission price), with the last one departing at 4pm. (☏212-219-0302; www.eldridgestreet.org; 12 Eldridge St, btwn Canal & Division Sts; adult/child $10/6; ⊙10am-5pm Sun-Thu, to 3pm Fri; S F to East Broadway)

St Mark's in the Bowery   CHURCH

6 ⊙ Map p66, B2

Though it's most popular with East Village locals for its cultural offerings – such as poetry readings hosted by the Poetry Project or cutting-edge dance performances by Danspace and the Ontological Hysteric Theater – this is also a historic site. This Episcopal church stands on the site of the farm, or *bouwerie,* owned by Dutch Governor Peter Stuyvesant, whose crypt lies under the grounds. (☏212-674-6377; www.stmarksbowery.org; 131 E 10th St, at Second Ave; ⊙10am-6pm Mon-Fri; S L to 3rd Ave, 6 to Astor Pl)

Essex Street Market   MARKET

7 ⊙ Map p66, D7

Founded in 1940, this market is the local place for produce, seafood, butcher-cut meats, cheeses, Latino grocery items, and even a barber's shop. Stop in Rainbo's for smoked fish or Saxelby Cheesemongers for artisanal cheese, smoked sausages and housemade pate. Pain d'Avignon bakes fresh breads, Boubouki whips up spinach pies and baklava, while Roni-Sue's Chocolates spreads sweet temptations. You can also nosh on site

Eldridge Street Synagogue

at Shopsin's General Store, Brooklyn Taco Company and Davidovich Bakery. (📞212-312-3603; www.essexstreetmarket.com; 120 Essex St, btwn Delancey & Rivington Sts; ⊗8am-7pm Mon-Sat; ⑤F to Delancey St, J/M/Z to Essex St)

ing hunting-cabin vibe – a charming escape from the bustle (when there isn't a crowd inside). (📞212-420-0012; www.freemansrestaurant.com; end of Freeman Alley; mains lunch $12-19, dinner $22-32; ⊗11am-11:30pm Mon-Fri, from 10am Sat & Sun; ⑤F to 2nd Ave)

Eating

Freemans   AMERICAN $$$

8 🍴 Map p66, B6

Tucked down a back alley, the charmingly located Freeman's draws a mostly hipster crowd who let their chunky jewelry clang on the wooden tables as they lean over to sip overflowing cocktails. Potted plants and taxidermic antlers lend an endear-

Hearth   ITALIAN $$$

9 🍴 Map p66, C1

A staple for finicky, deep-pocketed diners, Hearth has coziness down pat with its warm, brick-walled interior. Swill a soul-coaxing red and ponder the seasonal menu; an Italo-centric affair which might see roasted sturgeon paired with lentils and bacon, or rabbit papardelle with fava beans. (📞646-602-1300; www.restauranthearth.com;

403 E 12th St, at First Ave; mains $21-48; ⊘6-10pm Sun-Thu, to 11pm Fri, 11am-2pm & 6-11pm Sat, 11am-2pm Sun; ⑤L to 1st Ave; L, N/Q/R, 4/5/6 to 14th St-Union Sq)

Meatball Shop   ITALIAN $

10 Map p66, C6

Elevating the humble meatball to high art, the Meatball Shop serves up five varieties of juiciness (including a vegetable option). Order those balls on a hero, add mozzarella and spicy tomato sauce, and *voila,* you have a tasty, if happily downmarket, meal. The LES branch boasts a rock-and-roll vibe, with tattooed waitstaff and prominent beats. There are four other branches in NYC. (☎212-982-8895; www.themeatballshop.com; 84 Stanton St, btwn Allen & Orchard Sts; mains from $10; ⊘noon-2am Sun-Thu, to 4am Thu-Sat; ⑤2nd Ave; F to Delancey St; J/M/Z to Essex St)

Tacos Morelos   MEXICAN $

11 Map p66, D3

This famed food truck put down roots in a no-frills East Village storefront in 2013, quickly becoming one of Manhattan's favorite taco joints. Order them with chicken, steak, roast pork, beef tongue or vegetarian. Tip: pay the 50¢ extra for the homemade tortilla. (438 E 9th St, btwn First Ave & Ave A; tacos

PETER PTSCHELINZEW/GETTY IMAGES ©

Katz's Delicatessen

from $2.50; ⊙noon-midnight Sun-Thu, to 2am Fri & Sat; **S** L to 1st Ave)

Katz's Delicatessen   DELI $$

12 🍴   Map p66, D5

Though visitors won't find many remnants of the classic, old-world-Jewish Lower East Side dining scene, there are a few stellar holdouts, among them the famous Katz's Delicatessen, where Meg Ryan faked her infamous orgasm in the 1989 Hollywood flick *When Harry Met Sally,* and where, if you love classic deli grub like pastrami and salami on rye, it just might have the same effect on you. (📞212-254-2246; www. katzsdelicatessen.com; 205 E Houston St, at Ludlow St; pastrami on rye $17; ⊙8am-10:45pm Mon-Wed & Sun, to 2:45am Thu-Sat; **S** F to 2nd Ave)

Lavagna   ITALIAN $$

13 🍴   Map p66, E4

Flickering candles and the fiery glow from a somewhat open kitchen help make snug Lavagna a late-night hideaway for lovers. In love or not, prepare to fall for the food, from al dente pastas and thin-crust pizza to hearty, coaxing mains like tender baby rack of lamb. (📞212-979-1005; www.lavagnanyc. com; 545 E 5th St, btwn Aves A & B; mains $19-35; ⊙6-11pm Mon-Thu, to midnight Fri-Sun; 📷 🚻; **S** F to 2nd Ave)

Fat Radish   MODERN BRITISH $$$

14 🍴   Map p66, D8

The young and fashionable pack in to this dimly lit dining room with exposed white brick and industrial touches. There's a loud buzz and people checking each other out, but the mains, typical of the local-seasonal-haute pub fare fad, are worth your attention. Start off with big briny oysters before moving on to beetroot and Swiss chard crumble or Atlantic skate with honey crisp apples. Good vegetarian options. (17 Orchard St, btwn Hester & Canal Sts; mains $18-28; ⊙noon-3:30pm daily, 5:30pm-midnight Mon-Sat, to 10pm Sun; 📷; **S** F to East Broadway, B/D to Grand St)

Cafe Mogador   MOROCCAN, MIDDLE EASTERN $$

15 🍴   Map p66, C3

Family-run Mogador is a long-running NYC classic, serving fluffy piles of couscous, char-grilled lamb and merguez sausage over basmati rice and satisfying mixed platters of hummus and babaganoush. The standouts, however, are the tagines. A garrulous young crowd packs the space, spilling out onto the small cafe tables on warm days. Brunch (served weekends 9am to 4pm) is excellent. (📞212-677-2226; 101 St Marks Pl; mains lunch $8-14, dinner $17-21; ⊙9am-1am Sun-Thu, to 2am Fri & Sat; **S** 6 to Astor Pl)

Upstate
SEAFOOD **$$**

16 Map p66, C4

Small and often overlooked, Upstate nevertheless serves outstanding, market-fresh seafood dishes and craft beers. Celebrate all things surf with the likes of beer-steamed mussels, soul-coaxing seafood stew, sweet soft-shell crab and plump, silky oysters. (www.upstatenyc.com; 95 First Ave, btwn 5th & 6th Sts; mains $15-30; ☺5-11pm; **S** F to 2nd Ave)

Angelica Kitchen
VEGAN, CAFE **$$**

17 Map p66, B2

This enduring herbivore classic has a calming vibe – candles, tables both intimate and communal, and a mellow, longtime staff – and enough creative options to make your head spin. Some dishes get too-cute names (Goodnight Mushroom, Thai Mee Up), but all do wonders with tofu, seitan, spices and soy products, and sometimes an

Top Tip

Snagging Tables

A lot of the restaurants in this neck of the woods don't take reservations, so stop by the restaurant of your choosing in the early afternoon (2pm should do the trick) and place your name on the roster for the evening meal – chances are high that they'll take your name and you'll get seated right away when you return for dinner later on.

array of raw ingredients. (☎212-228-2909; www.angelicakitchen.com; 300 E 12th St, btwn First & Second Aves; dishes $11-19; ☺11:30am-10:30pm; ☑; **S** L to 1st Ave)

Calliope
FRENCH **$$**

18 Map p66, B4

This rustic-chic charmer serves French farmhouse comfort fare – though given a modern twist. The menu is small, and the dishes are surprisingly well executed: spicy mackerel with avocado and black sesame, beef tongue with pickled onions, delicate rabbit pappardelle, and a marvelously tender *tête du porc* (pig's head). Less adventurous eaters can opt for crispy roast chicken, Newport steak and mussels. (84 E 4th St, at Second Ave; mains lunch $12-17, dinner $26-39; ☺5-11pm Mon, 11am-2:30pm & 5-11pm Tue-Sat, 10:30am-3pm & 5-10pm Sun; **S** F to 2nd Ave)

Ippudo NY
NOODLES **$$**

19 Map p66, A2

In New York, the good folks from Ippudo have kicked things up a notch – they've taken their mouthwatering ramen recipe (truly, it's delish) and spiced it up with sleek surrounds (hello shiny black surfaces and streamers of cherry red) and blasts of rock-and-roll on the overhead speakers. (☎212-388-0088; www.ippudo.com/ny; 65 Fourth Ave, btwn 9th & 10th Sts; ramen $15-16; ☺Mon-Sat 11am-3:30pm, Mon-Thu 5pm-11:30pm, Fri & Sat 5pm-12:30am, Sun 11am-10:30pm; **S** N/R to 8th St-NYU, 4/5/6 to 14th St-Union Sq, 6 to Astor Pl)

Luzzo's

PIZZERIA $$

20 🍴 Map p66, C1

Fan favorite Luzzo's occupies a thin sliver of real estate in the East Village, which gets stuffed to the gills each evening as discerning diners feast on thin-crust pies, kissed with ripe tomatoes and cooked in a coal-fired stove. (📞212-473-7447; 211-213 First Ave, btwn 12th & 13th Sts; pizzas from $20; ⏲noon-11pm Tue-Sun, 5-11pm Mon; Ⓢ1st Ave)

Minca

NOODLES $

21 🍴 Map p66, E4

The epitome of an East Village hole-in-the-wall, Minca focuses all of its attention on the food: cauldronesque bowls of steaming ramen served with a recommended side order of fried gyoza. (📞212-505-8001; www.newyorkramen.com; 536 E 5th St btwn Aves A & B; ramen $11-14; ⏲noon-11:30pm; ⓈF to Second Ave, J/M/Z to Essex St, F to Delancey St)

Vanessa's Dumpling House

CHINESE $

22 🍴 Map p66, C8

Tasty dumplings – served steamed, fried or in soup (our favorite) – are whipped together in iron skillets at lightning speed and tossed into hungry mouths at unbeatable prices. (📞212-625-8008; 118 Eldridge St, btwn Grand & Broome Sts; dumplings $1-6; ⏲7:30am-10:30pm; ⓈB/D to Grand St, J to Bowery, F to Delancey St)

Clinton Street Baking Company

AMERICAN $

23 🍴 Map p66, E5

Mom-and-pop shop extraordinaire, Clinton Street Baking Company gets the blue-ribbon in so many categories – best pancakes (blueberry!), best muffins, best po'boys, best biscuits – that you're pretty much guaranteed a stellar meal no matter which time of day (or night) you stop by. Half-priced bottles of wine sweeten the deal on Mondays and Tuesdays. (📞646-602-6263; www.clintonstreetbaking.com; 4 Clinton St, btwn Stanton & Houston Sts; mains from $9-17; ⏲8am-4pm & 6-11pm Mon-Sat, 9am-6pm Sun; ⓈJ/M/Z to Essex St, F to Delancey St, F to Second Ave)

ChiKaLicious Dessert Club

DESSERT $

24 🍴 Map p66, B2

An ice cream served atop an éclair instead of a cone? We're in! Ever-popular ChiKaLicious takes traditional sweet-tooth standards and transforms them into inspired calorie concoctions. There's a second location across the street. (📞212-995-9511; www.chikalicious.com; 204 E 10th St, btwn First & Second Aves; desserts from $4; ⏲7am-midnight; ⓈL to 1st Ave, 6 to Astor Pl)

Abraço   CAFE $

25 🍴 Map p66, C3

With hardly room to move – let alone sit – Abraço is an East Village refuge where good coffee and good taste combine to form one of the finest cafes in the entire city. Slurp your perfectly crafted espresso while inhaling a slice of delicious olive cake. If you're stopping by with a friend you'll each need to order a slice – fights are known to break out over the last bite. (www.abraconyc.com; 86 E 7th St, btwn First & Second Aves; snacks $2-3; ⊙Tue-Sat 8am-4pm, Sun 9am-4pm; ⑤F to 2nd Ave, L to 1st Ave, 6 to Astor Pl)

Drinking

Death + Co   LOUNGE

26 🍺 Map p66, D3

'Death & Co' is scrawled in ornate cursive on the ground at Death's door, so to speak – the only hint that you're in the right place to try some of the most perfectly concocted cocktails in town. Relax amid dim lighting and thick wooden slatting, and let the bartenders – with their PhDs in mixology – work their magic as they shake, rattle and roll your blended poison of choice. (☎212-388-0882; www.deathandcompany.com; 433 E 6th St, btwn First Ave & Ave A; ⊙6pm-1am Mon-Thu & Sun, to 2am Fri & Sat; ⑤F to 2nd Ave, L to 1st Ave, 6 Astor Pl)

Angel's Share   BAR

27 🍺 Map p66, B3

Show up early and snag a seat at this gem, hidden behind a Japanese restaurant on the same floor. It's quiet and elegant with creative cocktails, but you can't stay if you don't have a table or a seat at the bar, and they tend to go fast. (☎212-777-5415; 2nd fl, 8 Stuyvesant St, near Third Ave & E 9th St; ⊙5pm-midnight; ⑤6 to Astor Pl)

Wayland   BAR

28 🍺 Map p66, E3

Whitewashed walls, weathered floorboards and salvaged lamps give this urban outpost a Mississippi flair, which goes just right with the live music on weekdays (bluegrass, jazz, folk). The drinks, though, are the real draw – in particular the 'I hear banjos', made of Apple pie moonshine, rye whiskey and applewood smoke, which tastes like a campfire (but slightly less burning). Decent drink specials and $1 oysters from 5pm to 7pm on weekdays. (700 E 9th St, cnr Ave C; ⊙5pm-4am; ⑤L to 1st Ave)

Golden Cadillac   BAR

29 🍺 Map p66, C5

This enticing new drinking spot pays homage to grittier, hard-drinking days of the 1970s, with glorious wood paneling, patterned wallpaper and groove-heavy '70s tunes playing overhead – plus 1970s Playboy covers in the bathroom. The tasty, tropical-themed cocktails (around $14 a pop) go down easy – try the Mezcal Mule (mezcal, passion fruit, ginger and cucumber). Vintage pub grub with a twist completes the retro tripping. (13 First Ave, cnr 1st St; ⊙5pm-2am Sun-Wed, to 4am Thu-Sat; **S**2nd Ave)

Ten Bells   TAPAS BAR

30 Map p66, D8

This tucked-away tapas bar has a grotto-like design, with flickering candles, dark tin ceilings, brick walls and a U-shaped bar that's an ideal setting for conversation with a new friend. The chalkboard menu hangs on both walls and features excellent wines by the glass, which go nicely with *boquerones* (marinated anchovies), *txipirones en su tinta* (squid in ink sauce), regional cheeses and refreshing oysters (just $1.25 before 7pm). (☎212-228-4450; 247 Broome St, btwn Ludlow & Orchard Sts; ⊙5pm-2am Mon-Fri, from 3pm Sat & Sun; **S**F to Delancey St, J/M/Z to Essex St)

Beauty & Essex   BAR

31 Map p66, D6

This newcomer's glamour is concealed behind a tawdry pawnshop front. Beyond lies 10,000-sq-ft of sleek lounge space, complete with leather sofas and banquettes, dramatic amber-tinged lighting and a curved staircase that leads to yet another lounge and bar area.

Ladies in need of a drink might want to bypass the bar and pay a visit

St Mark's Place (p68)

GARDEL BERTRAND/GETTY IMAGES ©

to the powder room, where there's complimentary champagne (sorry, fellas). (212-614-0146; www.beautyandessex. com; 146 Essex St, btwn Stanton & Rivington Sts; ⏱5pm-1am; **S**F to Delancey St, J/M/Z to Essex St)

Proletariat   BAR

32 ⊖ Map p66, C3

The cognoscenti of NYC's beer world pack this tiny, ten-stool bar just west of Tompkins Square Park. Promising 'rare, new and unusual beers', Proletariat delivers the goods with a changing line-up of brews you won't find elsewhere. Recent hits have included drafts from artisanal brewers like Hitachino Nest of Japan, Swiss-based BFM and Mahr's Bräu from Germany. (102 St Marks Pl, btwn First Ave & Ave A; ⏱5pm-2am; **S**L to 1st Ave)

Mayahuel   COCKTAIL BAR

33 ⊖ Map p66, B3

About as far from your typical Spring Break tequila bar as you can get – more like the cellar of a monastery. Devotees of the fermented agave can seriously indulge themselves experimenting with dozens of varieties (all cocktails $14); in between drinks, snack on *quesadillas* and *tamales*. (212-253-5888; 304 E 6th St, at Second Ave; ⏱6pm-2am; **S**L to 3rd Ave, L to 1st Ave, 6 to Astor Pl)

McSorley's Old Ale House   BAR

34 ⊖ Map p66, B3

Around since 1854, McSorley's feels far removed from the East Village veneer of cool: you're more likely to drink with firemen, Wall St refugees and a few tourists. It's hard to beat the cobwebs, sawdust floors and waiters who slap down two mugs of the house's ale for every one ordered. (212-474-9148; 15 E 7th St, btwn Second & Third Aves; ⏱11am-1am Mon-Sat, from 1pm Sun; **S**6 to Astor Pl)

Eastern Bloc   GAY

35 ⊖ Map p66, D3

Though the theme may be 'Iron Curtain,' the drapery is most definitely velvet and taffeta at this East Village gay bar. Hang your jacket at the 'Goat Czech' and spring forth into the cramped and crowded sea of boys – some flirting with the topless barkeeps, others pretending not to stare at the retro '70s porno playing on the TVs. (222-777-2555; www.easternblocnyc. com; 505 E 6th St, btwn Aves A & B; ⏱7pm-4am; **S**F to 2nd Ave)

Immigrant   WINE & BEER BAR

36 ⊖ Map p66, C2

Wholly unpretentious, these twin boxcar-sized bars could easily become your neighborhood local if you decide to stick around town. The staff are knowledgeable and kind, mingling with faithful regulars while dishing out tangy olives and topping up glasses with imported snifters. (☎212-677-2545; www.theimmigrantnyc.com; 341 E 9th St, btwn First & Second Aves; ⏱5pm-1am Mon-Wed & Sun, to 2am Thu, to 3am Fri & Sat; Ⓢ L to 1st Ave, 4/6 to Astor Pl)

Entertainment

Sweet
COMEDY

 37 Map p66, C6

There are tons of small comedy houses scattered around the city, but we're pretty sure you haven't heard of this one – a local gig hosted every Tuesday by Seth Herzog and his gang of friends (including his mother who loves to get up in front of the small crowd and discuss her weekly list of grievances). (The Slipper Room; ☎212-253-7246; www.slipperroom.com; 167 Orchard St, at Stanton St; admission $5; ⏱shows 9pm Tue; Ⓢ F to 2nd Ave, F to Delancey St, J/M/Z to Essex St)

La MaMa ETC
THEATER

 38 Map p66, B4

A long-standing home for onstage experimentation (the ETC stands for Experimental Theater Club), La MaMa is now a three-theater complex with a cafe, an art gallery and a separate studio building that features cutting-edge dramas, sketch comedy and readings of all kinds. (☎212-475-7710; www.lamama.org; 74A E 4th St; admission $10-20; Ⓢ F to Second Ave)

Slipper Room
BURLESQUE

39 Map p66, C6

Shuttered in 2010, the Slipper Room is back, and looking better than ever thanks to a major renovation. The two-story club hosts a wide range of performances, including Seth Herzog's popular variety show Sweet and several weekly burlesque shows, which feature a mash-up of acrobatics, sexiness, comedy and absurdity – generally well worth the admission. Tickets available online. (www.slipperroom.com; 167 Orchard St, entrance on Stanton St; admission $7-15; Ⓢ F to 2nd Ave)

New York Theater Workshop
THEATER

40 Map p66, B4

Recently celebrating its 25th year, this innovative production house is a treasure to those seeking cutting-edge, contemporary plays with purpose. It

Local Life
Art & Activism
Founded in 1980, **ABC No Rio** (☎212-254-3697; www.abcnorio.org; 156 Rivington St (Map p66, E6; between Suffolk & Clinton Sts); admission price varies; ⏱hours vary; Ⓢ F, J/M/Z to Delancey-Essex Sts) is an internationally known art and activism center which features weekly hard-core/punk and experimental music shows, as well as regular fine-arts exhibits, poetry readings and more.

was the originator of two big Broadway hits, *Rent* and *Urinetown,* and offers a constant supply of high-quality drama. (☎212-460-5475; www.nytw.org; 79 E 4th St, btwn Second & Third Aves; **S**F to 2nd Ave)

Bowery Ballroom   LIVE MUSIC

41 ⭐ Map p66, B7

This terrific, medium-sized venue has the perfect sound and feel for more blown-up indie-rock acts (The Shins, Stephen Malkmus, Patti Smith). (☎212-533-2111; www.boweryballroom.com; 6 Delancey St, at Bowery St; **S**J/Z to Bowery)

Landmark Sunshine Cinema   CINEMA

42 ⭐ Map p66, C5

A renovated Yiddish theater, the wonderful Landmark shows foreign and first-run mainstream art films on massive screens. It also has much-coveted stadium-style seating, so it doesn't matter what giant sits in front of you after the lights go out. (☎212-260-7289; www.landmarktheatres.com; 143 E Houston St, btwn Forsyth & Eldridge Sts; **S**F/V to Lower East Side-Second Ave)

Delancey   LIVE MUSIC

43 ⭐ Map p66, E7

Surprisingly stylish for the Lower East Side, the Delancey hosts some popular local bands for doting indie-rock crowds. A good early-evening spot to drink too, particularly from the palm-fringed 2nd-floor patio deck.

(☎212-254-9920; www.thedelancey.com; 168 Delancey St at Clinton St; **S**F to Delancey St, J/M/Z to Essex St)

Anthology Film Archives   CINEMA

44 ⭐ Map p66, B5

Opened in 1970, this theater is dedicated to the idea of film as an art form. It screens indie works by new filmmakers and also revives classics and obscure oldies, from Luis Buñuel to Ken Brown's psychedelia. (☎212-505-5181; www.anthologyfilmarchives.org; 32 Second Ave, at 2nd St; **S**F to 2nd Ave)

Amore Opera   OPERA

45 ⭐ Map p66, D4

This company, formed by several members of the now defunct Amato Opera, presents well-known works such as *The Magic Flute, La Bohème* and *The Mikado* and *Hansel and Gretel,* performed at its East Village theater. The appeal? Much cheaper tickets and a more intimate setting than most opera venues. (www.amore opera.org; Connelly Theater, 220 E 4th St, btwn Aves A & B; tickets $40; **S**F to 2nd Ave)

Sing Sing Karaoke   KARAOKE

46 ⭐ Map p66, B3

A chuckle-worthy reference to the nearby state prison, Sing Sing is exactly as it sounds – swing by to belt your heart out. (☎212-387-7800; www. karaokesingsing.com/page/home; 9 St Marks Pl; **S**N/R to 8th St-NYU, L to 3rd Ave, 6 to Astor Pl)

Shopping

Verameat   JEWELRY

47 🔒 Map p66, C2

Designer Vera Balyura creates exquisite little pieces with a dark sense of humor in this delightful little shop on 9th St. Tiny, artfully wrought pendants, rings, earrings and bracelets appear almost too precious, until a closer inspection reveals zombies, godzilla robots, animal heads, dinosaurs and encircling claws – bringing a whole new level of miniaturized complexity to the realm of jewelry. (📞212-388-9045; 315 E 9th St, btwn First & Second Aves; ⊙noon-8pm; 🚇6 to Astor Pl)

Obscura Antiques   ANTIQUES

48 🔒 Map p66, D1

This small cabinet of curiosities pleases both lovers of the macabre and inveterate antique hunters. Expect anything from taxidermy animal heads and butterfly displays in glass boxes, to German landmine flags (stackable so tanks could see them), old poison bottles, and Zippos from Vietnam soldiers. (📞212-505-9251; 207 Ave A, btwn 12th & 13th Sts; ⊙noon-8pm Mon-Sat, to 7pm Sun; 🚇L to 1st Ave)

Dinosaur Hill   CHILDREN

49 🔒 Map p66, B3

A small, old-fashioned toy store that's inspired more by imagination than Disney movies, this shop has loads of great gift ideas: Czech marionettes, shadow puppets, micro building blocks, calligraphy sets, toy pianos, art and science kits, kids' music CDs from around the globe and wooden blocks in half-a-dozen different languages, plus natural-fiber clothing for infants. (📞212-473-5850; www.dinosaurhill.com; 306 E 9th St; ⊙11am-7pm; 🚇6 to Astor Pl)

Top Hat   ACCESSORIES

50 🔒 Map p66, D8

This whimsical little shop is packed with intrigue from across the globe, whether it be vintage Italian pencils, handsome leather journals or beautifully carved wooden bird whistles. Need a toy clarinet, Japanese fabrics or a crumpled map of the night sky? Chances are you'll find it here. (📞212-677-4240; 245 Broome St, btwn Ludlow & Orchard Sts; ⊙noon-8pm; 🚇B/D to Grand St)

Tokio 7   CONSIGNMENT STORE

51 🔒 Map p66, C3

This revered, hip consignment shop, on a shady stretch of E 7th St, has good-condition designer labels for men and women at some fairly hefty prices. The Japanese-owned store often features lovely pieces by Issey Miyake and Yohji Yamamoto, as well as a well-curated selection of Dolce & Gabbana, Prada, Chanel and other top labels. (📞212-353-8443; www.tokio7.net; 83 E 7th St, near First Ave; ⊙noon-8pm; 🚇6 to Astor Pl)

Patricia Field
FASHION

52 🔒 Map p66, B5

The fashion-forward stylist for *Sex and the City,* Patricia Field isn't afraid of flash, with feather boas, pink jackets, disco dresses, graphic and color-block T-shirts and leopard-print heels, plus colored frizzy wigs, silver spandex and some wacky gift ideas for good measure. (📞212-966-4066; 306 Bowery St, at 1st St; ⏰11am-8pm Sun-Thu, to 9pm Fri & Sat; 🚇F to 2nd Ave)

Kiehl's
BEAUTY

53 🔒 Map p66, B1

Making and selling skincare products since it opened in NYC as an apothecary in 1851, this Kiehl's flagship store has doubled its shop size and expanded into an international chain, but its personal touch remains – as do the coveted, generous sample sizes. (📞212-677-3171; 109 Third Ave, btwn 13th & 14th Sts; ⏰10am-8pm Mon-Sat, 11am-6pm Sun; 🚇L to 3rd Ave)

By Robert James
FASHION

54 🔒 Map p66, D8

Rugged, beautifully tailored menswear is the mantra of Robert James, who sources and manufactures right here in NYC (the design studio in fact is just upstairs). The racks are lined with slim-fitting denim, handsome button-downs, and classic looking sports coats. (📞212-253-2121; www.byrobertjames. com; 74 Orchard St; ⏰noon-8pm Mon-Sat, to 6pm Sun; 🚇F to Delancey St, J/M/Z to Essex St)

Edith Machinist
VINTAGE

55 🔒 Map p66, D6

To properly strut about the Lower East Side, you've got to dress the part. Edith Machinist can help you get that rumpled but stylish look in a hurry – a bit of vintage glam via knee-high soft suede boots, 1930s silk dresses and ballet-style flats. (📞212-979-9992; 104 Rivington St, at Essex St; ⏰noon-7pm Tue-Sat, to 6pm Sun; 🚇F to Delancey St, J/M/Z to Essex St)

Sustainable NYC
CLOTHING

56 🔒 Map p66, D3

Across from Tompkins Square Park, this ecofriendly shop offers all sorts of home and office gear for living green. Organic T-shirts, wind-up radios and flashlights (no batteries required), soy and beeswax candles, recycled clocks made of vinyl records and Toms shoes are all on hand. There's a small cafe onsite. (📞212-254-5400; 139 Ave A, btwn St Marks Pl & 9th St; ⏰8am-10pm Mon-Fri, from 9am Sat & Sun; 🚇6 to Astor Pl)

John Varvatos
FASHION, SHOES

57 🔒 Map p66, B5

Set in the hallowed halls of former punk club CBGB, the John Varvatos Bowery store goes to great lengths to tie fashion with rock-and-roll, with records, '70s audio equipment and even electric guitars for sale alongside JV's denim, leather boots, belts and graphic tees. (📞212-358-0315; 315 Bowery, btwn 1st & 2nd Sts; ⏰noon-8pm Mon-Sat to 6pm Sun; 🚇F to 2nd Ave, 6 to Bleecker St)

PETER PTSCHELINZEW/GETTY IMAGES ©

Trash & Vaudeville

Trash & Vaudeville   CLOTHING

58 Map p66, B3

This two-story capital of punk-rocker-dom is the veritable costume closet for singing celebs like Debbie Harry, who found their groove in the East Village when it played host to a much grittier scene. On any day of the week you'll find everyone from drag queens to themed partygoers scouting out the most ridiculous shoes, shirts and hair dye. (4 St Marks Pl; ⊙noon-8pm Mon-Fri, 11:30am-9pm Sat, 1-7:30pm Sun; ⑤6 to Astor Pl)

Moo Shoes   SHOES

59 Map p66, D8

This earth- and animal-friendly boutique sells surprisingly stylish microfiber (faux leather) shoes, handbags and wallets. Look for elegant ballet flats from Love Is Mighty, rugged men's oxfords by Novacos and sleek Matt & Nat wallets. (☏212-254-6512; www.mooshoes.com; 78 Orchard St, btwn Broome & Grand Sts; ⊙11:30am-7:30pm Mon-Sat, noon-6pm Sun; ⑤F to Delancey St, J/M/Z to Essex St)

Explore

Greenwich Village, Chelsea & the Meatpacking District

There's a very good reason why this area is known as the Village: it kinda looks like one! Quaint, quiet lanes carve their way between brown-brick townhouses offering endless strolling fodder. The Meatpacking District – once filled with slaughterhouses and now brimming with sleek boutiques and roaring nightclubs – leads to Chelsea, studded with galleries and gay-friendly haunts.

The Sights in a Day

🔅 Wander along **The High Line** (p86) – an inviting emerald strand zipping over the gridiron – to get yourself oriented in this heart-stealing corner of the city. Exit at 14th St and lust over designer threads in the Meatpacking District, then slip into the West Village for more unique buys. Don't miss the **Strand Book Store** (p109) just beyond.

☀ An afternoon of art is in store for those who explore the Chelsea galleries, located in a swath of former warehouses. Fuel up at the gut-rumbling **Chelsea Market** (p92), or hit up one of the neighborhood eateries such as **Cookshop** (p98) or **Le Grainne** (p101).

🌙 Bluesy tunes often get tangled in the trees of **Washington Square Park** (p92) – swing by before a delicious dinner at one of the dozens of celebrated eateries, among them **Rosemary's** (p96) and **RedFarm** (p96). After dinner, channel Prohibition days at sneaky **Little Branch** (p101) or **Bathtub Gin** (p103), or opt for chuckles at comedy headquarters like the **Upright Citizens Brigade Theatre** (p105) or the **Comedy Cellar** (p106).

For a local's day in Chelsea, see p88.

◉ **Top Sights**

The High Line (p86)

○ **Local Life**

Chelsea Galleries (p88)

💜 **Best of New York City**

Eating

Jeffrey's Grocery (p97)

Rosemary's (p96)

RedFarm (p96)

Drinking

Little Branch (p101)

Top of the Standard (p102)

Jane Ballroom (p102)

Entertainment

Upright Citizens Brigade Theatre (p105)

Comedy Cellar (p106)

Getting There

Ⓢ **Subway** Take the A/C/E or 1/2/3 and disembark at 14th St (along either service) if you're looking for a good place to make tracks.

🚌 **Bus** Try the M14 or the M8 if you're traveling across town and want to access the westernmost areas of Chelsea and the West Village by public transportation.

Top Sights
The High Line

In the early 1900s, the area around western Chelsea was the largest industrial section of Manhattan and a set of elevated tracks were created to move freight off the cluttered streets below. The rails eventually became obsolete, and in 1999 a plan was made to convert the scarring strands of metal into a public green space. On June 9, 2009, part one of the city's most beloved urban renewal project opened with much ado. The final section is slated to be completed by late 2014, meandering from 30th up to 34th St.

Map p90, C3

212-500-6035

www.thehighline.org

Gansevoort St

admission free

7am-7pm

M11 to Washington St; M11, M14 to 9th Ave; M23, M34 to 10th Ave, S L, A/C/E to 14th St-8th Ave; C/E to 23rd St-8th Ave

Don't Miss

Public Art

In addition to being a haven of hovering green, The High Line is also an informal art space featuring a variety of installations, both site-specific and stand-alone. For detailed information about the public art on display at the time of your visit, check out art.thehighline.org.

Secret Staffers

As you walk along the High Line, you'll find dedicated staffers wearing shirts with the signature double-H logo who can point you in the right direction or offer you additional information about the converted rails. Free tours take place on Tuesday nights at 6:30pm in the warmer months. Sign up near the 14th St entrance.

The Industrial Past

It's hard to believe that The High Line – a shining example of brilliant urban renewal – was once a dingy rail line that anchored a rather unsavory district of thugs, trannies and slaughterhouses. The tracks that would one day become the High Line were commissioned in the 1930s when the municipal government decided to raise the street-level tracks after years of accidents that gave Tenth Ave the nickname 'Death Avenue.' The project drained over $150 million in funds (equivalent to around $2 billion by today's dime) and took roughly five years to complete. After two decades of effective use, a rise in truck transportation and traffic led to the eventual decrease in usage, and finally, in the 1980s, the rails became obsolete.

☑ Top Tips

▶ Beat the crowds by starting early at 30th St, wandering south and exiting at 14th St for a bite at Chelsea Market before exploring the West Village. If your tummy's grumbling, tackle The High Line in the reverse direction, gelato in hand.

▶ If you want to contribute financially to The High Line, become a member on the website. Members receive discounts at neighborhood establishments, such as Diane von Furstenberg's boutique and Amy's Bread in Chelsea Market.

✗ Take a Break

The High Line invites gastronomic establishments from around the city to set up stalls for to-go items. Expect a showing of the finest coffee and ice cream establishments during the warmer months.

A cache of eateries is stashed within the brick walls of Chelsea Market (p92) at the 14th St exit of The High Line.

Local Life
Chelsea Galleries

The High Line may be the big-ticket item in this part of town, but there's plenty going on underneath the strand of green. Chelsea is home to the highest concentration of art galleries in the city – and the number just keeps increasing. Most lie in the 20s, between Tenth and Eleventh Aves; wine-and-cheese openings for their new shows are typically held on Thursday evenings.

....

1 Greene Naftali
Edgy and youth-oriented, conceptually based **Greene Naftali** (212-463-7770; www.greenenaftaligallery.com; 526 W 26th St; 10am-6pm Tue-Sat; C/E to 23rd St) has a rotating display of art spanning all kinds of media: film/video, painting, drawing and performance art. The gallery is known for giving budding talent a break, including then-emerging Tracy Emin and Laura Owens.

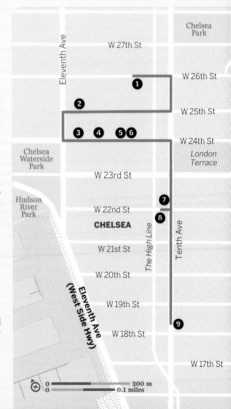

❷ Cheim & Read

Sculptures of every shape, size and material abound at **Cheim & Read** (☎212-242-7727; www.cheimread.com; 547 W 25th St btwn Tenth & Eleventh Aves; ☉10am-6pm Tue-Sat; Ⓢ C/E to 23rd St) and monthly rotations keep the exhibits fresh – expect blazing light installations and inspired photography displays.

❸ Gagosian

Gagosian (☎212-741-1111; www.gagosian. com; 555 W 24th St; ☉10am-6pm Tue-Sat; Ⓢ C/E to 23rd St) offers a different vibe from most of the one-off galleries, as it's part of a constellation of show-rooms that spreads across the globe. Also check out the 21st St location, which easily rivals some of the city's museums with large-scale installations.

❹ Mary Boone

Check out **Mary Boone Gallery** (www. maryboonegallery.com; 541 W 24th St; ☉10am-6pm Tue-Sat; Ⓢ C/E, 1 to 23rd St), whose owner found fame in the '80s with her eye for Jean-Michel Basquiat and Julian Schnabel – it's considered one of the main 'blue-chip' galleries in the area.

❺ Andrea Rosen

Oversized installations are the norm at **Andrea Rosen Gallery** (☎212-627-6000; www.andrearosengallery.com; 525 W 24th St; ☉10am-6pm Tue-Sat; Ⓢ C/E, 1 to 23rd St), where every inch of the space (and the annex Gallery 2 next door) is filled with intriguing ways. Represented artists include John Currin, Felix Gonzalez-Torres and Tetsumi Kudo.

❻ Barbara Gladstone

The curator of the eponymous **Barbara Gladstone Gallery** (☎212-206-9300; www.gladstonegallery.com; 515 W 24th St btwn Tenth & Eleventh Aves; ☉10am-6pm Tue-Sat, closed weekends Jul & Aug; Ⓢ C/E, 1 to 23rd St) has learned a thing or two after 30 years in the Manhattan art world. Ms Gladstone consistently puts together the most talked-about and well-critiqued displays around.

❼ Refuel, Spanish-Style

Wielding Spanish tapas amid closet-sized surrounds, **Tía Pol** (☎212-675-8805; www.tiapol.com; 205 Tenth Ave btwn 22nd & 23rd Sts; small plates $4-16; ☉noon-11pm Tue-Sun, from 5:30pm Mon; Ⓢ C/E to 23rd St) is the real deal, as the hordes of swarming locals can attest.

❽ Matthew Marks

Famous for exhibiting big names like Jasper Johns and Ellsworth Kelly, **Matthew Marks** (☎212-243-0200; www. matthewmarks.com; 522 W 22nd St; ☉10am-6pm Tue-Sat; Ⓢ C/E to 23rd St) is truly a Chelsea pioneer. There are three other nearby locations (on 22nd and 24th Sts) besides this one.

❾ Alexander & Bonin

Since moving to Chelsea from SoHo in 1997, the multi-level **Alexander & Bonin** (☎212-367-7474; www.alexanderandbonin. com; 132 Tenth Ave near 18th St; ☉10am-6pm Tue-Sat; Ⓢ C/E to 23rd St) has made excellent use of its airy space with a stellar roster of artists, including several prestigious Turner Prize winners.

A

Pier 66

Hudson River Park

1

Chelsea Waterside Park

B

W 27th St

Eleventh Ave

41

47

The High Line

Tenth Ave

C

Chelsea Park

CHELSEA

W 26th St

W 25th St

W 24th St

W 23rd St

Ninth Ave

D

45

25th St

23rd S

5

Eighth Ave

Chelsea Piers Complex

9

Pier 62

Pier 61

Pier 60

Pier 59

2

63

20

W 22nd St

W 21st St

29

W 20th St

W 19th St
38

W 18th St

W 17th St

16

56

57

Hudson River

3

Chelsea Market

2

W 16th St

W 15th St

W 14th St

8th Ave
14th St

5

Eleventh Ave (West Side Hwy)

Twelfth Ave
(West Side Hwy)

W 13th St

34

44

Little W 12th St
66

The High Line

**MEATPACKING
DISTRICT**

67

Gansevoort St

Horatio St

Jane St

Hudson St

Eighth Ave

23

**WEST
VILLAGE**

22

Abingdon
Sq

33

W 12th St

Bethune St

Bank St

Bleecker St

19

61

4

Hudson River Park

W 11th St

Perry St

Charles St

13

W 10th St

3

Hudson S

West Side Hwy

Washington St

Christopher St

Barrow St

Morton St

Greenwich St

5

Pier 45

5

12

11

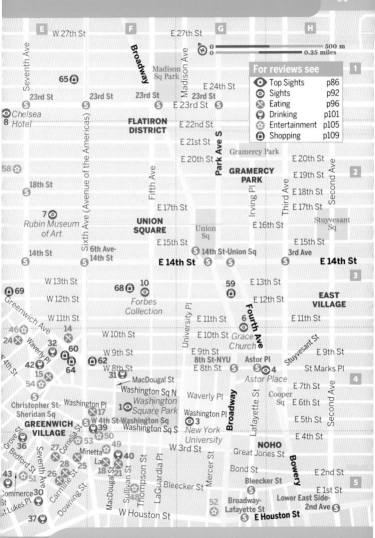

W 27th St

E 27th St

Broadway

Madison
Sq Park

E 24th St

65 🔒

E 23rd St

23rd St | 23rd St | 23rd St | 23rd St | E 23rd St

🅂

Seventh Ave

◉ Chelsea
8 Hotel

FLATIRON
DISTRICT

E 22nd St

E 21st St

Park Ave S

E 20th St

Gramercy Park

GRAMERCY
PARK

E 20th St

E 19th St

Second Ave

58 ☆

18th St

🅂

Fifth Ave

E 17th St

Irving Pl

Third Ave

E 18th St

E 17th St

Stuyvesant
Sq

7 ◉
Rubin Museum
of Art

UNION
SQUARE

Union
Sq

E 16th St

14th St

🅂

Sixth Ave (Avenue of the Americas)

6th Ave-
14th St

E 15th St

🅂 14th St-Union Sq

3rd Ave

E 15th St

🅂

E 14th St

🅂

E 14th St

E 14th St

W 13th St

E 13th St

EAST
VILLAGE

🔒 69

68 🔒

10
◉

59
🔒

E 12th St

W 12th St

W 11th St

Forbes
Collection

University Pl

E 11th St

Fourth Ave

6 ◉

E 11th St

Greenwich Ave

46 ❌

14

W 10th St

E 10th St Grace
Church

Stuyvesant St

E 9th St

24 ❌

32 ❌

60

W 9th St

8th St-NYU

🅂

Astor Pl

4

Waverly Pl

42 🔒

15

64

🔒 62

W 8th St

E 8th St

🅂

◉ 4

St Marks Pl

Second Ave

54 ❌

31 🔒

MacDougal St

Astor Place

E 7th St

Christopher St-
Sheridan Sq

Washington Sq N

Washington
Square Park

Waverly Pl

Cooper
Sq

E 6th St

Washington Pl

1 ◉

Broadway

Lafayette St

E 5th St

GREENWICH
VILLAGE

❌ 17

W 4th St-Washington Sq

Washington Sq S

Washington Pl

New York

NOHO

E 4th St

36

27

53

50

49

University

Great Jones St

Minetta
La

40

W 3rd St

Mercer St

Bond St

Bowery

E 2nd St

26

25

18

21

Sullivan St

Thompson St

LaGuardia Pl

Bleecker St

E 1st St

43

51

30

34

Carmine St

Downing St

Bleecker St

52

Broadway-
Lafayette St

🅂

Lower East Side-
2nd Ave 🅂

37

Commerce
St
St Lukes Pl

Seventh Ave

W Houston St

Grove St

Bedford St

Cornelia St

28

48

☆

E Houston St

500 m
0.25 miles

E | F | G | H

Sights

Washington Square Park   PARK

 Map p90, F4

What was once a potter's field and a square for public executions is now the unofficial town square of the Village. Washington Square Park plays host to everyone from lounging New York University (NYU) students and fire-eating street performers, to curious canines, their equally curious owners, and legions of speed-chess pros.

Encased in perfectly manicured brownstones and gorgeous twists of modern architecture (all owned by NYU), it's one of the most beautiful garden spaces in the city – especially when approached from the iconic Stanford White Arch on the north side of the green. (Fifth Ave at Washington Sq N; **S** A/C/E, B/D/F/M to W 4th St-Washington Sq; N/R to 8th St-NYU)

Chelsea Market   MARKET

 Map p90, C3

In a shining example of redevelopment and preservation, the Chelsea Market has taken a former factory of cookie giant Nabisco (creator of the Oreo) and turned it into an 800ft-long shopping concourse that keeps foodies purring. And that's only the lower part of a larger, million-sq-ft space that occupies a full city block – upstairs you'll find the current home of several TV channels, including the Food Network, Oxygen Network and NY1, the local news channel. (www.chelseamarket. com; 75 Ninth Ave at 15th St; ⏰7am-10pm Mon-Sat, 8am-9pm Sun; **S** A/C/E to 14th St; L to 8th Ave)

New York University   UNIVERSITY

 Map p90, G4

In 1831, Albert Gallatin, formerly Secretary of the Treasury, founded an intimate center of higher learning open to all students, regardless of race or class background. He'd scarcely recognize the place today, as it's swelled to a student population of more than 54,000. For a unique experience, sign up for a one-day class – from American history to photography – offered by the School of Professional Studies and Continuing Education. (NYU; ☎212-998-2222; www.nyu.edu; 50 W 4th St (information center); **S** A/C/E, B/D/F/M to W 4th St-Washington Sq; N/R to 8th St-NYU)

Astor Place   SQUARE

 Map p90, G4

This square is named after the Astor family, who built an early New York fortune on beaver pelts and lived on Colonnade Row, just south of the square. Originally Astor Place was the home of the Astor Opera House (now gone), which attracted the city's wealthy elite for regular performances in the mid-1800s. Today the square is largely known as the home of the *Village Voice* and the Cooper Union college. (8th St btwn Third & Fourth Aves; **S** N/R to 8th St-NYU; 6 to Astor Pl)

Understand

Gay in the Village

While the rough-and-ready Lower East Side had established quite a reputation for scandalous dancing halls, saloons and brothels by the 1890s, it was Greenwich Village that would ultimately play the leading role in NYC's long, illustrious queer history.

Village People

Writers and bohemians were already flocking to Greenwich Village in the early years of the 20th century. Their unconventional attitudes were not lost on the day's 'inverts', who flocked to the area to live a little more freely. A number of gay-owned businesses lined MacDougall St, among them the legendary Eve's Hangout at number 129. A tearoom run by Polish Jewish immigrant Eva Kotchever (Eve Addams), it was famous for two things: poetry readings and a sign on the door that read 'Men allowed but not welcome'.

Wowser Years

The relative transgression of the early 20th century was replaced with a new conservatism as the Great Depression, WWII and the Cold War took their toll. Conservatism was helped along by senator Joseph 'Joe' McCarthy, who declared that homosexuals in the State Department threatened America's security and children. Tougher policing aimed to eradicate queer visibility in the public sphere, forcing the scene further underground in the 1940s and '50s.

Gay Power

LGBT resentment reached boiling point on June 28, 1969, the day on which eight police officers raided the Stonewall Inn, a gay-friendly watering hole in Greenwich Village. Fed up with both the harassment and corrupt officers receiving payoffs from the bars' owners, they began bombarding the officers with coins, bottles, bricks and chants of 'Gay power' and 'We shall overcome'. They were also met by a line of high-kicking drag queens and their now legendary chant, 'We are the Stonewall girls, we wear our hair in curls, we wear no underwear, we show our pubic hair, we wear our dungarees, above our nelly knees...'. Their collective anger and solidarity was a turning point, forming the catalyst for the modern gay rights movement.

Local Life

Robert Hammond on The High Line

Co-founder and executive director of Friends of The High Line, Robert Hammond shares his High Line highlights: 'What I love most about The High Line are its hidden moments, like at the Tenth Ave cut-out near 17th St, most people sit on the bleachers, but if you turn the other way, you can see the Statue of Liberty far away in the harbor. Architecture buffs will love looking down 18th St, and up on 30th is my favorite moment – a steel cut-out where you can see the cars underneath.'

Pier 45   PIER

5 ◉ Map p90, C5

Known to many as the Christopher Street Pier, this 850ft-long finger of concrete dips into the mighty Hudson River. Pimped with a grass lawn, flowerbeds, an outdoor cafe, tented shade shelters and a stop for the New York Water Taxi, it's a magnet for downtowners of all stripes, from local families with toddlers in daylight to mobs of young gays looking to cruise. (W 10th St at Hudson River; S1 to Christopher St-Sheridan Sq)

Grace Church   CHURCH

6 ◉ Map p90, G3

Designed in 1843 by James Renwick Jr, this Gothic Revival Episcopal church was made of marble quarried by prisoners at 'Sing Sing,' the state penitentiary 30 miles away. After years of neglect, Grace Church is being spiffed up in a major way. Now it's a National Landmark, whose elaborate carvings, towering spire and verdant, and groomed yard are sure to stop you in your tracks as you make your way down this otherwise ordinary stretch of the Village. (📞212-254-2000; www. gracechurchnyc.org; 802 Broadway at 10th St; ⊙10am-5pm, services daily; S N/R to 8th St-NYU; 6 to Astor Pl)

Rubin Museum of Art   MUSEUM

7 ◉ Map p90, E2

This is the first museum in the Western world dedicated to the art of the Himalayas and surrounding regions. Its impressive collections include embroidered textiles from China, metal sculptures from Tibet, Pakistani stone sculptures and intricate Bhutanese paintings, as well as ritual objects and dance masks from various Tibetan regions, spanning from the 2nd to the 19th centuries. (📞212-620-5000; www. rmanyc.org; 150 W 17th St at Seventh Ave; adult/child $10/free, 6-10pm Fri free; ⊙11am-5pm Mon & Thu, to 9pm Wed, to 10pm Fri, to 6pm Sat & Sun; S1 to 18th St)

Chelsea Hotel   HISTORIC BUILDING

8 ◉ Map p90, E1

While the future of this infamous hotel remains unclear after being sold to a luxury developer in 2013, its legendary status remains unshakeable. Featuring ornate iron balconies and no fewer than seven plaques declaring its literary landmark status, the place has played a major role in pop-culture history.

It's here that Jack Kerouac allegedly crafted *On the Road,* and it's where Arthur C Clarke wrote *2001: A Space Odyssey.* Dylan Thomas died of alcohol poisoning while staying here in 1953, while Nancy Spungen died here after being stabbed by her Sex Pistols boyfriend Sid Vicious in 1978. (📞212-243-3700; 222 W 23rd St, btwn Seventh & Eighth Aves; Ⓢ1, C/E to 23rd St)

Chelsea Piers Complex   SPORTS

 Map p90, B2

This massive waterfront sports center caters to the athlete in everyone. You can set out to hit a bucket of golf balls at the four-level driving range, ice skate on the complex's indoor rink or rent in-line skates to cruise along the bike path on the Hudson River Park – all the way down to Battery Park.

The complex also features a bowling alley, Hoop City for basketball, a sailing school for kids, batting cages, a huge gym facility with an indoor pool (day passes for nonmembers are $50), indoor rock-climbing walls – the works. (📞212-336-6666; www.chelseapiers.com; Hudson River at end of W 23rd St; Ⓢ C/E to 23rd St)

Forbes Collection   MUSEUM

 Map p90, F3

These galleries, located in the lobby of the headquarters of *Forbes* magazine, house rotating exhibits and curios from the personal collection

---

Understand
The History of Washington Square Park

Although quite ravishing today, Washington Square Park has had a long and eclectic history. When the Dutch settled Manhattan to run the Dutch East India Company, they gave what is now the park to their freed black slaves. At the turn of the 19th century, it became a burial ground, quickly reaching capacity during an outbreak of yellow fever. Over 20,000 bodies remain buried under the park today. By 1830, the grounds were used for military parades, before quickly transforming into a park for the wealthy elite whose lavish townhouses began springing up on the surrounding streets.

Colloquially known as the Washington Square Arch, the iconic Stanford White Arch now dominates the park with its 72ft of beaming white Dover marble. Originally designed in wood to celebrate the centennial of George Washington's inauguration in 1889, the arch proved so popular that it was replaced with stone six years later. In 1916, artist Marcel Duchamp famously climbed to the top of the arch by its internal stairway and declared the park the 'Free and Independent Republic of Washington Square.'

of the late publishing magnate Malcolm Forbes. The eclectic mix of objects on display includes Fabergé eggs, toy boats, early versions of Monopoly and over 10,000 toy soldiers. (🖉212-206-5548; www.forbesgalleries. com; 62 Fifth Ave at 12th St; admission free; ⊙10am-4pm Tue-Sat; Ⓢ L, N/Q/R, 4/5/6 to 14th St-Union Sq)

Downtown Boathouse   KAYAKING

 11   Map p90, D5

New York's most active public boathouse offers free walk-up 20-minute kayaking (including equipment) in the protected embayment in the Hudson River on weekends and some weekday evenings. (www.downtownboathouse.org; Pier 40 near Houston St; tours free; ⊙10am-6pm Sat & Sun, 5-7pm Thu mid-May–mid-Oct; Ⓢ1 to Houston St)

New York Trapeze School   SPORTS

 12   Map p90, C5

Fulfill your circus dreams, like Carrie did on *Sex and the City,* flying trapeze to trapeze in this open-air tent by the river. It's open from May to September, on top of Pier 40. The school also has an indoor facility inside the Circus Warehouse in Long Island City, Queens, open October to April. (www.newyork.trapezeschool.com; Pier 40 at West Side Hwy; per class from $50; Ⓢ1 to Houston St)

Eating

RedFarm   FUSION $$$

13   Map p90, D4

RedFarm takes Eastern and Western flavors and merges them into palate-punching combos like fresh crab and eggplant bruschetta, juicy rib steak (marinated overnight in papaya, ginger and soy) and pastrami egg rolls. Waits can be long, so arrive early (no reservations), or plan on a few crafty cocktails at the lower-level bar. (🖉212-792-9700; www.redfarmnyc.com; 529 Hudson St btwn 10th & Charles Sts; mains $19-49; ⊙5-11:45pm Mon-Sat, to 11pm Sun & 11am-2:30pm Sat & Sun; Ⓢ A/C/E, B/D/F/M to W 4th St; 1 to Christopher St-Sheridan Sq)

Rosemary's   ITALIAN $$

14   Map p90, E4

West Village hotspot Rosemary's peddles high-end Italian flavors worth the hype. Tuck into generous serves of housemade pastas, rich salads and graze-friendly cheese and *salumi* (cured meat) boards. For a feast, order one of the family-style platters (*piatti unici*), like the *acqua pazza* (stewed seafood) or *carne misti* (pork ribs, lamb shoulder, half chicken). Arrive early or plan for crowds (no reservations). (🖉212-647-1818; rosemarysnyc. com; 18 Greenwich Ave at W 10th St; mains $12-26; ⊙8am-midnight; Ⓢ1 to Christopher St-Sheridan Sq)

Rubin Museum of Art (p94)

Jeffrey's Grocery

MODERN AMERICAN **$$**

15 Map p90, E4

Seafood shines at this lively West Village classic, complete with oyster bar. Turf options include a soulful roasted chicken with sunchokes, and a humble yet juicy pastrami burger. Brunch is fantastic, while the bar draws more drinkers than diners as the night wears on. (646-398-7630; jeffreysgrocery.com; 172 Waverly Pl at Christopher St; mains $18-35; 8am-11pm Sun-Wed, to 2am Thu-Sat; S 1 to Christopher St-Sheridan Sq)

Foragers City Table

MODERN AMERICAN **$$**

16 Map p90, D2

Owners of this Chelsea noshery run a 28-acre farm in the Hudson Valley, from which much of their menu is sourced. While we love the sustainability factor, we adore the end product – think heirloom squash soup with sunchokes and black truffles, or this season's harvest with toasted quinoa and a flavorful mix of vegetables. Brunch is another big draw. (www.foragerscitygrocer.com; 300 W 22nd St, cnr Eighth Ave; mains $22-28; 6pm-10pm Tue-Sat, from 10:30am Sat & Sun; ; S C/E, 1 to 23rd St)

Local Life
Eating At Chelsea Market

Boutique bakeries fill the renovated hallways of this foodie haven. **Eleni's** (Map p90, C3; ☑212-255-6804; Chelsea Market; ⑤A/C/E to 14th St, L to 8th Ave) is of special note – Eleni Gianopulos was one of the first tenants here and her expertly designed cookies are a big hit. Also worth a stop is Tuck Shop, serving Aussie-style savory pies, rolls, lamingtons and homemade sodas. Sweet-tooths will fawn over the icy outpost of l'Arte Del Gelato. Made fresh every day, its 20-plus flavors make for a perfect snack on your way up to the High Line.

Blue Hill   AMERICAN $$$

17 Map p90, F4

Darling of Slow Food junkies, Blue Hill was an early crusader in the local-is-better movement. Gifted chef Dan Barber, who hails from a farm family in the Berkshires, Massachusetts, uses harvests from that land, as well as from farms in upstate New York, to create lauded dishes like cod in almond broth or tender grass-fed lamb with white beans and fluffy new potatoes. (☑212-539-1776; www.bluehill farm.com; 75 Washington Pl btwn Sixth Ave & Washington Sq W; mains $32-38; ⊙ 5-11pm Mon-Sat, to 10pm Sun; ⑤A/C/E, B/D/F/M to W 4th St-Washington Sq)

Minetta Tavern   BISTRO $$

18 Map p90, F5

Book in advance, or come early on a weeknight to snag a table at the legendary Minetta, a snug mix of red-leather banquettes, dark-paneled walls and classic checkered floors. The menu is a flavor-packed bistro fare, spanning pan-seared marrow bones, big burgers and mustn't-miss French dip sandwiches. (☑212-475-3850; www.minettatavernny.com; 113 MacDougal St; mains $19-35; ⊙5:30pm-1am Mon & Tue, 11am-3pm & 5:30pm-1am Wed-Sun; ⑤A/C/E, B/D/F/M to W 4th St)

Spotted Pig   PUB $$

19 Map p90, D4

Villagers still flock to this Michelin-starred gastro-pub, famed for its hearty, upscale mains from Italy and the UK. Tuck into them on one of its two floors, sprinkled with nostalgic souvenirs. The downside: reservations are not taken, so expect to wait for a table. If you're the impatient kind, weekday lunch is less crowded. (☑212-620-0393; www.thespottedpig.com; 314 W 11th St at Greenwich St; mains $16-35; ⊙11am-2am; ☑ ⊞; ⑤A/C/E to 14th St; L to 8th Ave)

Cookshop   MODERN AMERICAN $$

20 Map p90, C2

A brilliant brunching pit stop before (or after) tackling the verdant High Line across the street, buzzing Cookshop knows its niche and does it well. Excellent service, eye-opening cocktails (good morning Bloody Maria!), a perfectly baked breadbasket and a cast of inventive egg mains make this a Chelsea winner on a Sunday afternoon. Dinner is a sure-fire win too. Ample outdoor seating on warm days seals the deal. (☎212-924-4440; www.cookshopny.com; 156 Tenth Ave btwn 19th & 20th Sts; mains $15-35; ☉11:30am-4pm & 5:30-11:30pm daily, from 10:30am Sat & Sun; ⑤L to 8th Ave; A/C/E to 23rd St)

Saigon Shack VIETNAMESE $

 21 Map p90, F5

Steaming bowls of *pho* (noodle soup), tangy *bahn mi* sandwiches and crunchy spring rolls nourish the masses at this ever-popular wood-lined noshery. Just a few strides from Washington Square Park, it's a big hit with penny-conscious NYU types, who love the price tag and prompt service. The only downside: you might have to wait for that table. (☎212-228-0588; saigonshacknyc.com; 114 MacDougal St btwn Bleecker & 3rd Sts; mains $7-10; ☉11am-11pm Sun-Thu, to 1am Fri & Sat; ⑤A/B/C, B/D/F/M to W 4th St)

Barbuto MODERN AMERICAN $$

22 Map p90, C4

Set inside a cavernous garage space with sweeping see-through doors that roll up during the warmer months, Barbuto slaps together a delightful assortment of nouveau Italian dishes like pork loin with polenta and apple, and bruschetta smeared with duck liver, pistachio and balsamic. (☎212-924-9700; www.barbutonyc.com; 775 Washington St btwn 12th & Jane Sts; mains $19-27; ☉noon-11pm Mon-Wed, to midnight Thu-Sat, to 10pm Sun; ⑤L to 8th Ave; A/C/E to 14th St; 1 to Christopher St-Sheridan Sq)

Café Cluny BISTRO $$

23 Map p90, D4

Civilized Café Cluny would sit perfectly in Paris' Le Marais, but Villagers are more than happy to see it sitting snugly in their hood. Adorned with a curious melange of stuffed songbirds and other natural-world knickknacks, its menu sings with clever bistro creations, from Montauk monkfish paired with French lentils and chorizo, to Tuscan kale gratin with aged gouda. (☎212-255-6900; www.cafecluny.com; 284 W 12th St; mains lunch $14-24, dinner $18-34; ☉8am-11:30pm Mon-Fri, 9am-11pm Sat & Sun; ⑤L to 8th Ave; A/C/E, 1/2/3 to 14th St)

Taïm ISRAELI $

24 Map p90, E4

Tiny Taïm whips up some of the best falafels in the city. You can order them Green (traditional style), Harissa (with Tunisian spices) or Red (with roasted peppers). Whichever you choose, you'll get them stuffed into pita with creamy tahini sauce and a generous dose of Israeli salad. You'll also find mixed platters, zesty salads and delicious smoothies – try the date, lime and banana. (☎212-691-1287; www.taimfalafel.com; 222 Waverly Pl btwn Perry & W 11th Sts; mains $6-12; ☉11am-10pm; ⑤1/2/3 to 14th St)

Joe's Pizza

PIZZA $

25 Map p90, E5

Swagging dozens of awards and accolades over the last three decades, lo-fi Joe's is a top spot to enjoy a slice of great NYC pizza. It's a 'come one, come all' kind of place, that pulls everyone from students and tourists, to celebrities (Kirsten Dunst and Bill Murray have eaten here). (212-366-1182; www.joespizzanyc.com; 7 Carmine St btwn Sixth Ave & Bleecker St; slices from $3; 10am-4:30am; S A/C/E, B/D/F/M to W 4th St; 1 to Christopher St-Sheridan Sq or Houston St)

Cafe Blossom

VEGAN $

26 Map p90, E5

Romantic, candlelit Blossom keeps punters glowing with its first-rate organic vegan grub. The focus is on creative sharing plates, from roasted oyster mushroom savory cakes and pizza with cashew, ricotta and smoked fennel, to agedashi crusted tofu with red Thai curry. Toast virtuously with an organic wine, beer or cocktail. (blossomnyc.com; 41 Carmine St btwn Bleecker & Bedford; small plates $8-16; 5-10pm Mon-Fri, noon-10pm Sat, to 9pm Sun; S A/C/E, B/D/F/M to W 4th St)

BARRY WINIKER/GETTY IMAGES ©

Chelsea Market (p92)

Murray's Cheese Bar CHEESE $$

27 Map p90, E5

New York's king of *fromage* celebrates all things creamy and artisanal, from gourmet mac and cheese to melted cheese sandwiches and French onion soup. Top pick are the cheese platters, especially the Cheesemongers Choice (with five to eight cheeses plus charcuterie items), best enjoyed with a drop from the cleverly curated wine list. (www.murrayscheesebar.com; 246 Bleecker St; mains $12-17, cheese platters $12-16; ⊗noon-10pm Sun-Tue, to midnight Wed-Sat; S A/C/E, B/D/F/M to W 4th St)

Victory Garden ICE CREAM $

28 Map p90, E5

If you've never tried goat's milk ice cream, you're in for a treat at this cute little cafe. Lick yourself silly on soft-serve ice cream with flavors like salted caramel, chocolate (made from Mexican stone-ground cocoa, naturally), and seasonal options spanning watermelon to roasted plum. Selections change weekly, with four or so available each day. (31 Carmine St btwn Bleecker & Bedford Sts; ice cream $4-6; ⊗noon-11pm Mon-Sat, to 10pm Sun; S A/C/E, B/D/F/M to W 4th St)

Le Grainne FRENCH $$

29 Map p90, C2

Tap the top of your French onion soup as you dream of that ingenue Amélie cracking open her crème brûlée; Le

Local Life
Eighth Ave Brunch
If you're a dude looking to meet (or at least look at) other dudes, but the cruise-y bar scene isn't your style, then opt for the weekend brunch scene along Eighth Ave. You'll spot piles of friendly Chelsea boys drinking their hangovers off in tight T-shirts and even tighter jeans.

Grainne transports the senses from the busy blocks of Chelsea to the back-streets of Paris. The tin-topped eatery excels at lunch time, when baguette sandwiches and savory crepes are scarfed down amid cramped quarters. (☏646-486-3000; www.legrainnecafe.com; 183 Ninth Ave btwn 21st & 22nd Sts; mains $10-24; ⊗8am-midnight; S C/E, 1 to 23rd St; A/C/E to 14th St)

Drinking

Little Branch COCKTAIL BAR

30 Map p90, E5

If it weren't for the casual bouncer dressed in slacks and suspenders, you'd never guess that one of New York's best drinking dens lurked beyond that plain metal door. When you get the go-ahead to enter, sink into a basement scene straight out of the '20s, complete with squeaky tunes and beautiful, old-school cocktails. (☏212-929-4360; 22 Seventh Ave at Leroy St; ⊗7pm-3am; S 1 to Houston St)

Stumptown Coffee Roasters

CAFE

31 Map p90, F4

Coffee snobs hail this cultish Portland roaster, its small-batch beans and artisan brewing techniques propelling NYC's coffee scene evolution. While we love the coffered ceiling and walnut bar, its the Joe that draws the crowds – velvety, complex and aromatic. If you're really lucky, you might score one of the few tables, usually colonized by laptop-toting types. (30 W 8th St at MacDougal St; ⏰7am-8pm; **S**A/C/E, B/D/F/M to W 4th St)

Bell Book & Candle

BAR

32 Map p90, E4

Twenty-somethings love this candlelit gastropub for strong, inventive libations (try the canela margarita, with cinnamon-infused tequila) and hearty nosh. Squeeze around the small, packed bar or try for a booth out the back. Either way, slurp on $1 oysters and happy hour drink specials early in the night, or tuck into more substantial gut-lining dishes, many made with vegetables from the aeroponic rooftop garden six flights up. (141 W 10th St btwn Waverley & Greenwich Ave; **S**A/B/C, B/D/F/M to W 4th St; 1 to Christopher St-Sheridan Sq)

Jane Ballroom

LOUNGE

33 Map p90, C4

The lounge inside the Jane Hotel is nothing short of outrageous: cue oversized disco ball, velour chairs, animal print fabrics and taxidermied critters. Low-key during the week, the place morphs into a full-blown party on weekends, complete with revelers dancing on the furniture. (Honey, you've been warned.) (113 Jane St cnr West St; **S**L to 8th Ave; A/C/E, 1/2/3 to 14th St)

Standard

BAR

34 Map p90, C3

Rising on concrete stilts over the High Line, the Standard attracts an A-list crowd, with a chichi lounge and nightclub on the upper floors – the Top of the Standard and Le Bain. There's also a grill, an eating-and-drinking plaza (that becomes a skating rink in winter) and an open-air beer garden with a classic German menu and frothy drafts. (📞212-645-4646, 877-550-4646; www.standardhotels.com; 848 Washington St; **S**A/C/E to 14th St; L to 8th Ave)

Top of the Standard

LOUNGE

Located at the Standard (see 34 Map p90, C3), the Top of the Standard has smooth beige surrounds, softer music and plenty of room to swig your top-shelf tipple. It is strictly VIP and the favored hangout for the vogue elite (and *Vogue* elite) – expect models, their photographers and the occasional celeb sighting. (📞212-645-4646; standardhotels.com/high-line; 848 Washington St btwn 13th & Little W 12th Sts; ⏰4pm-2am; **S**L to 8th Ave; 1/2/3, A/C/E to 14th St)

Employees Only
BAR

35 Map p90, D4

Duck behind the neon 'Psychic' sign to find this in-the-know hangout, which gets busier as the night wears on. The bartenders are top-tier mixologists, fizzing up crazy, addictive libations like the 'Ginger Smash' and the 'Mata Hari.' Great for late-night drinking, and eating, courtesy of the onsite restaurant that serves past midnight. (212-242-3021; 510 Hudson St near Christopher St; 6pm-4am; 1 to Christopher St-Sheridan Sq)

Buvette
WINE BAR

36 Map p90, E5

Delicate tin tiling, swooshing marble countertop and rustic-chic decor set an evocative scene at this brilliant gastrotèque, a top spot for a glass of vino no matter the time of day. For the full experience, grab a table and pair your Old World drop with a small, delectable dish or two. (212-255-3590; www.ilovebuvette.com; 42 Grove St btwn Bedford & Bleecker Sts; 8am-2am Mon-Fri, from 10am Sat & Sun; 1 to Christopher St-Sheridan Sq; A/C/E, B/D/F/M to W 4th St)

Clarkson
BAR

37 Map p90, E5

The horseshoe-shaped, polished wood bar at this svelte newbie is a solid spot for eyeing-up the garrulous crowd that gravitates here most nights. Observe over masterful cocktails or, if you're peckish, grab a table in the zebra-pattern side room for creative French grub. There's a late-night menu for owls on the town. (225 Varick St at Clarkson St; 11am-1:30am Mon, to 2:30am Tue-Sat, to 10pm Sun; 1 to Houston St)

Bathtub Gin
COCKTAIL BAR

38 Map p90, D2

Amid NYC's obsession with speakeasy-styled hangouts, Bathtub Gin pokes its head above the crowd with its super-secret front door, which doubles as a wall for an unassuming café. Inside, chill seating, soft background beats and kindly staff make it a great place to sling back a bespoke cocktail or three with friends, old or new. (646-559-1671; www.bathtubginnyc.com; 132 Ninth Ave btwn 18th & 19th Sts; 6pm-1:30am Sun-Tue, to 3:30am Wed-Sat; A/C/E to 14th St; L to 8th Ave; A/C/E to 23rd St)

Top Tip

Lost Like a Local

It's perfectly acceptable to arm yourself with a map (or rely on your smartphone) to get around the West Village's charming-but-challenging side streets. Even some locals have a tricky time finding their way! Just remember that 4th St makes a diagonal turn north – breaking away from the usual east–west street grid – and you'll quickly become a Village pro.

Vol de Nuit

PUB

39 Map p90, F4

Even all the NYU students can't ruin this: a cozy Belgian beer bar, with Delirium Tremens on tap and a few dozen bottle options – like Duvel and Lindemans Framboise (raspberry beer!). You can order *moules* (mussels) and *frites* (fries) to share at the front patio seats, the lounge, the communal wood tables or under the dangling red lights at the bar. (☎212-982-3388; 148 W 4th St; ☺4pm-1am Sun-Thu, to 3am Fri & Sat; ⑤A/C/E, B/D/F/M to W 4th St-Washington Sq)

124 Old Rabbit Club

BAR

40 Map p90, F5

You'll wanna pat yourself on the back when you find this cavernous, well-concealed bar (hint: look for the tiny words 'Rabbit Club Craft Beer Bar' over the door). Once inside, grab a seat at the dimly lit bar and reward yourself with a quenching stout or one of the dozens of imported brews. (☎212-254-0575; 124 MacDougal St; ☺6pm-4am; ⑤A/C/E, B/D/F/M to W 4th St; 1 to Houston St)

Eagle NYC

CLUB

41 Map p90, B1

A bi-level club full of hot men in leather, the Eagle is the choice for out-and-proud fetishists. Two levels and a roof deck offer plenty of room for drinking and dancing, both of which are done with abandon. Thursdays are 'code' nights (wear leather, or nada). Located in a renovated 19th-century stable, the inside joke is that 'the studs keep coming.' (☎646-473-1866; www.eaglenyc.com; 555 W 28th St btwn Tenth & Eleventh Aves; ☺10pm-4am Mon-Sat; ⑤C/E to 23rd St)

Julius Bar

GAY

42 Map p90, E4

One of the infamous originals – in fact, it's the oldest operating gay bar in NYC – Julius is a dive bar through and through. The only hint of its homo roots is the clientele, a mixed bag of faithful locals and the occasional debutant. It's refreshingly unpretentious and just steps away from the better-known Stonewall and Duplex. (☎212-243-1928; 159 W 10th St at Waverly Pl; ☺noon-2am Sun-Thu, to 4am Fri & Sat; ⑤A/C/E, B/D/F/M to W 4th St, 1 to Christopher St-Sheridan Sq)

Henrietta Hudson

LESBIAN

43 Map p90, E5

All types of cute young dykes, many from neighboring New Jersey and Long Island, storm this sleek lounge, where varying theme nights bring in spirited DJs playing particular genres (hip-hop, house, rock). The owner, Brooklyn native Lisa Canistraci, is a favorite promoter in the world of lesbian nightlife, and is often on hand to mix it up with her fans. (☎212-924-3347; 438 Hudson St; ☺5pm-2am Mon & Tue, 4pm-4am Wed-Fri, 2pm-4am Sat & Sun; ⑤1 to Houston St)

Spotted Pig (p98)

Cielo
CLUB

44 Map p90, C3

Long-running Cielo delivers a largely attitude-free crowd and an excellent sound system. While 'Deep House' Monday nights sees DJ François K spin dub and underground beats, other nights are dedicated to various Euro DJs spinning seductive sounds that pull everyone to their feet. (212-645-5700; www.cieloclub.com; 18 Little W 12th St; cover charge $15-25; 10:30pm-5am Mon-Sat; S A/C/E, L to 8th Ave-14th St)

Entertainment

Upright Citizens Brigade Theatre
COMEDY

45 Map p90, D1

Pros of comedy sketches and outrageous improvisations reign at this popular 74-seat venue, which gets drop-ins from casting directors. Getting in is cheap, and so is the beer and wine. You may recognize the pranksters on stage from late-night comedy shows. It's free Sundays after 9:30pm and Wednesdays after 11pm, when newbies take the stage. (212-366-9176; www.ucbtheatre.com; 307 W 26th St btwn Eighth & Ninth Aves; cover $5-10; S C/E to 23rd St)

Village Vanguard JAZZ

46 ⭐ Map p90, E4

Possibly the city's most prestigious jazz club, the Vanguard has hosted literally every major star of the past 50 years. It started as a home to spoken-word performances and occasionally returns to its roots, but most of the time it's just big, bold jazz all night long. (☎212-255-4037; www.villagevanguard.com; 178 Seventh Ave at 11th St; cover $25-30 plus 1-drink minimum; ⑤1/2/3 to 14th St)

Sleep No More THEATER

47 ⭐ Map p90, B1

One of the most immersive theater experiences ever conceived, Sleep No More is a loosely based retelling of *Macbeth* set inside a series of Chelsea warehouses. It's a choose-your-own adventure kind of experience where audience members are free to wander the elaborate rooms and interact with the actors. You'll need to check everything when you arrive (jackets, handbag, cellphone, etc), and wear a mask, a la *Eyes Wide Shut*. (www.sleepnomorenyc.com; McKittrick Hotel, 530 W 27th St; tickets from $106; ⏰7pm-midnight Mon-Sat; ⑤C/E to 23rd St)

Le Poisson Rouge LIVE MUSIC

48 ⭐ Map p90, F5

Push your boundaries at this high-concept art space (complete with dangling fish aquarium), famed for its highly eclectic lineup. Experimentation and cross-genre pollination between classical, ethnic folk music, opera and more is the norm, with past performers including Deerhunter, Marc Ribot and Cibo Matto. (☎212-505-3474; www.lepoissonrouge.com; 158 Bleecker St; ⑤A/C/E, B/D/F/M to W 4th St-Washington Sq)

Comedy Cellar COMEDY

49 ⭐ Map p90, F5

This long-established basement club in Greenwich Village features mainstream material and a good list of regulars (eg Colin Quinn, SNL's Darrell Hammond, Wanda Sykes), plus an occasional high-profile drop-in like Dave Chappelle. Its success continues: Comedy Cellar now boasts another location around the corner on W 3rd St. (☎212-254-3480; www.comedycellar.com; 117 MacDougal St btwn W 3rd & Minetta Ln; cover $12-24; ⏰shows start approx 9pm Sun-Fri, 7pm & 9:30pm Sat; ⑤A/C/E, B/D/F/M to W 4th St-Washington Sq)

Blue Note JAZZ

50 ⭐ Map p90, F5

This is by far the most famous (and expensive) of the city's jazz clubs. Most shows are $30 at the bar, $45 at a table, but can rise for the biggest jazz stars (there are also a few cheaper $20 shows, as well as jazz brunch on Sundays at 11:30am). Go on an off night, and be quiet – all attention is on the stage! (☎212-475-8592; www.bluenote.net; 131 W 3rd St btwn Sixth Ave & MacDougal St; ⑤A/C/E, B/D/F/M to W 4th St-Washington Sq)

Cherry Lane Theater THEATER

51 Map p90, E5

Started by poet Edna St Vincent Millay, this West Village classic has given a voice to numerous playwrights and actors over the years. It remains true to its mission of creating 'live' theater that's accessible to the public. Readings, plays and spoken-word performances rotate frequently. (☎212-989-2020; www.cherrylanetheater. org; 38 Commerce St; ⓢ1 to Christopher St-Sheridan Sq)

Angelika Film Center CINEMA

52 Map p90, G5

Angelika specializes in foreign and independent films and has some quirky charms (the rumble of the subway, long lines and occasionally bad sound). But its roomy cafe is a great place to meet and the beauty of its Stanford White–designed, beaux arts building is undeniable. (☎212-995-2570; www.angelikafilmcenter.com; 18 W Houston St at Mercer St; tickets $10-14; ♿; ⓢB/D/F/M to Broadway-Lafayette St)

IFC Center CINEMA

53 Map p90, E5

Slap bang in NYU-land, this arthouse film mecca serves up a solid lineup of new indies, cult classics and foreign flicks. Catch shorts, documentaries, '80s revivals, director-focused series, weekend classics and frequent special series, such as cult favorites (*The Shining, Taxi Driver, Aliens*) at midnight.

 Local Life
West 4th Street Basketball Courts

Also known as 'the Cage,' this small **basketball court** (Map p90, F4; Sixth Ave btwn 3rd & 4th Sts; ⓢA/C/E, B/D/F/V to W 4th St-Washington Sq) stands enclosed within chain-link fencing and is home to some of the best streetball in the country. Though it's more touristy than its counterpart, Rucker Park in Harlem, that's also part of its charm. Games held here draw massive, excitable crowds, who often stand 10-deep to hoot and holler for the skilled, competitive guys who play here.

(☎212-924-7771; www.ifccenter.com; 323 Sixth Ave at 3rd St; ⓢA/C/E, B/D/F/M to W 4th St-Washington Sq)

Duplex CABARET, KARAOKE

54 Map p90, E4

Cabaret, karaoke and campy dance moves are par for the course at the legendary Duplex. Pictures of Joan Rivers line the walls, and the performers like to mimic her sassy form of self-deprecation, while getting in a few jokes about audience members as well. It's a fun and unpretentious place, and certainly not for the bashful. (☎212-255-5438; www.theduplex. com; 61 Christopher St; cover $5-15, 2-drink minimum; ☺4pm-4am; ⓢ1 to Christopher St-Sheridan Sq)

Chelsea Bow Tie Cinema CINEMA

55 Map p90, D1

In addition to showing first-run films, this multiscreen complex hosts weekend midnight showings of the *Rocky Horror Picture Show,* as well as a great Thursday-night series, Chelsea Classics, which sees local drag star Hedda Lettuce hosting old-school camp fare from Joan Crawford, Bette Davis, Barbra Streisand and the like. (☏212-777-3456; www.bowtiecinemas.com; 260 W 23rd St btwn Seventh & Eighth Aves; Ⓢ C/E to 23rd St)

Atlantic Theater Company THEATER

 56 ⭐ Map p90, D2

Founded by David Mamet and William H Macy in 1985, the Atlantic Theater is a pivotal anchor for the off-Broadway community, hosting many Tony Award and Drama Desk winners over the last 25-plus years. (☏212-691-5919; www.atlantictheater.org; 336 W 20th St btwn Eighth & Ninth Aves; Ⓢ C/E to 23rd St, 1 to 18th St)

Joyce Theater DANCE

57 Map p90, D2

Occupying a renovated cinema, Joyce is a hit with dance fiends thanks to its offbeat dance offerings and good sightlines. The focus is on traditional modern companies such as Pilobolus, Stephen Petronio Company and Parsons Dance as well as global stars, such as DanceBrazil, Ballet Hispanico and MalPaso Dance Company. (☏212-242-0800; www.joyce.org; 175 Eighth Ave; Ⓢ C/E to 23rd St; A/C/E to Eighth Ave-14th St; 1 to 18th St)

New York Live Arts DANCE

58 ⭐ Map p90, E2

You'll find a program of more than 100 experimental, contemporary performances annually at this sleek dance center, led by artistic director Carla Peterson. International troupes from Serbia, South Africa, Korea and beyond bring fresh works to the stage; many shows include pre- or post-show discussions with choreographers or dancers. (☏212-924-0077; www.newyorklivearts.org; 219 W 19th St btwn Seventh & Eighth Aves; Ⓢ 1 to 18th St)

Local Life
Marie's Crisis

Aging Broadway queens, wide-eyed out-of-town gay boys, giggly tourist girls and other miscellaneous fans of musical theater assemble around the piano at **Marie's Crisis** (Map p90, E4; ☏212-243-9323; 59 Grove St btwn Seventh Ave & Bleecker St; ◷4pm-4am; Ⓢ 1 to Christopher St-Sheridan Sq), a one-time whorehouse, and take turns belting out campy numbers, often joined by the entire crowd. It's infectious, old-school fun, no matter how jaded you were when you went in.

Duplex (p107)

Shopping

Strand Book Store   BOOKS

59 🛍 Map p90, G3

Do not miss Gotham's most loved and famous bookstore. In operation since 1927, the Strand stocks new, used and rare titles, spreading an incredible 18 miles of books (over 2.5 million of them) among three labyrinthine floors. (📞212-473-1452; www.strandbooks.com; 828 Broadway at 12th St; ⏰9:30am-10:30pm Mon-Sat, from 11am Sun; Ⓢ L, N/Q/R, 4/5/6 to 14th St-Union Sq)

Personnel of New York   FASHION, ACCESSORIES

60 🛍 Map p90, E4

Good things come in small packages, including this clued-in fashion store. Pick up men's and women's designer clothing from unique East and West Coast labels, as well as in-the-know foreign brands. Keep an eye out for beautifully textured wovens by Ace & Jig, rugged menswear by Hiroshi Awai, couture pieces by Rodobjer and batik shirts by All Nations. (9 Greenwich Ave btwn Christopher & W 10th St; ⏰11am-8pm Mon-Sat, noon-7pm Sun; Ⓢ A/C/E, B/D/F/M to W 4th St; 1 to Christopher St-Sheridan Sq)

Monocle   ACCESSORIES, FASHION

61 Map p90, D4

Founded by style magazine guru Tyler Brûlé, bento-box-sized Monocle shops deals in stylish edits of well-made products for urbanites and global travelers, from leather-bound journals and elegant stationary, to passport holders, Japanese body soaps and swimming trunks. If by chance you haven't heard of Monocle magazine, pick up a copy here. (535 Hudson St at Charles St; ⊙11am-7pm Mon-Sat, noon-6pm Sun; **S**1 to Christopher St-Sheridan Sq)

CO Bigelow Chemists   HEALTH, BEAUTY

62 Map p90, F4

The 'oldest apothecary in America' is now a fantasyland for the beauty-product obsessed, its own line up of lip balms, hand and foot salves, shaving creams and rosewater looking good alongside lotions, shampoos, cosmetics and fragrances from names like Weleda, Yu-Be and Vichy. (☑212-473-7324; 414 Sixth Ave btwn 8th & 9th Sts; ⊙7:30am-9pm Mon-Fri, 8:30am-7pm Sat, 8:30am-5:30pm Sun; **S**1 to Christopher St-Sheridan Sq; A/C/E, B/D/F/M to W 4th St-Washington Sq)

Printed Matter   BOOKS

63 Map p90, C2

Printed Matter is a wondrous two-room treasure trove of limited-edition artist monographs and strange little zines. While you won't find anything carried by mainstream bookstores, you will stumble upon anything and everything from call-to-arms manifestos and critical essays on comic books, to flip books that reveal Jesus' face through barcodes. (☑212-925-0325; 195 Tenth Ave btwn 21st & 22nd Sts; ⊙11am-7pm Sat & Mon-Wed, to 8pm Thu-Fri; **S**C/E to 23rd St)

Aedes de Venustas   BEAUTY

64 Map p90, E4

Plush Aedes de Venustas ('Temple of Beauty' in Latin) offers over 40 brands of luxe European perfumes, including Hierbas de Ibiza, Mark Birley for Men, Costes, Odin and Shalini. Pair that perfect fragrance with skincare products by Susanne Kaufmann and Acqua di Rose, and scented candles from Diptyque. (☑212-206-8674; www.aedes.com; 9 Christopher St; ⊙noon-8pm Mon-Sat, 1-7pm Sun; **S**A/C/E, B/D/F/M to W 4th St; 1 to Christopher St-Sheridan Sq)

Antiques Garage Flea Market   ANTIQUES, MARKET

65 Map p90, E1

Set in a two-level parking garage, this weekend flea market sees over a 100 vendors peddling threads, shoes, records, books, globes, furniture, rugs, lamps, glassware, paintings, artwork and many other relics from the past. If you're an antique lover, dive in. (112 W 25th St at Sixth Ave; ⊙9am-5pm Sat & Sun; **S**1 to 23rd St)

Earnest Sewn
FASHION, ACCESSORIES

66 🔒 Map p90, C3

Earnest Sewn denim is legendary for its craftsmanship, and customers sign on to long waiting lists to order customized and tailored jeans. Denim aside, you'll find an eclectic mix of jewelry, outerwear and pocketknives among antique machinery. There's a second branch in the Lower East Side. (📞212-242-3414; www.earnestsewn. com; 821 Washington St; ⊙11am-7pm Sun-Fri, 11am-8pm Sat; Ⓢ A/C/E to 14th St; L to Eighth Ave)

Yoyamart
CHILDREN

67 🔒 Map p90, D3

Ostensibly geared toward the younger set, Yoyamart is a fun place to browse for adults – even if you're not packing a child. Sure, you'll find adorable apparel for babies and toddlers, but there are also cuddly robots, Gloomy Bear gloves, plush ninjas, build-your-own-ukulele kits, CD mixes and various anime-style amusement. (📞212-242-5511; www.yoyamart.com; 15 Gansevoort St; ⊙11am-7pm Mon-Sat, noon-6pm Sun; Ⓢ A/C/E to 14th St; L to Eighth Ave)

Beacon's Closet
THRIFT STORE

68 🔒 Map p90, F3

Plunder a satisfying selection of gently used, hipster-centric threads at only slightly higher prices than Beacon's sister store in Williamsburg. Thrift shops are thin on the ground in this area, which makes Beacon's even

more of a draw. Come mid-week or be prepared to brave the crowds. (10 W 13th St btwn Fifth & Sixth Aves; ⊙11am-8pm; Ⓢ L, N/R, 4/5/6 to Union Sq)

Bonnie Slotnick Cookbooks
BOOKS

Located near Julius Bar (see **42** 🔒 Map p90, E4), in what fees like grandma's pantry, owner Bonnie dotes on her customers on the hunt for the perfect cooking tome. Soaring shelves heave with some of the world's best recipes, from soulful Jewish soups to gay-themed bites. (📞212-989-8962; www. bonnieslotnickcookbooks.com; 163 W 10th St btwn Waverly Pl & Seventh Ave; Ⓢ 1/2 to Christopher St-Sheridan Sq; A/C/E, B/D/F/M to W 4th St)

Flight 001
TRAVEL GEAR

69 🔒 Map p90, E3

Travel is fun, sure – but the planning part is even more exhilarating. Daydream about your next adventure over Flight 001's super-cool luggage and bags, kitschy 'shemergency' kits (breath freshener, lip balm, stain remover, etc), pin-up-girl flasks, brightly colored passport holders and leather luggage tags, travel guidebooks and toiletry cases. All that's left is buying the ticket! (📞212-989-0001; www. flight001.com; 96 Greenwich Ave; ⊙11am-8pm Mon-Sat, noon-6pm Sun; Ⓢ A/C/E to 14th St; L to Eighth Ave)

Explore

Union Square, Flatiron District & Gramercy

The name 'Union Square' is quite apt since this neighborhood is the union of many disparate parts of the city; it's the urban glue linking unlikely cousins. Here, you'll feel the Village vibe, spilling over with quirky cafes, funky shops and dreadlocked loiterers, mingled with a distinct commercial feel replete with crowded lunch spots and after-work watering holes.

The Sights in a Day

☀️ Start the morning amid the colorful clash of personalities in **Union Square** (p115) – businessfolk dash to their offices and buskers juggle on the stone steps. If the **Union Square Greenmarket** (p124) is on, peruse freshly plucked produce from farms in the nearby Hudson Valley.

☀️ Wander by the ravishing **Flatiron Building** (p115) with its signature triangular shape, then check out **ABC Carpet & Home** (p124) for some serious souvenir shopping. Dine on-site at **ABC Kitchen** (p118) or try a classic New York carb at **Ess-a-Bagel** (p118). Wherever you decide to dine, make sure you wash it down with top-notch coffee at **Toby's Estate** (p122).

🌙 Take a sunset stroll around **Gramercy Park** (p116), then swing by the gourmet market at **Eataly** (p124) and take the elevator to the top to indulge in pork shoulder and hand-crafted brews at **Birreria** (p122), the lofted beer garden. Alternatively, crank up the culinary wow factor with a degustation feast at **Eleven Madison Park** (p117). Either way, cap the night with classic cocktails at **Flatiron Lounge** (p121).

💜 Best of New York City

Eating
Eleven Madison Park (p117)

Maialino (p118)

Birreria (p122)

Drinking
Flatiron Lounge (p121)

Raines Law Room (p121)

Boxers NYC (p123)

Shopping
ABC Carpet & Home (p124)

Idlewild Books (p125)

Books of Wonder (p125)

Getting There

S Subway A slew of subway lines converge below Union Square station, shuttling passengers up Manhattan's East Side on the 4, 5 and 6 lines, straight across to Williamsburg on the L, or up and over to Queens on the N, Q and R lines.

🚌 Bus The M14 and the M23 provide east–west service along 14th St and 23rd St respectively.

A

34th St-Herald Sq Ⓢ
W 34th St
Empire State Building
W 33rd St
W 32nd St (Korea Way)
KOREATOWN
W 31st St
W 30th St
W 29th St
W 28th St Ⓢ 28th St
W 27th St
W 26th St
W 25th St

Broadway

W 24th St **29** Ⓐ
23rd St Ⓢ
6◉ W 23rd St
Institute of Culinary Education

W 21st St
23Ⓟ **21**Ⓢ
14
18
Ⓧ Ⓟ W 20th St
W 19th St **31**Ⓐ
W 18th St **32**Ⓐ
W 17th St
19Ⓟ

Sixth Ave (Avenue of the Americas)

W 16th St **UNION SQUARE**
W 15th St
6th Ave-14th St Ⓢ
W 14th St
W 13th St
W 12th St
W 11th St

B

W 34th St
E 34th St
33rd St
E 33rd St Ⓢ
E 32nd St
E 31st St
E 30th St
E 29th St
28th St Ⓢ
E 28th St
E 27th St
E 26th St
E 25th St

Madison Ave

Madison Square Park
3◉ **7**Ⓧ
15Ⓧ
23rd St Ⓢ
◉ Flatiron Building **2**

FLATIRON DISTRICT
Theodore Roosevelt ◉ⓍⓍ**11**
Birthplace **5** **13**
28Ⓐ

Fifth Ave

E 17th St
E 16th St
E 15th St
14th St-Union Sq Ⓢ
33Ⓐ 14th St-Union Sq
E 13th St
E 12th St
E 11th St

Park Ave S

University Pl

Union Square
17Ⓧ
Union Square
1◉
Ⓢ Ⓢ
E 14th St Ⓢ

Broadway

Fourth Ave

C

E 33rd St

LITTLE INDIA
E 28th St

Lexington Ave

E 27th St
E 26th St
E 25th St

28th St Ⓢ
27Ⓐ

23rd St Ⓢ
E 23rd St

E 22nd St
8Ⓧ
4◉ Gramercy Park

E 21st St
GRAMERCY PARK
E 20th St
26Ⓟ **24**Ⓟ
30Ⓧ**12**
9Ⓧ
E 17th St

Third Ave

Irving Pl

E 16th St
E 15th St
3rd Ave
E 14th St Ⓢ
E 13th St
E 12th St
E 11th St

D

0 ◎ ───── 500 m
0 ───── 0.25 miles

For reviews see	
◉ Sights	p115
Ⓧ Eating	p117
Ⓟ Drinking	p121
Ⓐ Entertainment	p124
Ⓐ Shopping	p124

E 28th St
E 27th St
E 26th St
E 25th St

Second Ave

Mt Carmel Pl

First Ave

E 23rd St
GRAMERCY
10Ⓧ
E 21st St
E 20th St
E 19th St
E 18th St
E 17th St
Stuyvesant Sq E 16th St
E 15th St
20Ⓟ **22**Ⓟ 1st Ave Ⓢ
25ⓅⓍ**16**
E 13th St
E 12th St **EAST VILLAGE**
E 11th St

First Ave

RACHEL LEWIS/GETTY IMAGES ©

Flatiron Building

Sights

Union Square

SQUARE

1 ⊙ Map p114, B4

Union Sq is like the Noah's Ark of New York, rescuing at least two of every kind from the curling seas of concrete. In fact, one would be hard-pressed to find a more eclectic cross-section of locals gathered in one public place. Here, amid the tapestry of stone steps and fenced-in foliage, it's not uncommon to find denizens of every ilk: suited businessfolk gulping fresh air during their lunch breaks, dreadlocked loiterers tapping beats on their tabla, skateboarding punks flipping tricks on the southeastern stairs, rowdy college kids guzzling student-priced eats and throngs of protesting masses chanting fervently for various causes. (www.unionsquarenyc.org; 17th St btwn Broadway & Park Ave S; ⓢL, N/Q/R, 4/5/6 to 14th St-Union Sq)

Flatiron Building

LANDMARK

2 ⊙ Map p114, B3

Designed by Daniel Burnham and built in 1902, the 20-story Flatiron Building features a uniquely narrow triangular footprint that resembles the prow of a massive ship. It also features a traditional beaux arts limestone and terracotta facade that gets more complex and beautiful the longer you stare at it. Best viewed from the traffic island north of 23rd St between Broadway and Fifth Ave, the structure dominated the plaza back in the skyscraper era of the early 1900s. Indeed, until 1909 it was the world's tallest building. (Broadway cnr Fifth Ave & 23rd St; **S**N/R, F/M, 6 to 23rd St)

Madison Square Park
PARK

3 Map p114, B3

This park defined the northern reaches of Manhattan until the island's population exploded after the Civil War. These days, it's a much-welcome oasis from Manhattan's relentless pace, with locals unleashing their dogs in the popular dog-run area, children squealing giddily at the impressive playground and the hungry lining up at on-site burger joint Shake Shack (p120). (www.nycgovparks.org/parks/madisonsquarepark; 23rd to 26th Sts btwn Fifth & Madison Aves; ☉6am-11pm; **S**N/R, F/M, 6 to 23rd St)

Gramercy Park
PARK

4 Map p114, C3

This gorgeous, English-style park was created by Samuel Ruggles in 1831 after he drained the swamp in this area and laid out streets in a colonial style. It's one of the most inspired moments of calm in the city. It's a private park, so you can't enter, but it's well worth peering through the iron gates. (E 20th St btwn Park & Third Aves; **S**N/R, F/M, 6 to 23rd St)

Theodore Roosevelt Birthplace

HISTORIC SITE

5 Map p114, B4

This National Historic Site is a bit of a cheat, since the physical house where the 26th president was actually born was demolished in his own lifetime. But this building is a worthy reconstruction by his relatives, who joined it with another family residence next door.

If you're interested in Roosevelt's extraordinary life, which has been somewhat overshadowed by the enduring legacy of his younger cousin Franklin D, visit here – especially if you don't have the time to see his spectacular summer home in Long Island's Oyster Bay. Guided tours of the property last 30 minutes. (212-260-1616; www.nps.gov/thrb; 28 E 20th St, btwn Park Ave S & Broadway; adult/child $3/free; ☺guided tours 10am, 11am, 1pm, 2pm, 3pm & 4pm Tue-Sat; ⑤N/R/W, 6 to 23rd St)

Institute of Culinary Education

COOKING COURSE

6 Map p114, A3

Release your inner Jean Jacques with a cooking course at the Institute of Culinary Education (ICE). The center runs the country's biggest program of cooking, baking and wine appreciation courses, from 90-minute classes to multi-day sessions. The varied themes range from Tuscan cooking and Japanese street food, to Californian wines and coffee presentation. Restless foodies can choose from

Traffic on 14th Street
Human traffic can be overwhelming in Union Sq, especially along 14th St. If you're in a rush, or trying to hoof it on foot, then switch over to 13th St and you'll cover a lot more ground in much less time.

numerous culinary tours of the city. (ICE; http://recreational.ice.edu; 50 W 23rd St, btwn Fifth & Sixth Aves; courses $30-605; ⑤F/M, N/R, 6 to 23rd St)

Eating

Eleven Madison Park

MODERN AMERICAN $$$

7 Map p114, B3

Once overlooked in this star-studded town, this deco wonder has rocketed up the charts, coming in at number 5 in the 2013 San Pellegrino World's 50 Best Restaurants list. It's hardly surprising: this revamped poster child of modern, sustainable American cooking is also one of only seven NYC restaurants sporting three Michelin stars.

Behind the buzz is young-gun co-owner and chef Daniel Humm, who turns immaculate regional ingredients into indescribably pure, sublime statements. Book ahead. (212-889-0905; www.elevenmadisonpark.com; 11 Madison Ave, btwn 24th & 25th Sts; tasting menu $225; ☺noon-1pm Thu-Sat, 5:30-10pm Mon-Sun; ⑤N/R, F/M, 6 to 23rd St)

ABC Kitchen

MODERN AMERICAN $$$

Looking part gallery, part rustic farmhouse, sustainable ABC Kitchen is the culinary avatar of chi-chi home goods department store ABC Carpet & Home (see 28 Map p114, B4). Organic gets haute in dishes like vibrant raw diver scallops with market grapes and lemon verbena, or comforting roast suckling pig with braised turnips and smoked bacon marmalade. For a more casual bite, hit the scrumptious whole-wheat pizzas. (📞212-475-5829; www.abckitchennyc.com; 35 E 18th St, at Broadway; pizzas $15-19, dinner mains $24-34; ⊙noon-3pm & 5:30-10:30pm Mon-Wed, to 11pm Thu, to 11:30pm Fri, 11am-3:30pm & 5:30-11:30pm Sat, to 10pm Sun; 🚶; ⑤L, N/Q/R, 4/5/6 to Union Sq)

Maialino

ITALIAN $$$

8 Map p114, C3

Take your taste buds on a Roman holiday at this Danny Meyer must, humming away inside the forever-fashionable Gramercy Park Hotel. Created with greenmarket produce from nearby Union Sq, Maialino's iterations of rustic Italian fare are exquisite; one taste of the extraordinary *brodetto* (seafood stew), and we swear you'll agree.

The $35 prix-fixe lunch is great value, especially if you opt for the pricier items. (📞212-777-2410; www.maialinonyc.com; 2 Lexington Ave, at 21st St; mains lunch $19-26, dinner $28-72; ⊙ 7:30am-10:30pm Mon-Fri, from 10am Sat & Sun; ⑤6, N/R to 23rd St)

Casa Mono

TAPAS $$$

9 Map p114, C4

Another success story from Mario Batali and chef Andy Nusser, Casa Mono features a great, long bar where you can sit and watch your Michelin-starred tapas being made, as well as tables for more discrete conversation. Either way, get set for flavor-slamming bites like cauliflower crema with raw sea urchin and Vadouvan. Around the corner lies Batali's fun, communal **Bar Jamón**. (📞212-253-2773; www.casamononyc.com; 52 Irving Pl, btwn 17th & 18th Sts; small plates $9-24; ⊙noon-midnight; ⑤L, N/Q/R, 4/5/6 to Union Sq)

Ess-a-Bagel

DELI $

10 Map p114, D3

It's simply impossible to resist the billowy tufts of sesame-scented smoke that waft out onto First Ave. Inside, crowds of lip-smacking locals yell at the bagel mongers for their classic New York snack topped with generous gobs of cream cheese. And those gaudy, jewel-dripping chandeliers jammed into the Styrofoam ceiling? You stay classy, Ess-a-Bagel. (📞212-260-2252; www.ess-a-bagel.com; 359 First Ave, at 21st St; bagels from $1.65; ⊙6am-9pm Mon-Fri, to 5pm Sat & Sun; ⑤L, N/Q/R, 4/5/6 to Union Sq)

Gramercy Tavern

AMERICAN $$$

11 Map p114, B4

Seasonal, local ingredients drive Gramercy Tavern, a country-chic

Union Square Greenmarket (p124)

institution aglow with copper sconces, bright murals and dramatic floral arrangements. Choose from two spaces: the walk-in-only tavern and its a la carte menu, or the swankier dining room and its more ambitious prix-fixe and degustation feasts.

Either way, soulful dishes like pasture-raised chicken & sausage with apples, kohlrabi and buckwheat dumplings will leave you with a postprandial glow. (📞 212-477-0777; www.gramercytavern. com; 42 E 20th St, btwn Broadway & Park Ave S; tasting menu lunch/dinner $58/120; ⏰ tavern noon-11pm Sun-Thu, to midnight Fri & Sat; dining room noon-2pm & 5:30-10pm Mon-Thu, to 11pm Fri, 5:30-11pm Sat, 5:30-10pm Sun; Ⓢ N/R, 6 to 23rd St)

Pure Food & Wine   VEGETARIAN $$$

12 Map p114, C4

Smart and sophisticated, Pure achieves the impossible – churning out obscenely delicious creations made completely from raw organics put through blenders, dehydrators and the capable hands of its staff. The result is seductive, invigorating dishes like tomato-zucchini lasagna (sans cheese and pasta), Brazil-nut sea-vegetable croquettes, and a gorgeous lemon bar with almond coconut crust and zesty lemon custard. (📞 212-477-1010; www.oneluckyduck.com/purefoodand-wine; 54 Irving Pl, btwn 17th & 18th Sts; mains $19-26; ⏰ noon-4pm & 5:30-11pm; 📷; Ⓢ L, N/Q/R, 4/5/6 to 14th St-Union Sq)

Trattoria Il Mulino   ITALIAN $$$

13 🍴 Map p114, B4

That head chef Michele Mazza looks uncannily like the Italian film star Marcello Mastroianni seems apt – his beautifully prepared dishes personify Italian *dolce vita* (sweet life). The pasta dishes and wood-fired pizzas are particularly memorable, while cross-regional influences meet in the zingy, classic-with-a-twist limoncello tiramisu. Attentive service and a chic-yet-amiable vibe make this spot *perfetto* for a special feed. (📞212-777-8448; www.trattoriailmulino.com; 36 E 20th St, btwn Broadway & Park Ave; pasta dishes $24, mains $28-45; ☻11:30am-11pm Sun-Thu, to 2am Fri & Sat; ⑤6, N/R to 23rd St)

Boqueria Flatiron   TAPAS $$

14 🍴 Map p114, A4

A holy union between Spanish-style tapas and market-fresh fare, Boqueria woos the after-work crowd with a brilliant line up of small plates and larger *raciones*. Lick lips and fingers over the likes of sautéed wild mushrooms with Manchego cheese and thyme, or tender baby squid seared *a la plancha* with frisée, tomato confit and crispy scallions. (📞212-255-4160; www.boquerianyc.com; 53 W 19th St, btwn Fifth & Sixth Aves; dishes $5-22; ☻noon-10:30pm Sun-Wed, to 11:30pm Thu-Sat; ⑤F/M, N/R, 6 to 23rd St)

Shake Shack   BURGERS $

15 🍴 Map p114, B3

The flagship of chef Danny Meyer's gourmet burger chainlet, Shake Shack whips up hyper-fresh burgers, hand-cut fries and a rotating line-up of frozen custards. Veg-heads can dip into the crisp Portobello burger. Lines are long, but worth it. (📞212-989-6600; www.shakeshack.com; Madison Square Park, cnr 23rd St & Madison Ave; burgers from $3.60; ☻11am-11pm; ⑤N/R, F/M, 6 to 23rd St)

Artichoke Basille's Pizza   PIZZERIA $

16 🍴 Map p114, D5

Run by two Italian guys from Staten Island, the pizza here is authentic, tangy and piled high with all sorts of toppings. The signature pie is a rich, cheesy treat with artichokes and spinach; the plain Sicilian is thinner, with emphasis solely on the crisp crust and savory sauce. Lines usually form fast. (☏212-228-2004; www.artichokepizza.com; 328 E 14th St, btwn First & Second Aves; slice from $4.50; ⏱11am-5am; Ⓢ L to First Ave)

Republic

ASIAN $$

17 Map p114, B4

Eat-and-go Republic feeds the masses with fresh-n-tasty Asian staples. Slurp away on warming broth noodles, chomp on juicy pad thai or keep it light with a green papaya and mango salad. Located right on Union Square, it's a handy spot for a cheap, uncomplicated, walk-in bite. (www.thinknoodles.com; 37 Union Sq W; mains $12-15; ⏱11:30am-10:30pm Sun-Wed, to 11:30pm Thu-Sat; Ⓢ L, N/Q/R, 4/5/6 to 14th St-Union Sq)

Drinking

Flatiron Lounge

COCKTAIL BAR

18 Map p114, A4

Until time machines hit the market, this swinging cocktail den will do just fine. Head through a dramatic archway and into a dark, deco-inspired fantasy of lipstick-red booths, racy jazz tunes and sassy grown-ups downing seasonal drinks. The Beijing Mule (Jasmine vodka, lime juice, ginger syrup and pomegranate molasses) is scrumptious, while the genial 'Flight of the Day' (a trio of mini-sized cocktails) is head-spinning enlightenment. (www.flatironlounge.com; 37 W 19th St, btwn Fifth & Sixth Aves; ⏱4pm-2am Mon-Wed, to 3am Thu, to 4am Fri, 5pm-4am Sat, 5pm-2am Sun; Ⓢ F/M, N/R, 6 to 23rd St)

Raines Law Room

COCKTAIL BAR

19 Map p114, A4

A sea of velvet drapes and overstuffed leather lounge chairs, tin-tiled ceilings, the perfect amount of exposed brick, and expertly crafted cocktails using perfectly aged spirits – these guys are about as serious as a mortgage payment when it comes to amplified atmosphere. Walk through the unassuming entrance and let Raines Law Room transport you to a far more sumptuous era. (www.raineslawroom.com; 48 W 17th St, btwn Fifth & Sixth Aves; ⏱5pm-2am Mon-Thu, to 3am Fri & Sat, 8pm-1am Sun; Ⓢ F/M to 14th St, L to 6th Ave, 1 to 18th St)

Beauty Bar

THEME BAR

20 Map p114, D5

A kitschy favorite since the mid-90s, this homage to old-fashioned beauty parlors pulls in a cool local crowd with its gritty soundtrack, nostalgic vibe and US$10 manicures (with a free Blue Rinse margarita thrown in) from 6pm to 11pm on weekdays, and 3pm to 11pm on weekends. Nightly events range from comedy to karaoke. (☏212-539-1389; http://thebeautybar.com/home-new-york; 531 E 14th St, btwn Second & Third Aves; ⏱5pm-4am Mon-Fri, from 2pm Sat & Sun; Ⓢ L to 3rd Ave)

Birreria

BEER HALL

The crown jewel of Italian food emporium Eataly (see 29 Map p114, A3) is its rooftop beer garden tucked betwixt the Flatiron's corporate towers. A beer menu of encyclopedic proportions offers drinkers some of the best suds on the planet. If you're hungry, the signature pork shoulder is your frosty one's soul mate. (www.eataly.com/birreria; 200 Fifth Ave, at 23rd St; mains $17-26; ⏲11:30am-midnight Sun-Wed, to 1am Thu-Sat; **S**N/R, F/M, 6 to 23rd St)

Toby's Estate

CAFE

21 Map p114, A3

Sydney-born, Williamsburg-roasting Toby's Estate is further proof of Manhattan's evolving artisan coffee culture. Loaded with a custom-made Strada espresso machine, you'll find it tucked away in the Club Monaco store. Join coffee geeks for thick, rich brews, among them a geo-specific Flatiron Espresso Blend. Nibbles include pastries and sandwiches from local bakeries. (www.tobysestate.com; 160 Fifth Ave, btwn 20th & 21st Sts; ⏲7am-9pm Mon-Fri, 9am-9pm Sat, 10am-7pm Sun; **S**N/R, F/M, 6 to 23rd St)

Crocodile Lounge

LOUNGE

22 Map p114, D5

Hankering for Williamsburg but too lazy to cross the river? Then dive into Crocodile Lounge, outpost of Brooklyn success story Alligator Lounge. The lure of free pizza makes this hideout a big hit with East Village 20-somethings seeking a free feed. Slip on your skinny jeans and join them for on-tap microbrews, open mic sessions and some Skee-Ball. (☎212-477-7747; www.crocodileloungenyc.com; 325 E 14th St, btwn First & Second Aves; ⏲noon-4am; **S**L to 1st Ave)

Understand

Metronome

A walk around Union Sq reveals almost a dozen notable pieces of art – there's Rob Pruitt's 10ft homage to Andy Warhol and the imposing equestrian statue of George Washington. But on the south side of the square sits a massive art installation that either earns confused stares or simply gets overlooked by passersby. A symbolic representation of the passage of time, *Metronome* has two parts: a digital clock with a puzzling display of numbers and a wandlike apparatus with smoke puffing out of concentric rings. We'll let you ponder the latter while we give you the skinny on what exactly the winking orange digits denote. The 14 numbers must be split into two groups of seven. The seven from the left tell the current time (hour, minute, second, tenth-of-a-second) and the seven from the right are meant to be read in reverse order: they represent the remaining amount of time in the day.

Boxers NYC

GAY

23 Map p114, A3

Dave & Busters meets David Bowie at this self-proclaimed gay sports bar in the heart of the Flatiron District. There's football on the TV, buffalo wings at the bar, and topless wait staff keeping the pool cues polished. Monday's drag theme keeps everyone keenly aware that Boxers has a different definition of 'bromance'. (☎212-255-5082; www.boxersnyc.com; 37 W 20th St, btwn Fifth & Sixth Aves; ⏰4pm-2am Mon-Wed, to 4am Thu & Fri, 1pm-4am Sat, 1pm-2am Sun; 🖂F/M, N/R, 6 to 23rd St)

Pete's Tavern

BAR

24 Map p114, C4

This dark and atmospheric watering hole has all the earmarks of a New York classic – pressed tin, carved wood and an air of literary history. You can get a respectable burger here, and choose from 17 draft beers. The pub draws in everyone from post-theater couples and Irish expats to no-nonsense NYU students. (☎212-473-7676; www.petestavern. com; 129 E 18th St, at Irving Pl; ⏰11am-2am; 🖂L, N/Q/R, 4/5/6 to 14th St-Union Sq)

Nowhere

GAY

25 Map p114, D5

Dank and rife with amiable, flannel-clad fellas, Nowhere is everything your local gay dive bar should be (yes, there's a pool table to boot). The booze is priced for the '99%' and there's a pizza joint nearby, which keeps

Metronome, Union Square

crowds hanging out 'til the wee hours of the morn. (☎212-477-4744; www. nowherebarnyc.com; 322 E 14th St, btwn First & Second Aves; ⏰3pm-4am; 🖂L to First Ave)

71 Irving Place

CAFE

26 Map p114, C4

Few places take coffee more seriously than Irving Farm's quaint cafe just steps away from the peaceful Gramercy Park. Hand-picked beans are lovingly roasted on a farm in the Hudson Valley (about 90 miles from NYC), and imbibers can tell – this is one of the smoothest cups of joe you'll find in Manhattan. (Irving Farm Coffee Company; www.irvingfarm.com; 71 Irving Pl, btwn 18th & 19th Sts; ⏰7am-10pm Mon-Fri, from 8am Sat & Sun; 🖂4/5/6, N/Q/R to 14th St-Union Sq)

Entertainment

Peoples Improv Theater COMEDY

27 Map p114, C3

Aglow in red neon, this bustling comedy club serves up top-notch laughs at dirt-cheap prices (from free to a modest $20). The string of nightly acts range from stand-up to musical comedy, playing in either the main-stage theater or the basement lounge. (PIT; ☎212-563-7488; www.thepit-nyc.com; 123 E 24th St, btwn Lexington & Park Aves; 📶; S6, N/R, F/M to 23rd St)

Local Life
Union Square Greenmarket

Don't be surprised if you spot some of New York's top chefs examining the produce at the **Union Square Greenmarket** (Map p114, B4; Union Square, 17th St btwn Broadway & Park Ave S; ⊙8am-6pm Mon, Wed, Fri & Sat; S L, N/Q/R, 4/5/6 to 14th St-Union Sq). Straddling the west side of Union Square, it's arguably the city's most famous greenmarket and a fabulous spot to pick up some local edibles. Whet your appetite trawling the stalls, which peddle anything and everything from upstate fruit and vegetables, to artisan breads, cider, even honey produced on NYC rooftops.

Shopping

ABC Carpet & Home HOMEWARES, GIFTS

28 Map p114, B4

A mecca for home designers and decorators brainstorming ideas, this beautifully curated, six-level store heaves with all sorts of furnishings, large and small. Shop for easy-to-pack knickknacks, designer jewelry and global gifts, as well as statement furniture, slinky lamps and antique carpets. Come Christmas season the shop is a joy to behold. (☎212-473-3000; www.abchome.com; 888 Broadway, at 19th St; ⊙10am-7pm Mon-Wed, Fri & Sat, to 8pm Thu, noon-6pm Sun; S L, N/Q/R/, 4/5/6 to 14th St-Union Sq)

Eataly FOOD & DRINK

29 🔒 Map p114, A3

A 50,000-sq-ft tribute to the *dolce vita,* Mario Batali's food-filled wonderland is a New York version of those dreamy Tuscan markets you find in Diane Lane films. Decked stem to the stern with gourmet edibles, Eataly is a must for a picnic lunch – though make sure to leave room for some pork shoulder at the rooftop beer garden, Birreria (p122). (www.eatalyny.com; 200 Fifth Ave, at 23rd St; ⊙8am-11pm; S F/M, N/R, 6 to 23rd St)

Bedford Cheese Shop   FOOD

30 Map p114, C4

Whether you're after local raw cow-milk cheese washed in absinthe, or garlic-infused goat-milk cheese from Australia, chances are you'll find it among the 200-strong selection at this outpost of Brooklyn's most celebrated cheese vendor. Pair the cheesy goodness with artisanal charcuterie, deli treats and ready-to-eat sandwiches ($9), as well as a proud array of Made-in-Brooklyn edibles. (www.bedfordcheese shop.com; 67 Irving Pl, btwn 18th & 19th Sts; ⏰8am-9pm Mon-Sat, to 8pm Sun; ⑤L, N/Q/R, 4/5/6 to 14th St-Union Sq)

Idlewild Books   BOOKS

31 Map p114, A4

Named after JFK Airport's original moniker, this indie travel bookshop gets feet seriously itchy. Books are divided by region, and cover guidebooks as well as fiction, travelogues, history, cookbooks and other stimulating fare for delving into different corners of the world. Check the website for Idlewild's lineup of readings and book-launch parties. (☎212-414-8888; www.idlewildbooks.com; 12 W 19th St, btwn Fifth & Sixth Aves; ⏰noon-7.30pm Mon-Thu, to 6pm Fri & Sat, to 5pm Sun; ⑤L, N/Q/R, 4/5/6 to 14th St-Union Sq)

Books of Wonder   BOOKS

32 Map p114, A4

Kid or not, expect to fall head over heels for this colorful bookstore. Devoted to children's and young adult titles, it's a great place to take young ones on a rainy day, especially when a kids' author is giving a reading, or a storyteller is on hand. The impressive range of NYC-themed picture books make for great souvenirs. (☎212-989-3270; www.booksofwonder.com; 18 W 18th St, btwn Fifth & Sixth Aves; ⏰11am-7pm Mon-Sat, to 6pm Sun; ♿; ⑤F/M, L to 6th Ave-14th St)

Whole Foods   FOOD & DRINK

33 Map p114, B5

One of several locations of the healthy food emporium that has swept the city, Whole Foods is an excellent place to fill the picnic hamper. Drool over endless rows of gorgeous produce, both organic and non-organic, plus a butcher, a bakery, ready-to-eat dishes, a health and beauty section, and aisles packed with natural packaged goods. (☎212-673-5388; www.wholefoodsmarket. com; 4 Union Sq S; ⏰7.30am-11pm; 🛜; ⑤L, N/Q/R, 4/5/6 to 14th St-Union Sq)

Explore

Midtown

Midtown is the home of the NYC found on postcards: dazzling lights, Times Square billboards, glittering Broadway theaters, canyons of skyscrapers, endless streams of concrete roadways and bustling crowds that rarely thin. Scores of competitively priced hotels make it a great place to start and end your day during your New York foray.

The Sights in a Day

Midtown is big, bold and best seen on foot. The top end of Fifth Ave (around the 50s) makes for a fabled introduction – it's here you'll find glam icons like **Tiffany & Co** (p153), **Saks Fifth Ave** (p153) and the Plaza Hotel, not to mention the incredible **Museum of Modern Art** (p132). You could easily spend an entire day at the latter, ogling masterpieces, eating, drinking, catching a film and shopping for books and design objects.

Chow down on one of chef Danny Meyer's famous burgers at Shake Shack, then wander betwixt the city's signature skyscrapers, including the **Chrysler Building** (p136), **Rockefeller Center** (p136) and the almighty **Empire State Building** (p130).

Bright and blinding **Times Square** (p128) is most spectacular at night. Catch a Broadway show, such as **Kinky Boots** (p148), nibble on Michelin-starred tapas at **Danji** (p141), before dancing away the calories in Hell's Kitchen, best known for its kicking bars and gay hotspots, including **Industry** (p145), **Therapy** (p146), and **Flaming Saddles** (p146).

◉ Top Sights

Times Square (p128)

Empire State Building (p130)

Museum of Modern Art (p132)

Best of New York City

Entertainment
Kinky Boots (p148)

Book of Mormon (p148)

Playwrights Horizons (p150)

Museums
Museum of Modern Art (p132)

Architecture
Empire State Buildings (p130)

Chrysler Building (p136)

Grand Central Terminal (p136)

Getting There

S Subway Midtown's main interchange stations are Times Sq–42nd St, Grand Central–42nd St and 34th St–Herald Sq.

🚌 Bus Useful for the western and eastern extremes of Midtown. Routes include the 11 (running northbound on Tenth Ave and southbound on Ninth Ave) and the M15 (running northbound on First Ave and southbound on Second Ave).

Top Sights
Times Square

Love it or hate it, the intersection of Broadway and Seventh Ave (better known as Times Sq) is New York City's hyperactive heart: a restless, hypnotic torrent of glittering lights, bombastic billboards and raw urban energy. It's not hip, fashionable or in-the-know, and it couldn't care less. It's too busy pumping out iconic, mass-marketed NYC – yellow cabs, golden arches, soaring skyscrapers and razzle-dazzle Broadway marquees.

👁 Map p134, D4

www.timessquare.com

Broadway at Seventh Ave

S N/Q/R, S, 1/2/3, 7 to Times Sq-42nd St

Don't Miss

New Year's Eve Everyday

More than one million people gather in Times Sq every New Year's Eve (NYE) to watch a Waterford crystal ball descend at midnight. It's a mere 90-second spectacle that is arguably one of NYC's greatest anticlimaxes. Thankfully, you don't have to endure the crowds and cold to experience this short-lived thrill: the **Times Square Museum & Visitor Center** (Map p134, D3; 📞212-452-5283; www.timessquarenyc.org; 1560 Broadway, btwn 46th & 47th Sts, Midtown West; ⏱8am-8pm; 🄢N/Q/R, S, 1/2/3, 7 to Times Sq-42nd St) offers a simulated NYE light show every 20 minutes year-round, as well as a close-up look at the Centennial Dropping Ball used in 2007.

Broadway

New York's Theater District covers an area stretching from 40th St to 54th St between Sixth and Eighth Aves, with dozens of Broadway and off-Broadway theaters that show everything from blockbuster musicals to new and classic drama. Unless there's a specific show you're after, the best – and most affordable – way to score tickets in the area is at the **TKTS Booth** (Map p134, D3; www.tdf.org/tkts; Broadway at W 47th St, Midtown West; ⏱3-8pm Mon, Wed-Sat, 2-8pm Tue, 3-7pm Sun, also 10am-2pm Tue-Sat & 11am-3pm Sun during matinee performances; 🄢N/Q/R, S, 1/2/3, 7 to Times Sq-42nd St), where you can line up and get same-day half-price tickets for top shows.

Views From the TKTS Booth

The TKTS Booth is an attraction in itself, with its illuminated roof of 27 ruby-red steps rising a panoramic 16ft above 47th St. Needless to say, the view across Times Sq from the top is a crowd-pleaser, so good luck finding a spot to rest.

☑ Top Tips

▶ At the northwest corner of Broadway and 49th St, the Brill Building is arguably the most important generator of popular songs in the western world. By 1962, over 160 music businesses were based here, from songwriters and managers to promoters. It was a one-stop shop for artists, among them Carol King, Bob Dylan and Joni Mitchell.

✗ Take a Break

For a panoramic overview over the square, order a drink at the Renaissance Hotel's **R Lounge** (Map p134, D3; Renaissance Hotel; www.rloungetimessquare.com; Two Times Square, 714 Seventh Ave, at 48th St; ⏱11am-midnight Sun-Thu, 11:30am-1am Fri & Sat; 🄢N/Q/R to 49th St), which offers floor-to-ceiling glass windows of the neon-lit spectacle. It might not be the best-priced sip in town, but with a view like this, who's counting?

Top Sights
Empire State Building

The Chrysler Building may be prettier and One World Trade Center may now be taller, but the queen bee of the New York skyline remains the Empire State Building. It's Hollywood's tallest star, enjoying more than its fair share of close-ups in around one hundred films, from *King Kong* to *Independence Day*. No other building screams New York quite like it, and heading up to the top is as quintessential an experience as pastrami, rye and pickles at Katz's.

⊙ Map p134, E5

www.esbnyc.com

350 Fifth Ave, at 34th St

86th-fl observation deck adult/child $27/21, incl 102nd-fl observation deck $44/38

⊙8am–2am, last elevators up 1:15am

SB/D/F/M, N/Q/R to 34th St-Herald Sq

Don't Miss

Observation Decks

The Empire State Building has two observation decks. The open-air 86th-floor deck offers an alfresco experience, with coin-operated telescopes for close-up glimpses of the metropolis in action. Further up, the enclosed 102nd-floor deck is New York's highest – at least until the opening of the observation deck at One World Trade Center in 2015. Needless to say, the views over the city's five boroughs (and five neighboring states, weather permitting) are quite simply exquisite. Both decks are especially spectacular at sunset, when the city dons its nighttime cloak in dusk's afterglow.

Light Shows

Since 1976, the building's top 30 floors have been floodlit in a spectrum of colors each night, reflecting seasonal and holiday hues. Famous combos include red and pink sparkles for Valentine's Day; orange; red and green for Christmas; and the rainbow colors for Gay Pride weekend in June. For a full rundown of the color schemes, check the website.

Astounding Statistics

The statistics of Gotham's most iconic tower are astounding: 10 million bricks, 60,000 tons of steel, 6400 windows and 328,000 sq ft of marble. Built on the original site of the Waldorf-Astoria, construction took a record-setting 410 days, using seven million hours of labor. Coming in at 102 stories, it's 1472ft from top to bottom.

☑ Top Tips

▶ Alas, your passage to heaven will involve a trip through purgatory: the queues to the top are notorious. Getting here very early or very late will help you avoid delays – as will buying your tickets online ahead of time, where an extra $2 purchase charge is well worth the hassle it will save you.

▶ On the 86th floor between 10pm and 1am from Thursday to Saturday, the twinkling sea of lights below is accompanied by a live saxophone soundtrack (yes, requests are taken).

✕ Take A Break

Escape the maddening swarms of tourists and head to Koreatown, just a couple of blocks over, for some late-night grub after your sunset skyline viewing. Swing by darling dining destination Hangawi (p141) or try Gahm Mi Oak (p143) for midnight munchies.

Top Sights
Museum of Modern Art

Superstar of the modern art scene, MoMA's booty makes many other collections look...well... endearing. You'll find more A-listers here than at an Oscars after party: Van Gogh, Matisse, Picasso, Warhol, Lichtenstein, Rothko, Pollock, Bourgeois. Since its founding in 1929, the museum has amassed over 150,000 artworks, documenting the emerging creative ideas and movements of the late 19th century through to those that dominate today. For art buffs, it's Valhalla. For the uninitiated, it's a thrilling crash course in all that is beautiful and addictive about art.

MoMA

⊙ Map p134, E2

www.moma.org

11 W 53rd St, btwn Fifth & Sixth Aves

adult/child $25/free, 4-8pm Fri free

⊙10:30am-5:30pm Sat-Thu, to 8pm Fri; to 8pm Thu Jul-Aug

S E, M to 5th Ave-53rd St

Don't Miss

Collection Highlights

MoMA's permanent collection spans four levels. Many of the big hitters are on the last two levels, so tackle the museum from the top down before the fatigue sets in. Must-sees include Van Gogh's *The Starry Night,* Cézanne's *The Bather,* Picasso's *Les Demoiselles d'Avignon* and Henri Rousseau's *The Sleeping Gypsy,* not to mention iconic American works like Warhol's *Campbell's Soup Cans* and *Gold Marilyn Monroe,* Lichtenstein's equally poptastic *Girl With Ball* and Hopper's haunting *House by the Railroad.*

Abby Aldrich Rockefeller Sculpure Garden

With architect Yoshio Taniguchi's acclaimed reconstruction of the museum in 2004 came the restoration of the Sculpture Garden to the original, larger vision of Philip Johnson's 1953 design. Johnson described the space as a 'sort of outdoor room,' and on warm, sunny days, it's hard not to think of it as a soothing, alfresco lounge. Famous works include Aristide Maillol's *The River,* which sits among sculptures from greats including Auguste Rodin, Alexander Calder and Henry Moore. The Sculpture Garden is open free of charge from 9am to 10:15am daily, except in inclement weather and during maintenance.

Film Screenings

MoMA screens an incredibly well-rounded selection of celluloid gems from its collection of over 22,000 films, including the works of the Maysles Brothers. Expect anything from Academy-nominated documentary shorts and Hollywood classics to experimental works and international retrospectives. Best of all, your museum ticket will get you in for free.

☑ Top Tips

▶ To maximize your time and create a plan of attack, download the museum's free smartphone app from the website beforehand.

✖ Take A Break

For a casual vibe, nosh on Italian-inspired fare at MoMA's **Cafe 2** (⊙11am-5pm Sat-Mon, Wed & Thu, to 7.30pm Fri; **S** E, M to Fifth Ave-53rd St). For table service, opt for **Terrace Five** (mains $11-18; ⊙11am-5pm Sat-Mon, Wed & Thu, to 7:30pm Fri; **S** E, M to Fifth Ave-53rd St). If you're after a luxe feed, book a table at Michelin-starred **Modern** (☎212-333-1220; www.themodernnyc.com; 9 W 53rd St, btwn Fifth & Sixth Aves; 3-/4-course lunch $62/76, 4-course dinner $108; ⊙restaurant noon-2pm & 5-10:30pm Mon-Fri, 5-10:30pm Sat; bar 11:30am-10:30pm Mon-Sat, to 9:30pm Sun; **S** E, M to Fifth Ave-53rd St), famed for its contemporary, French-inspired creations.

For reviews see

⦿ Top Sights	p128
◉ Sights	p136
⊗ Eating	p141
✪ Drinking	p144
✪ Entertainment	p147
🔒 Shopping	p152

0 ———— 500 m
0 ———— 0.25 miles

The Pond
East Dr

E 61st St

E 49 🔒
5th Ave-59th St

F Lexington Ave-59th St
51 🔒
58
59th St

G
Roosevelt Island Tramway Station

E 60th St
Queensboro-59th St Bridge
H
E 59th St
E 58th St

54 🔒

50 🔒
57th St

53 🔒

Madison Ave
Park Ave
Lexington Ave
28
30
Lexington Ave-53rd St

Third Ave
E 57th St
E 56th St
E 55th St
E 54th St
E 53rd St

Second Ave
First Ave
Sutton Pl

East River

Museum of Modern Art

61 🔒 Fifth Ave-53rd St
Rockefeller Plaza

Fifth Ave
7 St Patrick's Cathedral

51st St

E 52nd St
E 51st St
E 50th St
E 49th St

20

Beekman Pl
Mitchell Pl

Franklin D Roosevelt Dr

52 🔒

Rockefeller Center

THE DIAMOND DISTRICT

E 48th St
E 47th St
E 46th St

12
Japan Society

29

Vanderbilt Ave
Grand Central Terminal
2
Grand Central Terminal

E 45th St
E 44th St
Chrysler Building
E 43rd St

9 United Nations

E 44th St
E 43rd St
5th Ave

42nd St
8
5
Bryant Park
New York Public Library

Third Ave
1
E 42nd St
42nd St-Grand Central
E 41st St

Second Ave

Tudor City Pl
Queens-Midtown Tunnel

First Ave
Franklin D Roosevelt Dr
East River

Fifth Ave
Madison Ave
Park Ave S
25

6
Morgan Library & Museum

Lexington Ave
E 40th St
E 39th St
E 38th St
E 37th St
E 36th St
E 35th St

MURRAY HILL

St Vartan Park

Empire State Building
KOREATOWN
33rd St
W 32nd St
(Korea Way)
31
19
16

E 34th St
E 33rd St
E 32nd St
E 31st St

Sights

Chrysler Building NOTABLE BUILDING

1 ◉ Map p134, F4

The 77-floor Chrysler Building makes most other skyscrapers look like uptight geeks. Designed by Willian Van Alen in 1930, it's a dramatic fusion of art deco and Gothic aesthetics, adorned with stern steel eagles and topped by a spire that screams Bride of Frankenstein. The building was constructed as the headquarters for Walter P Chrysler and his automobile empire. More than 80 years on, Chrysler's ambitious $15 million statement remains one of New York's most poignant symbols. (Lexington Ave at 42nd St, Midtown East; ◷lobby 8am-6pm Mon-Fri; ⓈS, 4/5/6, 7 to Grand Central-42nd St)

Grand Central Terminal NOTABLE BUILDING

2 ◉ Map p134, F3

New York's most breathtaking beaux arts building is more than just a station, it's an enchanted time machine; its swirl of chandeliers, marble, and historic bars and restaurants are a porthole into an era where train travel and romance were not mutually exclusive.

Don't miss a drink at the Grand Central's historic, chi-chi Campbell Apartment (p144). (www.grandcentral terminal.com; 42nd St at Park Ave, Midtown East; ◷5:30am-2am; ⓈS, 4/5/6, 7 to Grand Central-42nd St)

Rockefeller Center NOTABLE BUILDING

3 ◉ Map p134, E2

This 22-acre 'city within a city' debuted at the height of the Great Depression. Taking nine years to build, it was America's first multiuse retail, entertainment and office space – a modernist sprawl of 19 buildings (14 of which are the original art deco structures), outdoor plazas and big-name tenants. Developer John D Rockefeller Jr may have sweated over the cost (a mere $100 million), but it was all worth it – the Center was declared a National Landmark in 1987. (www.rockefellercenter.com; Fifth to Sixth Aves & 48th to 51st Sts; ◷24hr, times vary for individual businesses; ⓈB/D/F/M to 47th-50th Sts-Rockefeller Center)

Radio City Music Hall NOTABLE BUILDING

4 ◉ Map p134, D2

A spectacular art deco diva, this 5901-seat movie palace was the brainchild of vaudeville producer Samuel Lionel 'Roxy' Rothafel. Never one for understatement, Roxy launched his venue on 23 December 1932 with an over-the-top extravaganza that included a Symphony of the Curtains (starring... you guessed it...the curtains) and the high-kick campness of precision dance troupe the Roxyettes (wisely renamed the Rockettes). (www.radiocity.com; 1260 Sixth Ave, at 51st St; tours adult/child $20/15; ◷tours 11am-3pm; ⓈB/D/F/M to 47th-50th Sts-Rockefeller Center)

Understand

Midtown Skyscrapers: The Best of the Rest

Midtown's skyline is more than just the Empire State and Chrysler Buildings, with enough modernist and postmodern beauties to satisfy the wildest of high-rise dreams. Celebrate all things phallic with three of Midtown's finest.

Lever House

Upon its debut, 21-storey **Lever House** (Map p134, F2; 390 Park Ave, btwn 53rd & 54th Sts, Midtown East; **S**E, M to Fifth Ave-53rd St) was at the height of the cutting-edge, with only the UN Secretariat Building also boasting an innovative glass skin. The building's form was equally bold: two counter-posed rectangular shapes consisting of a slender tower atop a low-rise base. The open courtyard features marble benches by Japanese-American sculptor Isamu Noguchi, while the lobby exhibits contemporary art commissioned for the space.

Hearst Tower

Foster & Partners' **Hearst Tower** (Map p134, C1; 949 Eighth Ave, btwn 56th & 57th Ave, Midtown West; **S**A/C, B/D, 1 to 59th St-Columbus Circle) is hands down one of New York's most creative works of contemporary architecture. Its diagonal grid of trusses evokes a jagged glass-and-steel honeycomb, best appreciated up close and from an angle. The tower rises above the hollowed-out core of John Urban's 1928 cast-stone Hearst Magazine Building, itself originally envisioned as a skyscraper. In the lobby you'll find *Riverlines*, a mural by Richard Long.

Bank of America Tower

The crystal-shaped **Bank of America Tower** (Map p134, D4; Sixth Ave btwn 42nd & 43rd Sts; **S**B/D/F/M to 42nd St-Bryant Park) is lauded for its enviable green credentials. The stats are impressive: a clean-burning, on-site cogeneration plant provides around 65% of the tower's annual electricity requirements; CO_2-detecting air filters channel filtered air where needed; and the destination-dispatch elevators are designed to avoid empty car trips. Designed by Cook & Fox Architects, the 58-floor role model was awarded 'Best Tall Building in America' by the Council on Tall Buildings & Urban Habitat awards in 2010.

New York Public Library

CULTURAL BUILDING

5 ⊙ Map p134, E4

Loyally guarded by 'Patience' and 'Fortitude' (the famous marble lions overlooking Fifth Ave), this beaux arts show-off is one of NYC's best free attractions. When dedicated in 1911, New York's flagship library ranked as the largest marble structure ever built in the US. To this day, its Rose Main Reading Room will steal your breath with its lavish, coffered ceiling. (Stephen A Schwarzman Building; 📞917-275-6975; www.nypl.org; Fifth Ave at 42nd St; admission free; ⊙10am-6pm Mon & Thu-Sat, to 8pm Tue & Wed, 1-5pm Sun, guided tours 11am & 2pm Mon-Sat, 2pm Sun; ⑤B/D/F/M to 42nd St-Bryant Park, 7 to 5th Ave)

Morgan Library & Museum

MUSEUM

6 ⊙ Map p134, E4

Part of the 45-room mansion once owned by steel magnate JP Morgan, this sumptuous museum features a phenomenal array of manuscripts, tapestries, drawings, paintings, and books (with no fewer than three Gutenberg Bibles). Its lavish rooms include the extraordinary East Room library, with breathtaking ceiling murals by celebrated muralist Henry Siddons Mowbray. (www.morganlibrary. org; 29 E 36th St, at Madison Ave, Midtown East; adult/child $18/12; ⊙10:30am-5pm Tue-Thu, to 9pm Fri, 10am-6pm Sat, 11am-6pm Sun; ⑤6 to 33rd St)

Understand

A Brief History of Times Square

At the turn of last century, Times Sq was known as Longacre Sq, an unremarkable intersection far from the city's commercial epicenter of Lower Manhattan. This changed with a deal between subway pioneer August Belmont and *New York Times* publisher Adolph Ochs. Heading construction of the city's first subway line (from Lower Manhattan to the Upper West Side and Harlem), Belmont realized that a business hub along 42nd St would maximize profit and patronage on the route. He then approached Ochs, who had recently turned around the fortunes of the *New York Times,* arguing that moving the newspaper's operations to the intersection of Broadway and 42nd St would be a win-win for Ochs. Not only would an in-house subway station mean faster distribution of the newspaper, but the influx of commuters to the square would mean more sales right outside its headquarters. Belmont even convinced New York Mayor George B McClellan Jr to rename the square in honor of the broadsheet.

BARRY WINIKER/GETTY IMAGES ©

Radio City Music Hall (p136)

St Patrick's Cathedral CHURCH

7 🔘 Map p134, E2

When its face lift is complete and the scaffolding comes down in late 2015, America's largest Catholic cathedral will once more grace Fifth Ave with its neo-Gothic splendor. Built at a cost of nearly $2 million during the Civil War, the building did not originally include the two front spires, added in 1888. Highlights include the Louis Tiffany–designed altar and Charles Connick's stunning Rose Window. (www.saintpatrickscathedral.org; Fifth Ave btwn 50th & 51st Sts; ⊘6:30am-8:45pm; Ⓢ B/D/F/M to 47th-50th Sts-Rockefeller Center)

Bryant Park PARK

8 🔘 Map p134, E4

European coffee kiosks, alfresco chess games, summer film screenings and winter ice-skating: it's hard to believe that this leafy oasis was dubbed 'Needle Park' in the '80s. Nestled behind the show-stopping New York Public Library building, it's a handy spot for a little time-out from the Midtown madness. Opening hours are seasonal – check the website for details. (www.bryantpark.org; 42nd St btwn Fifth & Sixth Aves; ⊘7am-midnight Mon-Fri, to 11pm Sat & Sun Jun-Sep, shorter hrs rest of yr; Ⓢ B/D/F/M to 42nd St-Bryant Park, 7 to Fifth Ave)

United Nations

NOTABLE BUILDING

9 Map p134, H3

Welcome to the headquarters of the UN, a worldwide organization overseeing international law, international security and human rights. While the recently spruced-up, Le Corbusier–designed Secretariat building is off-limits, one-hour guided tours do cover the Security Council Chamber, the Trusteeship Council Chamber, the Economic and Social Council (ECOSOC) Chamber, as well as exhibitions about the UN's work and artworks given by member states. Weekday tours must be booked online (book at least two days ahead). (☎212-963-4475; http://visit.un.org/wcm/content; visitors' gate First Ave at 47th St, Midtown East; guided tour adult/child $20/11, children under 5yr not admitted, grounds access Sat & Sun

---

Local Life
Diamond District

Like Diagon Alley in Harry Potter, the **Diamond District** (Map p134, E3; www.diamonddistrict.org; 47th St btwn Fifth & Sixth Aves; S B/D/F/M to 47th-50th Sts-Rockefeller Center) is a world unto itself. A frenetic whirl of Hasidic Jewish traders, pesky hawkers and love-struck couples looking for the perfect rock, its 2600-plus businesses peddle all manner of diamonds, gold, pearls, gemstones and watches. In fact, the strip handles approximately 90% of the cut diamonds sold in the country. Marilyn, eat your heart out!

---

free; ⊘tours 9:15am-4:15pm Mon-Fri, visitor center also open 10am-5pm Sat & Sun; S S, 4/5/6, 7 to Grand Central-42nd St)

International Center of Photography

GALLERY

10 Map p134, D3

ICP is New York's paramount platform for photography, with a strong emphasis on photojournalism, and changing exhibitions on a wide range of themes. Past shows in the two-floor space have included work by Henri Cartier-Bresson, Man Ray and Robert Capa. The center is also a school, offering coursework (for credit) and a public lecture series.

Stop by the excellent gallery shop, great for instant cameras and photography tomes, cool little gifts and NYC souvenirs. (ICP; www.icp.org; 1133 Sixth Ave, at 43rd St; adult/child $14/free, by donation Fri 5-8pm; ⊘10am-6pm Tue-Thu, Sat & Sun, to 8pm Fri; S B/D/F/M to 42nd St-Bryant Park)

Museum at FIT

MUSEUM

11 Map p134, D5

The Fashion Institute of Technology (FIT) lays claim to one of the world's richest collections of garments, textiles and accessories. At last count, there were around 50,000 items spanning the 18th century to the present day. The school's museum is the place to catch a glimpse, its innovative, rotating exhibitions showcasing both permanent collection items and on-loan curiosities. (www.fitnyc.edu/museum; 227 W 27th St, at Seventh Ave, Midtown West;

admission free; ⏰noon-8pm Tue-Fri, 10am-5pm Sat; S1 to 28th St)

Japan Society
CULTURAL CENTER

12 Map p134, G3

Elegant exhibitions of Japanese art, textiles and design are the main draw at this cultural center. Its theater hosts a range of films and dance, music and theatrical performances, while those who want to dig deeper can browse through the 14,000 volumes of the research library or attend one of its myriad lectures. (www.japansociety.org; 333 E 47th St, btwn First & Second Aves, Midtown East; adult/child $12/free, 6-9pm Fri free; ⏰11am-6pm Tue-Thu, to 9pm Fri, to 5pm Sat & Sun; S S, 4/5/6, 7 to Grand Central-42nd St)

Eating

Le Bernardin
SEAFOOD $$$

13 Map p134, D2

The interiors may have been slightly sexed-up for a 'younger clientele' (the stunning storm-themed triptych is by Brooklyn artist Ran Ortner), but triple Michelin-starred Le Bernardin remains a luxe, fine-dining holy grail. At the helm is celebrity chef Eric Ripert, whose deceptively simple-looking seafood often borders on the transcendental. (📞212-554-1515; www.le-bernardin.com; 155 W 51st St, btwn Sixth & Seventh Aves, Midtown West; prix fixe lunch/dinner $76/135, tasting menus $155-198; ⏰noon-2:30pm & 5:15-10.30pm Mon-Fri, 5:15-11pm Sat; S1 to 50th St, B/D, E to 7th Ave)

Danji
KOREAN $$

14 Map p134, C2

Young-gun chef Hooni Kim has captured tastebuds with his Michelin-starred Korean 'tapas', served in a snug-and-slinky contemporary space. Top of the list are the sliders, a duo of *bulgogi* beef and spiced pork belly, each dressed with scallion vinaigrette and served on butter-grilled buns. Head in early or wait. (www.danjinyc.com; 346 W 52nd St, btwn Eighth & Ninth Aves, Midtown West; plates $6-20; ⏰noon-2:30pm & 5:15-11pm Mon-Thu, noon-2:30pm & 5:15-midnight Fri, 5:15-midnight Sat; S C/E to 50th St)

Betony
MODERN AMERICAN $$$

15 Map p134, E1

While industrial windows, exposed brickwork and a soaring bar make Betony's front section perfect for after-5 cocktails, request a table in the intimate, baroque-esque back dining room to savor chef Bryce Shuman's sophisticated albeit playful dishes. Book ahead. (📞212-465-2400; www.betony-nyc.com; 41 W 57th St, btwn Fifth & Sixth Aves; mains $27-38; ⏰5-10pm Mon-Thu, to 10:30pm Fri & Sat; SF to 57th St)

Hangawi
KOREAN $$

16 Map p134, E5

Leave your shoes at the entrance and slip into a soothing, zen-like space of meditative music, soft low seating and sublime Korean vegetarian fare. Showstoppers include the leek pancakes and a seductively smooth tofu claypot in ginger sauce. (☎212-213-0077; www. hangawirestaurant.com; 12 E 32nd St, btwn Fifth & Madison Aves; mains lunch $10-16, dinner $16-26; ◷noon-2:45pm & 5-10:15pm Mon-Thu, to 10:30pm Fri, 1-10:30pm Sat, 5-9:30pm Sun; ✎; Ⓢ B/D/F/M, N/Q/R to 34th St-Herald Sq)

Totto Ramen

JAPANESE $

17  Map p134, C2

Write your name and number of guests on the clipboard by the door and wait for your (cash-only) ramen revelation. Skip the chicken and go for the pork, which sings in dishes like miso ramen (with fermented soybean paste, egg, scallion, bean sprouts, onion and homemade chili paste). (www.tottoramen.com; 366 W 52nd St, btwn Eighth & Ninth Aves, Midtown West; ramen from $10; ◷noon-midnight Mon-Fri, noon-11pm Sat, 5-11pm Sun; Ⓢ C/E to 50th St)

Burger Joint

BURGERS $

18  Map p134, D1

With only a small neon burger as your clue, this speakeasy burger hut loiters behind the curtain in the lobby of the Le Parker Meridien hotel. Find it and you'll stumble onto a thumping scene of graffiti-strewn walls, retro booths, and attitude-loaded staff slapping up beef-n-patty brilliance. (www.burger jointny.com; Le Parker Meridien, 119 W 56th St, btwn Sixth & Seventh Aves, Midtown West;

SIEGFRIED LAYDA/GETTY IMAGES ©

42nd St theaters

burgers from $8; ⏲11am-11:30pm Sun-Thu, to midnight Fri & Sat; **S**F to 57th St)

NoMad
NEW AMERICAN **$$$**

19 Map p134, E5

Carved up into a series of distinctly different spaces – including a see-and-be-seen Atrium, Victoriana parlor and snacks-only Library – hotspot NoMad is the hipper, (slightly) more relaxed sibling of Michelin-starred Eleven Madison Park (p117). The menus are eclectic, Eurocentric and – true to chef Daniel Humm's reputation – just a little fun. (☏347-472-5660; www.thenomadhotel.com/#!/dining; NoMad Hotel, 1170 Broadway, at 28th St; mains $20-37; ⏲noon-2pm & 5:30-10:30pm Mon-Thu, to 11pm Fri, 11am-2pm & 5:30-11pm Sat, 11am-3pm & 5:30-10pm Sun; **S**N/R, 6 to 28th St; F/M to 23rd St)

Smith
AMERICAN **$$**

20 Map p134, G2

The Smith has sexed-up dining in the far eastern throws of Midtown with its industrial-chic interior, buzzing bar and well-executed brasserie grub. With much of the food made from scratch on-site, the emphasis is on regional produce, and retro American and Italian-inspired flavors. (☏212-644-2700; www.thesmithnyc.com; 956 Second Ave, at 51st St, Midtown East; mains $17-33; ⏲7:30am-midnight Mon-Wed, to 1am Thu & Fri, 10am-1am Sat, 10am-midnight Sun; ☏; **S**6 to 51st St)

 Local Life

Koreatown

For kimchi and karaoke, it's hard to beat **Koreatown** (Map p134, E5; 31st to 36th Sts & Broadway to Fifth Ave; **S**B/D/F/M, N/Q/R to 34th St-Herald Sq). Mainly concentrated on 32nd St, with some spillover into the surrounding streets both south and north of this strip, it's a Seoul-ful mix of Korean-owned restaurants, shops, salons and spas. Authentic barbecue is available around the clock at many of the all-night spots on 32nd St, some with microphones, video screens and Manic Monday at the ready.

Marseille
FRENCH, MEDITERRANEAN **$$$**

21 Map p134, C3

Looking somewhere between an old cinema lobby and an art deco brasserie, this Hell's Kitchen classic is a fabulous spot to kick back with a Le Pamplemousse cocktail and nibble on flavor-packed French-Med fare like Provencal goat cheese tart or Tuscan chicken with truffle jus. (www.marseillenyc.com; 630 Ninth Ave at 44th St; mains $20-29; ⏲11:30am-11pm Sun-Tue, to midnight Wed-Sat; **S**A/C/E to 42nd St-Port Authority)

Gahm Mi Oak
KOREAN **$$**

22 Map p134, E5

If you're craving *yook hwe* (raw beef and Asian pear matchsticks) at 3am, this Koreatown savior has you covered. The shtick here is authenticity, shining through in dishes like the house specialty *sul long tang* (a milky broth of ox bones, boiled for 12 hours and pimped with brisket and scallion). (43 W 32nd St, btwn Broadway & Fifth Ave; dishes $10-22; ⊘24hr; **S**N/Q/R, B/D/F/M to 34th St-Herald Sq)

Shake Shack   BURGERS $

23 Map p134, C3

Yet another branch of Danny Meyer's cultishly popular burger chain, a fry-flick away from Times Square and Broadway theaters. Join the queue for butter-soft buns stuffed with top-notch fillings, hand-cut fries and frozen custards. (www.shakeshack.com; 691 Eighth Ave at 44th St; burgers from $3.60; ⊘11am-midnight; **S**A/C/E to 42nd Street-Port Authority, N/Q/R, S, 1/2/3, 7 to Times Sq-42nd St)

El Margon   CUBAN $

24 Map p134, D3

It's still 1973 at this ever-packed Cuban lunch counter, where orange Laminex and greasy goodness never went out of style. Go for gold with its legendary cubano sandwich (a pressed panino jammed with rich roast pork, salami, cheese, pickles, mojo and mayo). (136 W 46th St, btwn Sixth & Seventh Aves, Midtown West; sandwiches from $4, mains $9-15; ⊘7am-5pm; **S**B/D/F/M to 47-50th Sts-Rockefeller Center)

Drinking

Top of the Strand   COCKTAIL BAR

25 Map p134, E4

For that 'Oh my God, I'm in New York' feeling, head to the Strand Hotel's rooftop bar, order a martini (extra dirty) and drop your jaw (discreetly). Sporting slinky cabanas and a sliding glass roof, its view of the Empire State Building is unforgettable. (www.topofthestrand.com; Strand Hotel, 33 W 37th St, btwn Fifth & Sixth Aves; ⊘5pm-midnight Mon & Sun, to 1am Tue-Sat; **S**B/D/F/M to 34th St)

Campbell Apartment   COCKTAIL BAR

Party like it's 1928! This sublime, deliciously snooty gem in Grand Central (see 2 Map p134, F3) was once the office of a '20s railroad magnate fond of Euro eccentricities: think Florentine-style carpets, decorative wooden ceiling beams and a soaring leaded glass window. Suitably tucked away from the hordes, reach it from the lift beside the Oyster Bar or the stairs to the West Balcony. (www.hospitalityholdings.com; Grand Central Terminal, 15 Vanderbilt Ave, at 43rd St; ⊘noon-1am Mon-Thu, to 2am Fri, 2pm-2am Sat, noon-midnight Sun; **S**S, 4/5/6, 7 to Grand Central-42nd St)

Rum House   COCKTAIL BAR

26 Map p134, C3

Not long ago, this was Hotel Edison's crusty old piano bar. Enter the capable team from Tribeca bar Ward III, who

ripped out the grubby carpet, polished
up the coppertop bar and revived
this slice of old New York. You'll still
find a nightly pianist (Wednesday to
Monday), but he's now accompanied
by well-crafted drinks and an enviable
medley of whiskeys and rums. (www.
edisonrumhouse.com; 228 W 47th St, btwn
Broadway & Eighth Ave, Midtown West; ⏱1pm-
4am; **S**N/Q/R to 49th St)

Industry
GAY

27 Map p134, C2

What was once a parking garage is
now one of the hottest gay bars in
Hell's Kitchen – a slick 4000-sq-ft
watering hole with handsome lounge
areas, a pool table and a stage for
top-notch drag divas. Head in between
4pm and 9pm for the two-for-one
drinks special or squeeze in later to
groove with the hordes. Cash only.
(www.industry-bar.com; 355 W 52nd St, btwn
Eighth & Ninth Aves, Midtown West; ⏱4pm-
4am; **S**C/E, 1 to 50th St)

Little Collins
CAFE

28 Map p134, F2

Little Collins emulates the celebrated
cafes of Melbourne, Australia: understatedly cool, welcoming spaces serving
superlative coffee and equally tasty
grub. The cafe is home to New York's
very first Modbar; high-tech, under-
the-counter brewers that look like
sleek chrome taps. (http://littlecollinsnyc.
com; 667 Lexington Ave, btwn 55th & 56th Sts,
Midtown East; ⏱7am-6pm Mon-Fri, 9am-4pm
Sat & Sun; **S**E, M to 53rd St, 4/5/6 to 59th St)

Lantern's Keep
COCKTAIL BAR

29 Map p134, E3

Cross the lobby of the Iroquois hotel
and slip into this dark, intimate
cocktail salon. Its specialty is pre-
Prohibition libations, shaken and
stirred by passionate mixologists.
(☎212-453-4287; www.thelanternskeep.
com; Iroquois Hotel, 49 W 44th St, btwn Fifth
& Sixth Aves; ⏱5pm-midnight Mon-Fri, 6pm-
1am Sat; **S**B/D/F/M to 42nd St-Bryant Park)

PJ Clarke's
BAR

30 Map p134, F2

This lovingly worn wooden saloon has
been straddling the scene since 1884;
Buddy Holly proposed to his future
wife here, and Old Blue Eyes pretty
much owned table 20. Choose a juke-
box tune, order the knockout burger
and settle in with a come-one-and-all
crowd of collar-and-tie colleagues,
college students and nostalgia-craving
urbanites. (www.pjclarkes.com; 915 Third
Ave, at 55th St, Midtown East; ⏱11:30am-
4am; **S**E, M to Lexington Ave-53rd St)

Stumptown Coffee Roasters
CAFE

31 Map p134, E5

Hipster baristas in fedora hats brewing killer coffee? No, you're not in
Williamsburg, you're at the Manhattan
outpost of Portland's most celebrated
coffee roaster. The queue is a small
price to pay for proper espresso in
Midtown, so count your blessings. It's
standing-room only, though weary

punters might find a seat in the adjacent Ace Hotel lobby. (www.stumptown coffee.com; 18 W 29th St, btwn Broadway & Fifth Ave; ⏰6am-8pm Mon-Fri, from 7am Sat & Sun; ⓢN/R to 28th St)

Robert
COCKTAIL BAR

32 🚇 Map p134, C1

Perched on the 9th floor of the Museum of Arts & Design, '60s-inspired, pink-tastic Robert is technically a high-end, modern American restaurant. Ditch the food and head in late afternoon or post-dinner, find a sofa and gaze out over Central Park with a MAD Manhattan (Bourbon, Blood Orange Vermouth and liquored cherries). (www.robertnyc.com; Museum of Arts & Design, 2 Columbus Circle, btwn Eighth Ave & Broadway; ⏰11:30am-10pm Mon, 11:30am-midnight Tue-Fri, 11am-midnight Sat, 11am-10pm Sun; ⓢA/C, B/D, 1 to 59th St-Columbus Circle)

Flaming Saddles
GAY

33 🚇 Map p134, B2

Butter my butt and call me a biscuit, a country and western gay bar in Midtown! *Coyote Ugly* meets *Calamity Jane* at this Hell's Kitchen hangout, complete with studly bar-dancing barmen, aspiring urban cowboys and a rough 'n' ready vibe. So slip on them Wranglers and hit the Saddle, partner. You're in for a wild and boozy ride. (www.flamingsaddles.com; 793 Ninth Ave, btwn 52nd & 53rd Sts, Midtown West; ⏰4pm-4am Mon-Fri, noon-4am Sat & Sun; ⓢC/E to 50th St)

Culture Espresso
CAFE

34 🚇 Map p134, D4

Culture peddles single-origin espresso that's nutty, complex and creamy, as well as Third Wave options like Chemex and cold brew varieties (we're addicted to the Kyoto-style iced coffee). Tasty edibles include gourmet panini (with combos like prosciutto, fig jam and arugula), baked treats from local artisans, and Culture's very own super-gooey choc-chip cookies. (www.cultureespresso.com; 72 W 38th St, at Sixth Ave; ⏰7am-7pm Mon-Fri, from 8am Sat & Sun; 🛜; ⓢB/D/F/M to 42nd St-Bryant Park)

Rudy's
DIVE BAR

35 🚇 Map p134, B3

The big pantless pig in a red jacket out front marks Hell's Kitchen's best divey mingler, with cheap pitchers of Rudy's two beers, half-circle booths covered in red duct tape, and free hot dogs. A mix of folks come to flirt or watch muted Knicks games as classic rock plays. (www.rudysbarnyc.com; 627 Ninth Ave, at 44th St, Midtown West; ⏰8am-4am Mon-Sat, noon-4am Sun; ⓢA/C/E to 42nd St-Port Authority Bus Terminal)

Therapy
GAY

Located near Totto Ramen (see 17 ❌ Map p134, C2), Multilevel Therapy was the first gay man's lounge/club to draw throngs to Hell's Kitchen and it still pulls a crowd with its nightly shows (from music to Broadway bingo) and decent grub Sunday to Friday (chicken skewers, burgers, hummus, salads). Drink monikers team with the theme: Oral Fixation and Size Queen, to name a few. (www.therapy-nyc.com; 348 W 52nd St, btwn Eighth & Ninth Aves, Midtown West; ⊙5pm-2am Sun-Thu, to 4am Fri & Sat; ⑤C/E, 1 to 50th St)

XL Nightclub
GAY

36 🚇 Map p134, B4

Muscle boys pack this mega dance club, a hedonistic playpen featuring two dance floors, cabaret theater, lounge bar, and the prerequisite quota of go-go boys and pin-up bartenders. The venue hosts some great shows, from camp comedy to cheeky drag revues. (www.xlnightclub.com; 512 W 42nd St, btwn Tenth & Eleventh Aves, Midtown West; ⊙10pm-4am; ⑤A/C/E to 42nd St-Port Authority Bus Terminal)

Entertainment

Jazz at Lincoln Center
JAZZ

Perched high atop the Time Warner Center (see 59 🔒 Map p134), Jazz at Lincoln Center consists of three state-of-the-art venues: the midsized Rose Theater; the panoramic, glass-backed Allen Room; and the intimate, atmospheric Dizzy's Club Coca-Cola. It's the last one you're likely to visit given its regular, nightly shows. The talent is often exceptional, as are the dazzling Central Park views. (🎟tickets to Dizzy's Club Coca-Cola 212-258-9595, tickets to Rose Theater & Allen Room 212-721-6500; www.jazzatlincolncenter.org; Time Warner Center, Broadway at 60th St; ⑤A/C, B/D, 1 to 59th St-Columbus Circle)

Understand
The Early Days of Broadway

The Broadway of the 1920s was well-known for its lighthearted musicals, commonly fusing vaudeville and music hall traditions, and producing classic tunes like George Gershwin's *Rhapsody in Blue* and Cole Porter's *Let's Misbehave*. At the same time, Midtown's theater district was evolving as a platform for new American dramatists. One of the greatest was Eugene O'Neill. Born in Times Sq at the long-gone Barrett Hotel (1500 Broadway) in 1888, the playwright debuted many of his works here, including Pulitzer Prize winners *Beyond the Horizon* and *Anna Christie*. O'Neill's success on Broadway paved the way for other American greats like Tennessee Williams, Arthur Miller and Edward Albee. This surge of serious talent led to the establishment of the annual Tony Awards in 1947, Broadway's answer to Hollywood's Oscars.

Carnegie Hall
LIVE MUSIC

37 Map p134, D1

This legendary music hall may not be the world's biggest, nor grandest, but it's definitely one of the most acoustically blessed venues around. Opera, jazz and folk greats feature in the Isaac Stern Auditorium, with edgier jazz, pop, classical and world music in the hugely popular Zankel Hall. The intimate Weill Recital Hall hosts chamber music concerts, debut performances and panel discussions. ([☎]212-247-7800; www.carnegiehall.org; W 57th St at Seventh Ave, Midtown West; tours adult/child $15/5; [⊙]tours 11:30am, 12:30pm, 2pm & 3pm Mon-Fri, 11:30am & 12:30pm Sat, 12:30pm Sun Oct-May; [S]N/Q/R to 57th St-7th Ave)

✓ Top Tip

Budget Broadway

Many of the hottest shows – including *Kinky Boots* and *Book of Mormon* – run ticket lotteries, entered at the theater 2½ hours before the performance. If your name is drawn, the show is yours for less than $40. The bad news: tickets are limited and in high demand. Other shows, such as *Chicago* offer a limited number of general rush tickets, available each morning when the box office opens. Again, tickets are limited and in high demand, translating into early-morning queues and long waits.

Signature Theatre
THEATER

38 Map p134, B4

Looking fine in its Frank Gehry–designed home – complete with three theaters, bookshop and cafe – Signature Theatre devotes entire seasons to the body of work of its playwrights-in-residence, both past and present. Featured dramatists have included Tony Kushner, Edward Albee and Athol Fugard. Aim to book shows one month in advance. ([☎]tickets 212-244-7529; www.signaturetheatre.org; 480 W 42nd St, btwn Ninth & Tenth Aves, Midtown West; [S]A/C/E to 42nd St-Port Authority Bus Terminal)

Kinky Boots
THEATER

39 ⭐ Map p134, C3

Adapted from a 2005 British indie film, Harvey Fierstein and Cyndi Lauper's smash hit tells the story of a doomed English shoe factory unexpectedly saved by Lola, a business-savvy drag queen. Its solid characters and electrifying energy have not been lost on critics; the musical won six Tony Awards, including Best Musical in 2013. (Hirschfeld Theatre; [☎]tickets 212-239-6200; www.kinkybootsthemusical.com; 302 W 45th St, btwn Eighth & Ninth Aves, Midtown West; [S]A/C/E to 42nd St-Port Authority Bus Terminal)

Book of Mormon
THEATER

40 ⭐ Map p134, C3

Subversive, obscene and ridiculously hilarious, this cutting musical satire is the work of *South Park* creators Trey Parker and Matt Stone and *Avenue Q*

Allen Room, Jazz at Lincoln Center (p147)

composer Robert Lopez. Winner of nine Tony Awards, it tells the story of two naive Mormons on a mission to 'save' a Ugandan village. (Eugene O'Neill Theatre; ☑ tickets 212-239-6200; www.bookofmormonbroadway.com; 230 W 49th St, btwn Broadway & Eighth Ave, Midtown West; S N/Q/R to 49th St, 1 to 50th St, C/E to 50th St)

Chicago   THEATER

41 ⭐ Map p134, C3

This beloved Bob Fosse/Kander & Ebb classic – a musical about showgirl Velma Kelly, wannabe Roxie Hart, lawyer Billy Flynn and the fabulously sordid goings-on of the Chicago underworld – has made a great comeback. This version, revived by director Walter

Bobbie, is seriously alive and kicking. (Ambassador Theater; ☑ tickets 212-239-6200; www.chicagothemusical.com; 219 W 49th St, btwn Broadway & Eighth Ave, Midtown West; S N/Q/R to 49th St, 1, C/E to 50th St)

Matilda   THEATER

42 ⭐ Map p134, D3

Giddily subversive, this multi-award-winning musical is an adaptation of Roald Dahl's classic children's tale. Star of the show is a precocious five-year-old who uses wit, intellect and a little telekinesis to tackle parental neglect, unjust punishment, even the Russian mafia.

The nightly ticket lottery – held at the theater 2½ hours before showtime – offers a limited number of $27 tickets. (Shubert Theatre; ☎ tickets 212-239-6200; http://us.matildathemusical.com; 225 W 44th St, btwn Seventh & Eighth Aves, Midtown West; S N/Q/R, S, 1/2/3, 7 to Times Sq-42nd St, A/C/E to 42nd St-Port Authority Bus Terminal)

Playwrights Horizons   THEATER

44 ⭐ Map p134, B4

This veteran 'writers' theater' is dedicated to fostering contemporary American works. Notable past productions include Bruce Norris' Tony Award-winning *Clybourne Park,* as well as *I Am My Own Wife* and *Grey Gardens,* both of which moved on to Broadway. (☎ tickets 212-279-4200; www.playwrightshorizons.org; 416 W 42nd St, btwn Ninth & Tenth Aves, Midtown West; S A/C/E to 42nd St-Port Authority Bus Terminal)

Birdland   JAZZ, CABARET

44 ⭐ Map p134, C3

Off Times Sq, this bird's got a slick look, not to mention the legend – its name dates from bebop legend Charlie Parker (aka 'Bird'), who headlined at the previous location on 52nd St, along with Miles, Monk and just about everyone else (you can see their photos on the walls). The lineup is always stellar. (☎ 212-581-3080; www.birdlandjazz.com; 315 W 44th St, btwn Eighth & Ninth Aves, Midtown West; admission $20-50; ⊗ 5pm-1am; 🛜; S A/C/E to 42nd St-Port Authority Bus Terminal)

Understand
TV Tapings

If you want to be part of a live studio audience for a TV taping, NYC is the place to do it. Just follow the instructions below.

For more show ticket details, visit the websites of individual TV stations, or try www.tvtickets.com.

▶ **Saturday Night Live** Known for being difficult to get into. Try your luck in the fall lottery by sending an email to snltickets@nbcuni.com in August. Or line up by 7am the day of the show on the 49th St side of Rockefeller Plaza for standby tickets.

▶ **Late Show with David Letterman** Request tickets for a specific date online at www.cbs.com/lateshow or submit a request in person by showing up at the theater (1697 Broadway between 53rd and 54th Sts) between 9:30am and noon Monday to Thursday, and 10am and 6pm Saturday and Sunday. Try for a standby ticket by calling ☎ 212-247-6497 at 11am on the day of the taping. Letterman will be retiring in 2015 and will be replaced by Stephen Colbert – at the time of writing, it was undecided if Colbert will continue to film in the same location. Check the website for updates.

Caroline's on Broadway COMEDY

45 ⭐ Map p134, D2

You may recognize this big, bright, mainstream classic from comedy specials filmed here on location. Expectantly, it's a top spot to catch US comedy big guns and sitcom stars. (📞212-757-4100; www.carolines.com; 1626 Broadway, at 50th St; 🚇N/Q/R to 49th St, 1 to 50th St)

Don't Tell Mama CABARET

46 ⭐ Map p134, C3

Piano bar and cabaret venue extraordinaire, Don't Tell Mama is an unpretentious little spot that's been around for more than 25 years and has the talent to prove it. Its regular roster of performers aren't big names, but true lovers of cabaret who give each show their all and don't mind a little singing help from the audience sometimes. (📞212-757-0788; www.dont tellmamanyc.com; 343 W 46th St, btwn Eighth & Ninth Aves, Midtown West; 🕐4pm-3am Mon-Thu, to 4am Fri-Sun; 🚇N/Q/R, S, 1/2/3, 7 to Times Sq-42nd St)

New York City Center DANCE

47 ⭐ Map p134, D2

This Moorish, red-domed wonder hosts dance troupes (including the Alvin Ailey American Dance Theater), theater productions, the New York Flamenco Festival in February or March, and the Fall for Dance Festival in September or October. (📞212-581-1212; www.nycitycenter.org; 131 W 55th St, btwn Sixth & Seventh Aves, Midtown West; 🚇N/Q/R to 57th St-7th Ave)

Madison Square Garden STADIUM

48 ⭐ Map p134, C5

NYC's major performance venue delivers big-arena performers, from Kanye West to Madonna. It's also a sports arena, with New York Knicks and New York Rangers games, as well as boxing matches and events like the Annual Westminster Kennel Club Dog Show. (www.thegarden.com; Seventh Ave btwn 31st & 33rd Sts, Midtown West; 🚇1/2/3 to 34th St-Penn Station)

HIROYUKI MATSUMOTO/GETTY IMAGES ©

Busker outside Carnegie Hall (p148)

Shopping

Barneys
DEPARTMENT STORE

49 🔒 Map p134, E1

Serious fashionistas swipe their plastic at Barneys, respected for its spot-on collections of savvy labels like Holmes & Yang, Kitsuné and Derek Lam. For (slightly) less expensive deals geared to a younger market, shop street-chic labels on the 8th floor. (www.barneys.com; 660 Madison Ave, at 61st St, Midtown East; ⊙10am-8pm Mon-Fri, to 7pm Sat, 11am-6pm Sun; §N/Q/R to 5th Ave-59th St)

Local Life
Garment District

Centered on Seventh Ave between 34th St and Times Sq, the famed **Garment District** (Map p134, D4; §N/Q/R, S, 1/2/3 & 7 to Times Sq-42nd St) is where you'll find a huge selection of fabrics, sequins and lace. Check out the sidewalk when you hit Seventh and 39th St and you'll catch the Fashion Walk of Fame, honoring the likes of Betsey Johnson, Marc Jacobs, Halston and other fashion visionaries. It's on the same corner as Claes Oldenburg's sculpture of the world's largest button, held upright by a 31ft-tall steel needle.

Bergdorf Goodman
DEPARTMENT STORE

50 🔒 Map p134, E1

Not merely loved for its Christmas windows (the city's best), plush BG leads the fashion race, with its fashion director Linda Fargo considered an Anna Wintour of sorts. Drawcards include exclusive collections of Tom Ford and Chanel shoes, an expanded women's shoe department, and the biggest collection of Thom Browne clothing for men and women. (www.bergdorfgoodman.com; 754 Fifth Ave, btwn 57th & 58th Sts; ⊙10am-8pm Mon-Fri, to 7pm Sat, noon-6pm Sun; §N/Q/R to 5th Ave-59th St, F to 57th St)

Bloomingdale's
DEPARTMENT STORE

51 🔒 Map p134, F1

Blockbuster 'Bloomie's' is something like the Metropolitan Museum of Art to the shopping world: historic, sprawling, overwhelming and packed with bodies. Raid the racks for clothes and shoes from a who's who of US and global designers, including an increasing number of 'new-blood' collections. (www.bloomingdales.com; 1000 Third Ave, at E 59th St, Midtown East; ⊙10am-8:30pm Mon-Sat, 11am-7pm Sun; 📶; §4/5/6 to 59th St, N/Q/R to Lexington Ave-59th St)

MoMA Design & Book Store
BOOKS, GIFTS

The flagship store at the Museum of Modern Art (see ◎ Map p134, E2) is a fab spot to souvenir shop in one fell swoop. You'll find art books, prints and posters, and one-of-a-kind knick-knacks. For furniture, lighting, homewares, jewelry, bags, and MUJI merchandise, head to the MoMA Design Store across the street. (www.momastore.org; 11 W 53rd St, btwn Fifth & Sixth Aves; ⊙9:30am-6:30pm Sat-Thu, to 9pm Fri; **S** E, M to 5th Ave-53rd St)

Saks Fifth Ave DEPARTMENT STORE

52 🔒 Map p134, E2

Graced with vintage elevators, Saks' 10-floor flagship store is home to the 'Shoe Salon', NYC's biggest women's shoe department (complete with express elevator and zip code). Other strengths include the cosmetics and men's departments. The store's January sale is legendary. (www.saksfifthavenue.com; 611 Fifth Ave, at 50th St; ⊙10am-8pm Mon-Sat, 11am-7pm Sun; **S** B/D/F/M to 47th-50th Sts-Rockefeller Center, E/M to 5th Ave-53rd St)

Tiffany & Co JEWELRY, HOMEWARES

53 🔒 Map p134, E1

This fabled jeweler, with its trademark clock-hoisting Atlas over the door, has won countless hearts with its luxe diamond rings, watches, silver Elsa Peretti heart necklaces, crystal vases and glassware. Swoon, drool, but whatever you do, don't harass the elevator attendants with tired 'Where's the breakfast?' jokes. (www.tiffany.com; 727 Fifth Ave, at 57th St; ⊙10am-7pm Mon-Sat, noon-6pm Sun; **S** F to 57th St, N/Q/R to 5th Ave-59th St)

Statue of *Atlas* at Rockefeller Center (p136)

FAO Schwarz CHILDREN

54 🔒 Map p134, E1

The toy store giant, where Tom Hanks played footsy piano in the movie *Big*, is number one on the NYC wish list of most visiting kids. Why not indulge them? The magical (over-the-top consumerist) wonderland, with dolls up for 'adoption', life-size stuffed animals, gas-powered kiddie convertibles, air-hockey sets and much more, might even thrill you, too. (www.fao.com; 767 Fifth Ave, at 58th St; ⊙10am-8pm Sun-Thu, to 9pm Fri & Sat; **S** 4/5/6 to 59th St, N/Q/R to 5th Ave-59th St)

B&H Photo Video
ELECTRONICS

55 Map p134, C5

Visiting NYC's most popular camera shop is an experience in itself – it's massive and crowded, and bustling with black-clad (and tech-savvy) Hasidic Jewish salesmen bussed in from communities in distant Brooklyn neighborhoods. Your chosen item is dropped into a bucket, which then moves up and across the ceiling to the purchase area (which requires a second queue). (www.bhphotovideo.com; 420 Ninth Ave, btwn 33rd & 34th Sts, Midtown West; ⏰9am-7pm Mon-Thu, to 1pm Fri, 10am-6pm Sun; ⑤A/C/E to 34th St-Penn Station)

Drama Book Shop
BOOKS

56 Map p134, C4

Nirvana for Broadway fans, this expansive bookstore has taken its theater (both plays and musicals) seriously since 1917. You'll find scripts, books on costume, stage design and other elements of performance, as well as industry journals and magazines. Check the website for in-store events. (www.dramabookshop.com; 250 W 40th St, btwn Seventh & Eighth Aves, Midtown West; ⏰11am-7pm Mon-Wed, Fri & Sat, 11am-8pm Thu, noon-6pm Sun; ⑤A/C/E to 42nd St-Port Authority Bus Terminal)

FRANZ MARC FREI/GETTY IMAGES ©

Window display at Bergdorf Goodman (p152)

Macy's
DEPARTMENT STORE

57 🔒 Map p134, D5

Fresh from a much-needed facelift, the world's largest department store covers most bases, with fashion, furnishings, kitchenware, sheets, cafes, hair salons and even a branch of the Metropolitan Museum of Art gift store. It's more 'mid-priced' than 'exclusive', with mainstream labels and big-name cosmetics. (www.macys.com; 151 W 34th St, at Broadway; ⏰9am-9:30pm Mon-Fri, 10am-9:30pm Sat, 11am-8:30pm Sun; S B/D/F/M, N/Q/R to 34th St-Herald Sq)

Argosy
BOOKS, MAPS

58 🔒 Map p134, F1

Since 1925, this landmark used book-store has stocked antiquarian items such as leatherbound books, old maps, art monographs and other classics picked up from high-class estate sales and closed antique shops. There's interesting Hollywood memorabilia, from personal letters and signed books, to contracts and autographed publicity stills. Prices range from cost-ly to clearance. (www.argosybooks.com; 116 E 59th St, btwn Park & Lexington Aves, Midtown East; ⏰10am-6pm Mon-Fri year-round, to 5pm Sat late Sep-late May; S 4/5/6 to 59th St, N/Q/R to Lexington Ave-59th St)

Time Warner Center
MALL

59 🔒 Map p134

A great add-on to an adventure in Central Park, the Time Warner Center has a line-up of upscale vendors including Coach, Stuart Weitzman, Williams-Sonoma, True Religion, Se-phora and J Crew. For delectable pic-nic fare, visit the Whole Foods in the basement. (www.theshopsatcolumbuscircle. com; Time Warner Center, 10 Columbus Circle; S A/C, B/D, 1 to 59th St-Columbus Circle)

Nepenthes New York
FASHION, ACCESSORIES

60 🔒 Map p134, C4

Occupying an old sewing shop in the Garment District, this cult Japanese collective stocks in-the-know labels like Engineered Garments and Needles, known for their quirky detailing and artisanal production value. While there's a small edit of women's pieces, the focus is on menswear. Accessories include bags and satchels, gloves and footwear. (www.nepenthesny.com; 307 W 38th St, btwn Eighth & Ninth Aves, Midtown West; ⏰noon-7pm Mon-Sat, to 5pm Sun; S A/C/E to 42nd St-Port Authority Bus Terminal)

Uniqlo
FASHION

61 🔒 Map p134, E2

Uniqlo is Japan's answer to H&M and this is its showstopping 89,000-sq-ft flagship megastore. Grab a mesh bag at the entrance and let the elevators woosh you up to the 3rd floor to begin your retail odyssey. The forte here is afford-able, fashionable, quality basics, from tees and undergarments, to Japanese denim, cashmere sweaters and super-light, high-tech parkas. (www.uniqlo.com; 666 Fifth Ave, at 53rd St; ⏰10am-9pm Mon-Sat, 11am-8pm Sun; S E, M to Fifth Ave-53rd St)

Explore

Upper East Side

High-end boutiques line Madison Ave and sophisticated mansions run parallel along Fifth Ave, which culminates in an architectural flourish called Museum Mile – one of the most cultured strips in the city, if not the world. It's here that you'll find the gigantic Metropolitan Museum of Art holding court with its learned siblings – Guggenheim, Whitney and Frick – in orbit.

The Sights in a Day

A day on the Upper East Side can easily be devoted to the Big Apple's clutch of world-class museums – it's a great neighborhood to explore on days with unfavorable weather. Start at the **Metropolitan Museum of Art** (p158), the mothership of museums. You could very well spend the entire day here, but its best to cut yourself off after two hours if you're going to fit in the opulent **Frick Collection** (p165) and the stunning **Neue Galerie** (p166).

Join the 'ladies who lunch' crowd with a late bite at **Via Quadronno** (p170) or **Café Sabarsky** (p170), then recaffeinate at **Sant Ambroeus** (p170) before filling the afternoon with a medley of contemporary wonders, starting at the **Guggenheim Museum** (p162) and finishing at the **Whitney Museum of American Art** (p165).

Return to the Met for a round of pre-dinner drinks at the **Metropolitan Museum Roof Garden Café & Martini Bar** (p171), then soak up the alcohol at Brit-cool **James Wood Foundry** (p168). End the night with laughs at **Comic Strip Live** (p173) or (if it's Monday) jazz with Woody Allen at **Café Carlyle** (p172).

👁 Top Sights

Metropolitan Museum of Art (p158)

Guggenheim Museum (p162)

💜 Best of New York City

Eating
Tanoshi (p168)

James Wood Foundry (p168)

ABV (p169)

Museums
Metropolitan Museum of Art (p158)

Guggenheim Museum (p162)

Frick Collection (p165)

Neue Galerie (p166)

Architecture
Whitney Museum of American Art (p165)

Temple Emanu-El (p167)

Getting There

S Subway The sole subway lines here are the 4/5/6, which travel north and south on Lexington Ave.

🚌 Bus The M1, M2, M3 and M4 buses make the scenic drive down Fifth Ave along the eastern edge of Central Park. The M15 is handy for getting around the far east side.

Top Sights
Metropolitan Museum of Art

This sprawling encyclopedic museum, founded in 1870, houses one of the biggest art collections in the world. Its permanent collection has more than two million individual objects, from Egyptian temples to American paintings. Known colloquially as 'The Met,' the museum attracts over six million visitors a year to its 17 acres of galleries – making it the largest single-site attraction in New York City. (Yup, you read that right: 17 acres.) In other words, plan on spending some time here.

◉ Map p164, A2

☏ 212-535-7710

www.metmuseum.org

1000 Fifth Ave at 82nd St

recommended admission adult/child $25/free

🕓 10am-5:30pm Sun-Thu, to 9pm Fri & Sat

Ⓢ 4/5/6 to 86th St

Temple of Dendur

Don't Miss

Egyptian Art

The museum has an unrivaled collection of ancient Egyptian art, some of which dates back to the Paleolithic era. Located to the north of the Great Hall, the 39 Egyptian galleries open dramatically with one of the Met's prized pieces: the Mastaba Tomb of Perneb (c 2300 BC), an Old Kingdom burial chamber crafted from limestone. From here, a web of rooms is cluttered with funerary stele, carved reliefs and fragments of pyramids. (Don't miss the intriguing Models of Meketre, clay figurines meant to help in the afterlife, in Gallery 105.) These eventually lead to the Temple of Dendur (Gallery 131), a sandstone temple to the goddess Isis that resides in a sunny atrium gallery with a reflecting pool – a must-see for the first-time visitor.

European Paintings

On the museum's 2nd floor, the European Paintings' galleries display a stunning collection of masterworks. This includes more than 1700 canvases from the roughly 500-year-period starting in the 13th century, with works by every important painter from Duccio to Rembrandt. In fact, everything here is, literally, a masterpiece. In Gallery 621 are several Caravaggios, including the masterfully painted *The Denial of St Peter*. Gallery 611, to the west, is packed with Spanish treasures, including El Greco's famed *View of Toledo*. Continue south (to Gallery 632) to see various Vermeers, including the *Young Woman with a Water Pitcher*. Nearby (in Gallery 634) gaze at Rembrandts, including a 1660 *Self-Portrait*. Altogether more modern beauties include Van Gogh's *Wheat Field with Cypresses* (Gallery 823), Renoir's *By the Seashore* (Gallery 824),

☑ Top Tips

▶ A desk inside the Great Hall has audio tours in several languages ($7), while docents offer guided tours of specific galleries. These are free with admission. Check the website or information desk.

▶ The museum crowds can often be overbearing. If you're looking for a bit of calm, it's best to avoid the Met on weekends.

▶ The most popular galleries with children are generally the Egyptian, African and Oceania galleries, and the collection of medieval arms and armor. You can grab a special museum brochure and map made specifically for tykes.

✖ Take a Break

In the warmer months (April to October), wander up to the roof garden for brilliant views of Central Park and its abutting skyscrapers. You'll also find the Roof Garden Café & Martini Bar (p171), the best place in the museum for a sip — especially at sunset.

and a young Picasso's pensive *Seated Harlequin* (Gallery 830). And that's just the beginning. You could spend hours exploring this veritable sea of powerful works.

Art of Arab Lands

On the 2nd floor you'll find the Islamic galleries with 15 incredible rooms showcasing the museum's extensive collection of art from the Middle East and Central and South Asia. In addition to garments, secular decorative objects and manuscripts, you'll find gilded and enameled glassware (Gallery 452) and a magnificent 14th-century *mihrab*, or prayer niche, lined with elaborately patterned polychrome tilework (Gallery 455). There is also a superb array of Ottoman textiles (Gallery 459), a medieval-style Moroccan court (Gallery 456) and an 18th-century room from Damascus (Gallery 461). Individual highlights include the lavishly colored Indian painting *A King Offers to Make Amends to a Bereaved Mother* (Gallery 465). Attributed to the artist Miskin and dating back to the late 16th century, it's especially interesting for its fusion of Islamic and Western aesthetics.

American Wing

In the museum's northwest corner, the revamped American galleries showcase a wide variety of decorative and fine art from throughout US history, including Hudson River School masterpieces. The rich hues of Louis Comfort Tiffany's leaded glass grace several galleries, his works including *Window* (Gallery 702), *Dogwood*, and *Magnolias and Irises* (Gallery 743). Highlights from the colonial portraiture collection include John Singleton Copley's 18th-century *Mrs. John Winthrop* (Gallery 748), the painting's reflective tabletop attesting to the artist's technical prowess. Hard to miss is Emanuel Leutze's massive canvas of *Washington Crossing the Delaware* (Gallery 760), while lovers of landscape painting will lose themselves in the rhythmic paintings

© THE METROPOLITAN MUSEUM OF ART, NEW YORK

14th-century *mihrab* (prayer niche)

of Childe Hassam, among them *Surf, Celia Thaxter's Garden, Isles of Shoals, Maine* and *The Water Garden* (Gallery 769). Nearby hangs John Singer Sargent's unbearably sexy *Madame X* (Gallery 771), a painting laden with more self-confidence and attitude than a Hollywood gala.

Greek & Roman Art

The 27 galleries devoted to classical antiquity are another Met doozy, some of which are dramatically illuminated by natural daylight. Among the extraordinary objects is a pair of late 7th-century-BC bronze helmets from Crete (Gallery 152), one of them adorned with *repoussé* winged youths and panthers, the other with horses and lions. Further along, Gallery 159 houses beautiful examples of ancient Greek pottery. Especially interesting are the white-ground funerary vases, in which the deceased and mourners are depicted on a distinctive white background. From the Great Hall, a passageway takes viewers through a barrel-vaulted room flanked by the chiseled torsos of Greek figures. This spills right into one of the Met's loveliest spaces: the airy Roman sculpture court (Gallery 162), full of marble carvings of gods and historical figures. The statue of a bearded Hercules from AD 68–98 is particularly awe-inspiring.

Armor of Henry II of France

Roof Garden

One of the best spots in the entire museum is the roof garden, which features rotating sculpture installations by contemporary and 20th century artists. (Jeff Koons, Andy Goldsworthy and Imran Qureshi have all shown here.) Yet its finest features are the views it offers of the city and Central Park. It's also home to the Roof Garden Café & Martini Bar, an ideal spot for a drink — especially at sunset. The roof garden is open from April to October.

Top Sights
Guggenheim Museum

A sculpture in its own right, architect Frank Lloyd Wright's building almost overshadows the collection of 20th-century art within. Completed in 1959, the inverted ziggurat structure was initially derided by some critics, but the swishing spirals of white quickly became a beloved architectural icon, featuring on countless postcards, TV programs and films.

◉ Map p164, A1

☎212-423-3500

www.guggenheim.org

1071 Fifth Ave, at 89th St

adult/child $22/free, by donation 5:45-7:45pm Sat

⌚10am-5:45pm Sun-Wed & Fri, to 7:45pm Sat

⑤4/5/6 to 86th St

Don't Miss

Permanent Collection Galleries

Although the Museum of Modern Art has garnered a reputation in New York City for having a more robust collection of oeuvres, the Guggenheim is very much a heavy hitter as well, boasting a variety of art from the 20th and 21st centuries. Hanging on the white-washed walls are works by the likes of Kandinsky, Picasso, Chagall, Jackson Pollock, Van Gogh, Monet, Magritte and Degas. Much of the Guggenheim's art is made up of several personal collections, including those of Justin Thannhauser, Peggy Guggenheim and the Robert Mapplethorpe Foundation, which generously bequeathed 200 photographs, making the museum the single-most important public repository of his work.

Exterior Views of the Facade

An architectural marvel from the outside and within, the Guggenheim didn't always garner the praise it does today. In fact, in 1959, when it opened, the structure was savaged by the *New York Times,* which lambasted it as 'a war between architecture and painting in which both come out badly maimed.' Beyond early criticism, the edifice itself was a logistical nightmare to build. Construction was delayed for almost 13 years due to budget constraints, the outbreak of WWII and outraged neighbors who weren't all that excited to see an architectural spaceship land in their midst. Construction was completed in 1959, after both Wright and Guggenheim had passed away.

☑ Top Tips

▶ The line to get in to the museum can be brutal at any time of the year. You'll save a lot of time if you purchase your tickets in advance on the website.

✗ Take a Break

There are two good on-site food options: **Wright** (☎212-427-5690; www.thewrightrestaurant.com; mains $23-28; ☺11:30am-3:30pm Sun-Wed, to 6pm Sat; ⑤4/5/6 to 86th St), at ground level, a space-age eatery serving steamy risotto and classic cocktails, and **Cafe 3** (www.guggenheim.org; sandwiches $9-10; ☺10:30am-5pm Fri-Wed; ⑤4/5/6 to 86th St), on the 3rd floor, which offers sparkling views of Central Park and excellent coffee and light snacks.

A

1
Jacqueline Kennedy Onassis Reservoir

National Academy Museum

4 Jewish Museum

9 Cooper-Hewitt National Design Museum

5

Guggenheim Museum

Neue Galerie

B

E 93rd St
E 92nd St
E 91st St
E 90th St
E 89th St
E 88th St
E 87th St
E 86th St

C

25
26

YORKVILLE

First Ave

D

For reviews see

⊙	Top Sights	p158
⊙	Sights	p165
✕	Eating	p168
⊙	Drinking	p171
☆	Entertainment	p172
⊕	Shopping	p174

0   400 m
0   0.2 miles

2
Metropolitan Museum of Art

31
18
33

21

E 85th St
E 84th St
E 83rd St
E 82nd St
E 81st St
E 80th St

24
29
19

Carl Schurz Park

East End Ave

Madison Ave
Park Ave
Lexington Ave
Third Ave
Second Ave
York Ave

79th St Transverse

Central Park

Conservatory Water

32

UPPER EAST SIDE

16
23
20 35
15

77th St

30
17
14

E 79th St
E 78th St
E 77th St
E 76th St
E 75th St
E 74th St
E 73rd St

11

22
27

John Jay Park

Franklin D Roosevelt Dr

East River

10

East End Ave

72nd St Transverse

The Mall

Frick Collection

Whitney Museum of American Art

2

Asia Society & Museum

8

E 72nd St
E 71st St
E 70th St
E 69th St
E 68th St
E 67th St

First Ave

York Ave

Roosevelt Island

65th St Transverse

East Dr

The Pond

Central Park South

6

Temple Emanu-El

Lexington Ave-63rd St

5th Ave-59th St

Fifth Ave
Madison Ave
Park Ave
Lexington Ave

Lexington Ave-59th St
59th St
E 59th St

68th St-Hunter College

E 66th St
E 65th St
E 64th St
E 63rd St
E 62nd St
E 61st St
E 60th St

Third Ave
Second Ave

Roosevelt Island Tramway Station

Rockefeller University

Eighth Ave

Ed Koch Queensboro Bridge

Temple Emanu-El (p167)

Sights

Whitney Museum of American Art
MUSEUM

1  Map p164, B3

The Whitney makes no secret of its mission to provoke, which starts with its imposing Brutalist building, a structure that houses works by 20th-century masters Edward Hopper, Jasper Johns, Georgia O'Keeffe and Mark Rothko. In addition to rotating exhibits, there is a biennial on even years, an ambitious survey of contemporary art that rarely fails to generate controversy. The museum is set to move into a new Renzo Piano–designed structure in the Meatpacking District in 2015. Check the website for updates. (☎ 212-570-3600; www.whitney. org; 945 Madison Ave, cnr 75th St; adult/child $20/free, by donation 6-9pm Fri; ☺ 11am-6pm Wed, Thu, Sat & Sun, 1-9pm Fri; ⑤ 6 to 77th St)

Frick Collection
GALLERY

2  Map p164, A4

This spectacular art collection sits in a mansion built by prickly steel magnate Henry Clay Frick, one of the many such residences that made up Millionaires' Row. The museum has over a dozen splendid rooms displaying masterpieces by Titian, Vermeer, Gilbert Stuart, El Greco and Goya. A demure Portico Gallery displays decorative works and sculpture. The museum is generally not crowded and feels refreshingly intimate. Children

Sculpture of Ganesh, Asia Society & Museum

metics magnate Ronald Lauder for a whopping $135 million. Children under 12 are not admitted. (212-628-6200; www.neuegalerie.org; 1048 Fifth Ave, cnr E 86th St; admission $20, free 6-8pm 1st Fri of every month; ⊙11am-6pm Thu-Mon; **S**4/5/6 to 86th St)

Jewish Museum

MUSEUM

4 ◉ Map p164, A1

This New York City gem is tucked into a French-Gothic mansion from 1908, which houses 30,000 items of Judaica, as well as sculpture, paintings and decorative arts. It is well regarded for its thoughtful temporary exhibits, featuring retrospectives on influential figures such as Chaim Soutine and sprawling examinations of socially conscious photography in New York. (212-423-3200; www.jewishmuseum.org; 1109 Fifth Ave, at 92nd St; adult/child $15/free, Sat free, by donation 5-8pm Thu; ⊙11am-6pm Fri-Tue, to 8pm Thu; 👪; **S**6 to 96th St)

National Academy Museum

GALLERY

5 ◉ Map p164, A1

Co-founded by painter/inventor Samuel Morse in 1825, the National Academy Museum is comprised of an incredible permanent collection of paintings by figures such as Will Barnet, Thomas Hart Benton and George Bellows, including some highly compelling self-portraits. It is housed in a beaux arts structure designed by Ogden Codman and featuring a

under 10 are not admitted. (212-288-0700; www.frick.org; 1 E 70th St, at Fifth Ave; admission $20, by donation 11am-1pm Sun, ⊙10am-6pm Tue-Sat, 11am-5pm Sun; **S**6 to 68th St-Hunter College)

Neue Galerie

MUSEUM

3 ◉ Map p164, A2

This restored Carrère and Hastings mansion from 1914 is a resplendent showcase for German and Austrian art, featuring works by Paul Klee, Ernst Ludwig Kirchner and Egon Schiele. In pride of place on the 2nd floor is Gustav Klimt's golden 1907 portrait of Adele Bloch-Bauer – which was acquired for the museum by cos-

marble foyer and spiral staircase. (☎212-369-4880; www.nationalacademy.org; 1083 Fifth Ave, at 89th St; adult/child $15/free; ⊙11am-6pm Wed-Sun; **S**4/5/6 to 86th St)

Temple Emanu-El SYNAGOGUE

 Map p164, A4

Founded in 1845 as the first Reform synagogue in New York and completed in 1929, this temple is now one of the largest Jewish houses of worship in the world. An imposing Romanesque structure, it is more than 175ft long and 100ft tall, with a brilliant, hand-painted ceiling that contains details in gold. (☎212-744-1400; www.emanuelnyc.org; 1 E 65th St, cnr Fifth Ave; ⊙10am-4:30pm Sun-Thu; **S**6 to 68th St-Hunter College)

Museum of the City of New York MUSEUM

 Map p164, A1

Step inside this colonial Georgian-style mansion to explore New York City's past, present and future. Don't miss the 22-minute film *Timescapes* (on the second floor), which charts Gotham's growth from a tiny native trading post to a burgeoning metropolis.

One of the museum's star attractions is the 12-room mansion dollhouse fabricated by Carrie Stettheimer over 25 years at the turn of the 20th century – replete with tiny art works (including miniatures of pieces by Marcel Duchamp and Gaston Lach-

aise). (☎212-534-1672; www.mcny.org; 1220 Fifth Ave, btwn 103rd & 104th Sts; suggested admission adult/child $10/free; ⊙10am-6pm; **S**6 to 103rd St)

Asia Society & Museum MUSEUM

 Map p164, B4

Founded in 1956 by John D Rockefeller (an avid collector of Asian Art), this cultural center hosts fascinating exhibits (such as pre-Revolutionary art of Iran, retrospectives of leading Chinese artists or block prints of Edo-era Japan), as well as Jain sculptures and Nepalese Buddhist paintings. There are tours (offered free with admission) at 2pm on Tuesdays year-round and at 6:30pm Fridays (excluding summer months). (☎212-288-6400; www.asiasociety.org; 725 Park Ave, at E 70th St; admission $12, 6-9pm Fri mid-Sep–Jun free; ⊙11am-6pm Tue-Sun, to 9pm Fri mid-Sep–Jun; **S**6 to 68th St-Hunter College)

Local Life
Road Runners

The long-time club and organizer of the New York City Marathon, the **New York Road Runners Club** (Map p164, A1; www.nyrr.org; 9 E 89th St btwn Madison & Fifth Aves; ⊙10am-8pm Mon-Fri, to 5pm Sat, to 3pm Sun; **S**4/5/6 to 86th St) coordinates runs throughout the year, including a midnight fun run on New Year's Eve.

Cooper-Hewitt National Design Museum   MUSEUM

9 Map p164, A1

Part of the Smithsonian Institution in Washington, DC, this house of culture is the only museum in the country dedicated to both historic and contemporary design. The collection is housed in the 64-room mansion built by billionaire Andrew Carnegie in 1901. The museum closed for an extensive renovation and expansion, and is slated to reopen in 2014. Check the website for updates. (☑212-849-8400; www.cooperhewitt.org; 2 E 91st St, at Fifth Ave; ⑤4/5/6 to 86th St)

Eating

Tanoshi   SUSHI $$$

10 Map p164, D3

It's not easy to snag one of the ten stools at this small, humble, wildly

Top Tip

In Search of Cheap Eats

The Upper East Side is ground zero for all things luxurious, especially the area that covers the blocks from 60th to 86th Sts between Park and Fifth Aves. As a general rule, if you're looking for eating and drinking spots that are easier on the wallet, head east of Lexington Ave. First, Second and Third Aves are lined with less pricey neighborhood spots.

popular sushi spot, but boy is it worth it. From the Hokkaido scallops and Atlantic shad, to the seared salmon belly and mouth-watering *uni* (sea urchin), everything is obscenely fresh. Only sushi is on offer and only *omakase*, the chef's selection of whatever is particularly outstanding that day. It's BYO beer, sake or whatnot. Book well in advance. (☑646-727-9056; 1372 York Ave, btwn 73rd & 74th Sts; 12-piece sushi $50; ⊗6-10pm Tue-Sat; ⑤6 to 77th St)

James Wood Foundry   BRITISH $$

11 Map p164, C3

What was once an ironworks is now a Brit-inspired gastropub peddling first-rate beer-battered fish and chips, bangers and mash, lamb and rosemary pie and other comfort classics from across the pond. If the weather is on your side, grab a table on the enclosed courtyard patio. (☑212-249-2700; 401 E 76th St, btwn First & York Aves; mains lunch $10-24, dinner $18-32; ⊗11am-2am; ☜; ⑤6 to 77th St)

Earl's Beer & Cheese   AMERICAN $

12 Map p164, B1

Chef Corey Cova's tiny comfort-food outpost channels a hipster hunting vibe with its giant deer in the woods mural and mounted buck's head. Basic grilled cheese is a paradigm shifter, served with pork belly, fried egg and kimchi. You'll also find mac 'n' cheese (with goat's cheese and shredded chicken) and tacos (featuring braised pork shoulder and *queso fresco*), best

Neue Galerie (p166)

washed down with a smooth craft beer. (www.earlsny.com; 1259 Park Ave, btwn 97th & 98th Sts; grilled cheese $6-8; ⊙4pm-midnight Mon & Tue, 11am-midnight Wed-Thu & Sun, to 2am Fri & Sat Sat & Sun; [S]6 to 96th St)

ABV   MODERN AMERICAN $$

 13   Map p164, B1

On the borderline of East Harlem, ABV draws a young, laid-back crowd tucking into eclectic sharing plates (fish tacos, foie gras mousse, scallops, veal sweetbreads), wine ($9 to $12 per glass) and craft beers. Soaring ceilings and cozy brick walls invite lingering, and there's live music on Monday nights (from 9pm), except during football season. (☏212-722-8959; 1504 Lexington Ave, at 97th St; mains $10-24; ⊙5pm-midnight Mon-Thu, 4pm-1am Fri, from 11am Sat & Sun; ☏; [S]6 to 96th St.)

JG Melon   PUB $

14   Map p164, B3

JG's is a loud, old-school, melon-themed pub that has been serving basic burgers on tea plates since 1972. It's a local favorite for both eating and drinking (the Bloody Marys are excellent) and it gets crowded in the after-work hours. If you're feeling claustrophobic, try lunchtime instead. (☏212-744-0585; 1291 Third Ave, at 74th St; burgers $10.50; ⊙11:30am-4am; [S]6 to 77th St)

Café Sabarsky

AUSTRIAN $$

The lines get long at this popular cafe at Neue Galerie (see 3 Map p164, A2), which evokes opulent turn-of-the-century Vienna. Thankfully the well-rendered Austrian specialties make the wait well worth it. Channel Central Europe with smoked trout crepes, goulash soup and creamed *spätzle* (a type of German noodle). Adding temptation is a long list of specialty sweets, including a divine *sachertorte* (dark chocolate cake laced with apricot preserves). (📞212-288-0665; www.kg-ny.com/wallse; 1048 Fifth Ave, at E 86th St; mains $15-30; ⊗9am-6pm Mon & Wed, to 9pm Thu-Sun; 🍴👶; Ⓢ4/5/6 to 86th St)

Via Quadronno

CAFE $

15 Map p164, A3

If you're pining for Rome, slip into this cozy cafe-bistro, famed for its exquisite *caffè* (coffee) and just-like-mamma dishes. The mind-boggling selection of sandwiches features a decadent wild boar prosciutto and Camembert combo, while other menu options include soulful soups, pastas and a daily lasagna. (📞212-650-9880; www.viaquadronno.com; 25 E 73rd St, btwn Madison & Fifth Aves; sandwiches $8-15, mains $23-38; ⊗8am-11pm Mon-Fri, 9am-11pm Sat, 10am-9pm Sun; 🍴; Ⓢ6 to 77th St)

Sant Ambroeus

CAFE, ITALIAN $$$

16 Map p164, A3

Slip on those Prada shoes and strike a pose at this classic Milanese cafe-cum-bistro. While the front bar dispenses pastries, panini and velvety cappuccinos, the elegant back dining room is a northern Italian affair. Book a table and tuck into decadent classics, from saffron risotto to breaded veal chop. Don't bypass the famed gelato. (📞212-570-2211; www.santambroeus.com; 1000 Madison Ave, btwn 77th & 78th St; panini $12-18, mains $23-64; ⊗7am-11pm; 🍴; Ⓢ6 to 77th St)

Candle Cafe

VEGAN $$

17 Map p164, B3

The moneyed yoga set piles into this attractive vegan cafe serving a long list of sandwiches, salads, comfort food and market-driven specials. The specialty here is the house-made seitan. There is a juice bar and a gluten-free menu.

For a more upscale take on the subject, check out its sister restaurant, **Candle 79**, two blocks away on 79th St. (📞212-472-0970; www.candlecafe.com; 1307 Third Ave, btwn 74th & 75th Sts; mains $15-21; ⊗11:30am-10:30pm Mon-Sat, to 9:30pm Sun; 🍴; Ⓢ6 to 77th St)

William Greenberg Desserts

BAKERY $

18 Map p164, A2

Make a pitstop here for New York City's finest black-and-white cookies, soft vanilla discs dipped in white sugar and dark chocolate glazes. Takeout only. (www.wmgreenbergdesserts.com; 1100 Madison Ave, btwn E 82nd & 83rd Sts; baked goods from $2; ⊗8am-6:30pm Mon-Fri, to 6pm Sat, 10am-4pm Sun; 👶; Ⓢ4/5/6 to 86th St)

Sandro's

ITALIAN $$

19 Map p164, C2

This neighborhood trattoria serves up fresh Roman dishes and homemade pastas by chef Sandro Fioriti. Specialties include crisp fried artichokes and sea urchin ravioli. (☏212-288-7374; www.sandrosnyc.com; 306 E 81st St, near Second Ave; mains $20-40; ⏰4:30-11pm Mon-Sat, to 10pm Sun; S6 to 77th St)

Café Boulud

FRENCH $$$

20 Map p164, A3

This Michelin-starred bistro – part of Daniel Boulud's gastronomic empire – attracts a staid crowd with its globetrotting French cuisine. Seasonal menus include classic dishes such as coq au vin, as well as more inventive fare such as scallop *crudo* (raw) with white miso. Foodies on a budget will be interested in the three-course, $43 prix fixe lunch. (☏212-772-2600; www.danielnyc.com/cafebouludny.html; 20 E 76th St, btwn Fifth & Madison Aves; mains $24-48; ⏰breakfast, lunch & dinner; ☍; S6 to 77th St)

Drinking

Metropolitan Museum Roof Garden Café & Martini Bar

COCKTAIL BAR

21 Map p164, A2

The sort of setting you can't get enough of (even if you are a jaded local). The roof garden's bar sits right above Central Park's tree canopy, allowing for splendid views of the park and the city skyline all around. Sunset is when you'll find fools in love – then again, it could all be those martinis. (www.metmuseum.org; 1000 Fifth Ave, at 82nd St; ⏰10am-4:30pm Sun-Thu, to 8pm Fri & Sat, Martini Bar 5:30-8pm Fri & Sat May-Oct; S4/5/6 to 86th St)

JBird

BAR

22 Map p164, C3

This rare uptown creature serves craft cocktails and seasonal pub grub in a screen-free environment that feels more downtown than uptown. Grab a seat at the marble bar or arrive early and sink into a dark leather banquette. Peckish? Nibble on pork sliders or garlic fries while sipping complex libations. (☏212-288-8033; 339 E 75th St, btwn First & Second Aves; ⏰5:30pm-2am Mon-Thu, to 4am Fri & Sat; S6 to 77th St)

Bemelmans Bar

LOUNGE

23 Map p164, B3

It's still 1940-something at this fabled bar – the sort of place where the waiters wear white jackets, a baby grand is always tinkling and the ceiling is 24-carat gold leaf. Note the charming murals by Ludwig Bemelman, famed creator of *Madeline*. Show up before 9pm if you don't want to pay a cover (per person $15 to $30). (☏212-744-1600; www.thecarlyle.com/dining/bemelmans_bar; Carlyle Hotel, 35 E 76th St, at Madison Ave; ⏰noon-2am Mon-Sat, to 12:30am Sun; S6 to 77th St)

The Penrose · BAR

24 Map p164, C2

The Penrose brings a much-needed dose of cool to the Upper East Side, with craft beers, vintage mirrors, floral wallpaper, reclaimed wood details and friendly bartenders. There's Duvel and Murphy's on draft, a decent selection of Irish whiskeys (no surprise, given the owners hail from Cork) and plenty of good pub grub to boot. (☎212-203-2751; 1590 Second Ave, btwn 82nd & 83rd Sts; ⊙3pm-4am Mon-Thu, noon-4am Fri, 10:30am-4am Sat & Sun; **S**4/5/6 to 86th St)

Vinus and Marc · LOUNGE

25 Map p164, C1

Red walls, vintage fixtures and a long dark wood bar set a decadent stage at Vinus and Marc. Cocktails range from the elegantly creative – try the spicy Baby Vamp (tequila, mescal, strawberry and habandero bitters) – to Prohibition-era classics like the Scofflaw (Rye whiskey, dry vermouth and housemade grenadine).

Solid bistro fare includes mussels, shrimp and grits, and a succulent Angus beef tenderloin sandwich. (☎646-692-9015; 1825 Second Ave, btwn 95th & 94th Sts; ⊙3pm-1am Sun-Tue, to 2am Wed & Thu, to 3am Fri & Sat; **S**6 to 96th St)

Drunken Munkey · LOUNGE

26 Map p164, C1

Playful Drunken Munkey channels colonial-era Bombay with its yesteryear wallpaper, cricket ball door handles and jauntily attired waitstaff. The monkey chandeliers may be pure whimsy, but the cocktails and sharing-sized curries are serious business. Gin, not surprisingly, is the drink of choice. Try the Bramble, with Bombay gin, blackberry liqueur, fresh lemon juice and blackberries. (338 E 92nd St, btwn First & Second Aves; ⊙11am-2am Mon-Thu, to 3am Fri-Sun; **S**6 to 96th St)

Oslo Coffee Roasters · CAFE

27 Map p164, C3

Headquartered in Williamsburg (where they do their roasting), Oslo whips up magnificent brews, espressos and lattes – all fair trade and organic, of course. (422 E 75th St, btwn York & First Aves; coffee from $2; ⊙7am-6pm Mon-Fri, from 8am Sat, 8am-3pm Sun; **S**6 to 77th St)

Entertainment

Café Carlyle · JAZZ

This swanky spot sits at the Carlyle Hotel along with Bemelman's Bar (see **23** Map p164, B3), and draws top-shelf talent, including Woody Allen, who plays his clarinet here with the Eddy Davis New Orleans Jazz Band on Mondays at 8:45pm (September through May). Bring bucks: the cover doesn't include food or drinks. (www.thecarlyle.com/dining/cafe_carlyle; Carlyle Hotel, 35 E 76th St, at Madison Ave; cover $110-185; **S**6 to 77th St)

Frick Collection

Frick Collection CLASSICAL MUSIC

Once a month, this opulent mansion-museum (see 2 Map p164, A4) hosts a 5pm Sunday concert that showcases world-renowned performers such as cellist Yehuda Hanani and violinist Thomas Zehetmair. Check the museum website for details. (www.frick.org; 1 E 70th St, at Fifth Ave; admission $35; S 6 to 68th St-Hunter College)

92nd St Y CULTURAL CENTER

28 Map p164, B1

In addition to its wide spectrum of concerts, dance performances and literary readings, this nonprofit cultural center hosts an excellent lecture and conversation series. Playwright Edward Albee, cellist Yo-Yo Ma, funnyman Steve Martin and novelist Gary Shteyngart have all taken the stage. (www.92y.org; 1395 Lexington Ave, at 92nd St; ; S 6 to 96th St)

Comic Strip Live COMEDY

29 Map p164, C2

Chris Rock, Adam Sandler, Jerry Seinfeld and Eddie Murphy have all performed at this club. Not recently, mind – but you're sure to find somebody stealing their acts here most nights. Reservations required. (212-861-9386; www.comicstriplive.com; 1568 Second Ave, btwn 81st & 82nd Sts; cover charge $15-30 plus 2-drink min; shows 8:30pm Sun-Thu; 8:30pm, 10:30pm & 12:30pm Fri; 8pm, 10:30pm & 12:30am Sat; S 4/5/6 to 86th St)

Shopping

Housing Works Thrift Shop

VINTAGE

30  Map p164, B3

As at the other Housing Works around town, shopping here can be a bit hit-or-miss. On good days, you might score a designer jacket, flattering jeans or a haute handbag. The threads are generally in excellent condition – if not new – and sold at mere-mortal prices. Extras include books, CDs and housewares. It gets crowded on weekends. (202 E 77th St, btwn Second & Third Aves; ⏱11am-7pm Mon-Fri, 10am-6pm Sat, noon-5pm Sun; **S** 6 to 77th St)

Encore

CLOTHING

31 🔒 Map p164, A2

This A-list consignment store has been emptying out Upper East Side closets since the 1950s. (Jacqueline Kennedy Onassis used to sell her clothes here.) Expect a gently worn string of high-end couture from the likes of Louboutin, Fendi and Dior. Prices are high but infinitely better than retail. (www.encoreresale.com; 1132 Madison Ave, btwn 84th & 85th Sts; ⏱10:30am-6:30pm Mon-Sat, noon-6pm Sun; **S** 4/5/6 to 86th St)

Shopfronts, Madison Avenue

PANORAMIC IMAGES/GETTY IMAGES ©

Michael's
CLOTHING

32 Map p164, B3

Another '50s veteran, this vaunted Upper East Side resale shop is strong on high-end labels, including Chanel, Gucci and Prada. Almost everything on display is less than two years old. It's pricey, but cheaper than shopping the flagship boutiques on Madison Ave. (www.michaelsconsignment.com; 2nd fl, 1041 Madison Ave, btwn 79th & 80th Sts; ⊘9:30am-6pm Mon-Sat, to 8pm Thu; S 6 to 77th St)

Crawford Doyle Booksellers
BOOKS

33 Map p164, A2

Bookworms are free to browse at this genteel Upper East Side book shop, with stacks devoted to art, literature and the history of New York – not to mention plenty of first editions. A wonderful place to while away a chilly afternoon. (1082 Madison Ave, btwn 81st & 82nd Sts; ⊘10am-6pm Mon-Sat, noon-5pm Sun; S 6 to 77th St)

Blue Tree
FASHION, HOMEWARES

34 Map p164, B1

Owned by actress Phoebe Cates Kline of *Fast Times at Ridgemont High*, charming Blue Tree peddles a dainty, elegant edit of women's clothing, cashmere scarves, Lucite objects, whimsical accessories and quirky home design. (www.bluetreenyc.com; 1283 Madison Ave, btwn 91st & 92nd Sts; ⊘10am-6pm Mon-Fri, from 11am Sat & Sun; S 4/5/6 to 86th St)

Zitomer
BEAUTY

35 Map p164, B3

Refresh your skin at this multi-story retro pharmacy, a veritable treasure trove of premium, all-natural skincare products from the likes of Kiehl's, Clarins, Kneipp, Mustela and Ahava (made from rejuvenating Dead Sea minerals). Hit the third floor for kids' clothes and toys. (www.zitomer.com; 969 Madison Ave, btwn 75th & 76th Sts; ⊘9am-8pm Mon-Fri, to 7pm Sat, 10am-6pm Sun; S 6 to 77th St)

Explore

Upper West Side & Central Park

New York's antidote to the endless stretches of concrete, Central Park is a verdant escape from honking horns and sunless sidewalks. The Upper West Side lines the park with inspired residential towers, each one higher than the next. This area is most notably home to Lincoln Center, largely considered to hold the greatest concentration of performance spaces in town.

The Sights in a Day

☼ Start things off at the **American Museum of Natural History** (p184), where you can zoom through outer space in the planetarium or gaze at the reassembled bones of a Tyrannosaurus Rex. Afterwards, walk over to **Zabar's** (p186) to pack a gourmet picnic hamper.

☼ When the weather's in your favor, fill the rest of the day in **Central Park** (p178). Spread a blanket on a patch of green, then take in the park's myriad sights, like the Bethesda Fountain, the Central Park Zoo and the Great Lawn. Pause for a drink at the **Loeb Boathouse** (p187), then hire a paddle boat for a quick jaunt around the lake.

☾ As the sun begins to tuck behind the fortress of highrises lining the four corners of the park, it's time to head to **Lincoln Center** (p184) – the city's unofficial headquarters for performance pursuits – to visit the city's other 'Met', the **Metropolitan Opera House** (p191). Enjoy a late-night dinner at one of the neighborhood's all-star eateries, such as **Dovetail** (p187).

◉ **Top Sights**

Central Park (p178)

♥ **Best of New York City**

Local Eats
Zabar's (p186)

Gray's Papaya (p188)

Entertainment
Lincoln Center (p184)

Film Society of Lincoln Center (p191)

Escape
Central Park (p178)

Getting There

Ⓢ **Subway** On the Upper West Side, the 1/2/3 subway lines are good for destinations along Broadway and points west, while the B and C trains are best for points of interest and access to Central Park.

🚌 **Bus** The M104 bus runs north to south along Broadway and the M10 plies the scenic ride along the western edge of the park.

Top Sights
Central Park

Vast and majestic, Central Park is 843 acres filled with picturesque meadows, tranquil ponds and hidden architectural treasures. The rolling green isn't simply the space of the island that wasn't developed, it is – believe it or not – one of the biggest architectural feats in the entire city. In fact, it took over 20 years to convert the land from swamps and farms into the beautiful retreat you see today.

◉ Map p182, D5

www.centralparknyc.org

59th & 110th Sts, btwn Central Park West & Fifth Ave

⊙ 6am-1am

Don't Miss

Strawberry Fields

This tear-shaped **garden** (www.centralparknyc.org/
visit/things-to-see/south-end/strawberry-fields.html;
Central Park, at 72nd St on the west side; 🚻; **S** A/C, B to
72nd St) serves as a memorial to former Beatle
John Lennon, who was shot dead outside the
Dakota building on December 8, 1980. The
building stands across the street at 1 West 72nd
Street. The garden itself is composed of a grove of
stately elms and a tiled mosaic that reads, simply,
'Imagine.' Appropriately, the memorial sits at the
level of 72nd St on the west side of the park.

Bethesda Terrace & the Mall

The arched walkways of Bethesda Terrace, crowned
by the magnificent Bethesda Fountain (at the level
of 72nd St), have long been a gathering area for
New Yorkers of all flavors. Indeed, the area has
featured in numerous films and TV shows, including the 1970s musical *Godspell*. To the south is the
Mall (featured in countless movies), a promenade
shrouded in mature North American elms. The
southern stretch, known as Literary Walk, is
flanked by statues of famous authors.

Central Park Zoo

Officially known as the Central Park Wildlife Center, this small **zoo** (📞212-861-6030; www.centralparkzoo.
com; Central Park, 64th St, at Fifth Ave; adult/child $12/7;
🕙10am-5:30pm Apr-Nov, to 4:30pm Nov-Apr; 🚻; **S** N/Q/R
to 5th Ave-59th St) is home to penguins, snow leop-
ards, dart poison frogs and red pandas. Feeding
times in the sea lion and penguin tanks make for
a rowdy spectacle. The attached **Tisch Children's
Zoo** (www.centralparkzoo.com/animals-and-exhibits/ex-
hibits/tisch-childrens-zoo.aspx; Central Park, at 65th & Fifth
Ave), a petting zoo, has alpacas and mini-Nubian
goats and is perfect for small children.

☑ Top Tips

▶ Free and custom
walking tours are avail-
able via the **Central
Park Conservancy**
(www.centralparknyc.org/
walkingtours), the
nonprofit organization
that supports park
maintenance.

▶ Crosstown MTA buses
at 66th, 72nd, 79th, 86th
and 96th Sts take you
through the park, but it's
important to note that
they pick up and drop off
passengers at the edge
of the park – not inside.

✕ Take a Break

Consider packing a
picnic from the assort-
ment of gourmet good-
ies at Zabar's (p186) in
the heart of the Upper
West Side.

Class things up at the
Loeb Boathouse (p187)
with a round of crab
cakes and a smooth
afternoon martini.

Understand
Central Park

In the 1850s, the area now graced by Central Park was occupied by pig farms, a garbage dump, a bone-boiling operation and an African American village. It took thousands of laborers to shift 10 million cartloads of soil to transform swamp and rocky outcroppings into the 'people's park' of today. Featuring more than 24,000 trees, 136 acres of woodland, 21 playgrounds and seven bodies of water, this giant green lung attracts more than 38 million visitors a year.

José de Creeft's sculpture, *Alice in Wonderland*

Conservatory Water & Alice in Wonderland Statue

North of the zoo at the level of 74th St is the Conservatory Water, where model sailboats drift lazily and kids scramble about on a toadstool-studded statue of Alice in Wonderland. There are Saturday story hours at the Hans Christian Andersen statue to the west of the water (at 11am June to September).

Great Lawn

The Great Lawn is a massive emerald carpet at the center of the park and is surrounded by ball fields and London plane trees. (This is where Simon & Garfunkel played their famous 1981 concert.) Immediately to the southeast is Delacorte Theater, home to an annual Shakespeare in the Park festival, as well as Belvedere Castle (p184), a birdwatching lookout.

The Ramble

South of the Great Lawn, between 72nd and 79th Sts, is the leafy Ramble, a popular birding destination (and legendary gay pick-up spot). On the southeastern end is the Loeb Boathouse (p184), home to a waterside restaurant that offers rowboat and bicycle rentals.

Jacqueline Kennedy Onassis Reservoir

This reservoir takes up almost the entire width of the park at the level of 90th St and serves as a gorgeous reflecting pool for the city skyline. It is surrounded by a 1.58-mile track that draws legions of joggers in the warmer months. Nearby, at Fifth Ave and 90th St, is a statue of New York City Marathon founder Fred Lebow peering at his watch.

Conservatory Garden

If you want a little peace and quiet (as in, no runners, cyclists or boom boxes), the six-acre Conservatory Garden serves as one of the park's official quiet zones. And it's beautiful to boot: bursting with crabapple trees, meandering boxwood and, in the spring, lots of flowers. It's located at 105th St off Fifth Ave. Otherwise, you can catch maximum calm (and maximum bird life) in all areas of the park just after dawn.

DENNIS K. JOHNSON/GETTY IMAGES ©

John Lennon memorial at Strawberry Fields

North Woods & Blockhouse

The North Woods, on the west side between 106th and 110th Sts, is home to the park's oldest structure, the Blockhouse, a military fortification from the War of 1812.

Summer Happenings in Central Park

During the warm months, Central Park is home to countless cultural events, many of which are free. The two most popular are Shakespeare in the Park (p221), which is managed by the Public Theater, and **SummerStage** (www.summerstage.org; admission free), a series of free concerts. Check out the websites for more information.

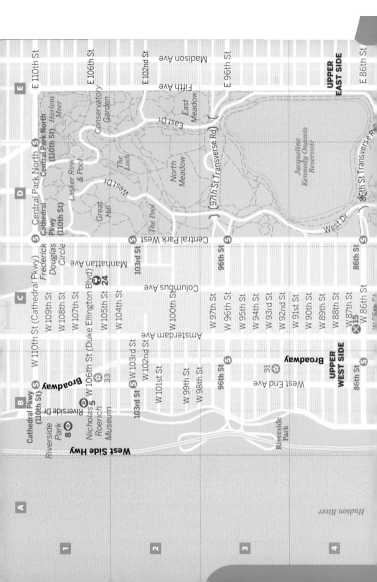

Sights

Lincoln Center CULTURAL CENTER

1 🎯 Map p182, C8

This stark arrangement of gleaming Modernist temples contains some of Manhattan's most important performance spaces: Avery Fisher Hall (home to the New York Philharmonic), David H Koch Theater (site of the New York City ballet) and the iconic Metropolitan Opera House, whose interior walls are dressed with brightly saturated murals by painter Marc Chagall. Various other venues are tucked in and around the 16-acre campus, including a theater, two film screening centers and the renowned Juilliard School. (📞212-875-5456; http://lc.lincolncenter.org; Columbus Ave btwn 62nd & 66th Sts; public plazas free, tours adult/student $18/15; 🚻; ⑤1 to 66th St-Lincoln Center)

American Museum of Natural History MUSEUM

2 🎯 Map p182, C5

Founded in 1869, this classic museum contains a veritable wonderland of more than 30 million artifacts, including lots of menacing dinosaur skeletons, as well as the Rose Center for Earth & Space, with its cutting-edge planetarium. From October through May, the museum is home to the Butterfly Conservatory, a glass house featuring 500-plus butterflies from all over the world. (📞212-769-5100; www.amnh.org; Central Park West, at 79th St; suggested donation adult/child $22/12.50; ⑳10am-5:45pm, Rose Center to 8:45pm Fri, Butterfly Conservatory Oct-May; 🚻; ⑤B, C to 81st St-Museum of Natural History, 1 to 79th St)

Loeb Boathouse KAYAKING, CYCLING

3 🎯 Map p182, E6

Central Park's boathouse has a fleet of 100 rowboats plus three kayaks available for rent from April to November. In the summer, there is also a Venetian-style gondola that seats up to six (per 30 minutes $30). Bicycles are available from April to November. Rentals require an ID and credit card and are weather permitting. Helmets included. (📞212-517-2233; www.thecentralparkboathouse.com; Central Park, btwn 74th & 75th Sts; boating per hr $12, bike rentals per hr $9-15; ⑳10am-dusk Apr-Nov; 🚻; ⑤B, C to 72nd St, 6 to 77th St)

Belvedere Castle BIRDWATCHING

4 🎯 Map p182, D5

For a DIY birding expedition with kids, pick up a 'Discovery Kit' at Belvedere Castle in Central Park. It comes with binoculars, a bird book, colored pencils and paper – a perfect way to get the tykes excited about birds. Picture ID required. (📞212-772-0210; Central Park, at 79th St; admission free; ⑳10am-3pm Tue-Sun; 🚻; ⑤B, C, 1/2/3 to 72nd St)

Nicholas Roerich Museum MUSEUM

5 🎯 Map p182, B1

This compelling little museum, housed in a three-story townhouse

Blue whale, American Museum of Natural History

from 1898, is one of the city's best-kept secrets. It contains more than 200 paintings by the prolific Nicholas Konstantinovich Roerich (1874–1947), a Russian-born poet, philosopher and painter. His most remarkable works are his stunning depictions of the Himalayas, where he often traveled. (www.roerich.org; 319 W 107th St, btwn Riverside Dr & Broadway; suggested donation $5; ⊙noon-5pm Tue-Fri, from 2pm Sat & Sun; S 1 to Cathedral Pkwy)

Wollman Skating Rink   ICE SKATING

6 ⊙ Map p182, D8

Larger than Rockefeller Center skating rink and allowing all-day skating, this rink is at the southeastern edge of Central Park and offers nice views. It's open mid-October through April. Cash only. (☏212-439-6900; www.wollmanskatingrink.com; Central Park, btwn 62nd & 63rd Sts; adult Mon-Thu/Fri-Sun $11/18, child $6, skate rentals $8, lock rental $5, spectator fee $5; ⊙Nov-Mar; ♿; S F to 57 St, N/Q/R to 5th Ave-59th St)

New-York Historical Society   MUSEUM

7 ⊙ Map p182, C6

As the antiquated hyphenated name implies, the Historical Society is the city's oldest museum, founded in 1804 to preserve the city's historical and cultural artifacts. Its collection of more than 60,000 objects is quirky and fascinating and includes everything from George Washington's inauguration chair to a 19th century Tiffany ice cream dish (gilded, of course). (www.nyhistory.org; 2 W 77th St at Central Park West; adult/child $18/6, by donation 6-8pm Fri, library free; ⏰10am-6pm Tue-Thu & Sat, to 8pm Fri, 11am-5pm Sun; Ⓢ B, C to 81st St-Museum of Natural History)

Riverside Park

OUTDOORS

 8 ⦿ Map p182, B1

A classic beauty designed by Central Park creators Frederick Law Olmsted and Calvert Vaux, this waterside spot, running north on the Upper West Side and banked by the Hudson River from 59th to 158th Sts, is lusciously leafy. Plenty of bike paths and playgrounds make it a family favorite.

From late March through October (weather permitting), a rowdy waterside restaurant, the West 79th Street Boat Basin Café, serves a light menu at the level of 79th St. (☎212-870-3070; www.riversideparknyc.org; Riverside Dr, btwn 68th & 155th Sts; ⏰6am-1am; 🚻; Ⓢ1/2/3 to any stop btwn 66th & 157th Sts)

American Folk Art Museum

MUSEUM

 9 ⦿ Map p182, C7

This tiny institution contains a couple of centuries' worth of folk and outsider art treasures, including pieces by Henry Darger (known for his girl-filled battlescapes) and Martín Ramírez (producer of hallucinatory *caballeros* on horseback). There is also an array of wood carvings, paintings, hand-tinted photographs and decora-

tive objects. There are guitar concerts on Wednesdays and free music on Fridays. (www.folkartmuseum.org; 2 Lincoln Sq, Columbus Ave, at 66th St; admission free; ⏰noon-7:30pm Tue-Sat, to 6pm Sun; Ⓢ1 to 66th St-Lincoln Center)

Zabar's

MARKET

 10 ⦿ Map p182, B5

Gourmet goes kosher at this sprawling local market, which dates back to the 1930s. Drool over heavenly cheeses, meats, olives, caviar, smoked fish, pickles, dried fruits, nuts and baked goods. Don't miss the pillowy, fresh-out-of-the-oven *knishes* (Eastern European–style potato dumplings wrapped in dough), an enlightening antidote to the frozen, stock-standard industrial variety sold by street vendors across the city. (www.zabars.com; 2245 Broadway, at 80th St; ⏰8am-7:30pm Mon-Fri, to 8pm Sat, 9am-6pm Sun; Ⓢ1 to 79th St)

Eating

Café Luxembourg

FRENCH $$$

 11 ✕ Map p182, B7

This quintessential French bistro is generally crowded with locals and it's no mystery why: the setting is elegant, the staff friendly, and the menu outstanding. The classics – salmon tartare, cassoulet and *steak frites* – are all deftly executed, and its proximity to Lincoln Center makes it a perfect pre-performance destination. There is a lighter lunch menu and decadent brunch offerings (try the lobster Benedict). (☎212-873-7411; www.cafeluxembourg.com; 200 W 70th St, btwn

Broadway & West End Ave; lunch mains $18-29, dinner mains $25-36; ⊘breakfast, lunch & dinner daily, brunch Sun; **S**1/2/3 to 72nd St)

Loeb Boathouse

AMERICAN **$$$**

Perched on the northeastern tip of the Central Park Lake and sporting views of the skyline, the Loeb Boathouse (see 3 ⊙ Map p182, E6) delivers one of Gotham's dreamiest dining settings. That said, what you're paying for is the location. While the food is generally good (the crab cakes are the standout), the downside is the somewhat indifferent service. To experience the location without the big bucks, hit the adjacent **Bar & Grill**, which offers a limited bar menu (plates $16), where you can still get crabcakes and a cinematic backdrop. (☏212-517-2233; www.thecentralparkboathouse.com; Central Park Lake, Central Park, at 74th St; mains $24-47; ⊘restaurant noon-4pm & 5:30-9:30pm Mon-Fri, 9:30am-4pm & 6-9:30pm Sat & Sun; **S**A/C, B to 72nd St, 6 to 77th St)

Dovetail

MODERN AMERICAN **$$$**

12 Map p182, C6

Michelin-starred Dovetail flies high with delectable seasonal dishes: think striped bass with sunchokes and burgundy truffle, or venison with bacon, golden beets and foraged greens. On Mondays, chef John Fraser offers a four-course vegetarian tasting menu ($58) that is winning over carnivores with the likes of plump hen of the woods mushrooms with d'anjou pears and green peppercorns. (☏212-362-

3800; www.dovetailnyc.com; 103 W 77th St, cnr Columbus Ave; tasting menu $88, mains $36-58; ⊘5:30-10pm Mon-Sat, 11:30am-10pm Sun; ☝; **S**A/C, B to 81st St-Museum of Natural History, 1 to 79th St)

Kefi

GREEK **$$**

13 Map p182, C5

Whitewashed Kefi is the domain of chef Michael Psilakis, whose rustic Hellenic cooking could make the toughest Greek weep. Swoon over winners like spicy lamb sausage, sheep-milk dumplings and succulent grilled octopus. The four-spread platter is finger-licking good, as is the flat pasta with braised rabbit. Toast to the old country with a comprehensive selection of Greek vintages (from $24 per bottle). (www.kefirestaurant.com; 505 Columbus Ave, btwn 84th & 85th Sts; small sharing plates $7-10, mains $13-20; ⊘noon-3pm & 5-10pm Mon-Fri, from 11am Sat & Sun; ☝; **S**B, C to 86th St)

Jacob's Pickles

AMERICAN **$$**

14 Map p182, C5

Jacob's elevates the humble pickle to dizzying highs. Aside from briny cukes and other preserves, you'll find heaping portions of upscale comfort food, such as catfish tacos, wine-braised turkey leg dinner, and mushroom mac and cheese. The biscuits and regional craft beers are top notch too. (☏212-470-5566; 509 Amsterdam Ave, btwn 84th & 85th; mains $14-21; ⊘11am-2am Mon-Thu, to 4am Fri, 9am-4am Sat, to 2am Sun)

Barney Greengrass

DELI $$

15 🍴 Map p182, C4

Self-proclaimed 'King of Sturgeon' Barney Greengrass serves up the same heaping dishes of eggs and salty lox, luxuriant caviar, and melt-in-your mouth chocolate babkas that first made it famous when it opened a century ago. Pop in to fuel up in the morning or for a quick lunch; there are rickety tables set amid the crowded produce aisles. (www.barney-greengrass.com; 541 Amsterdam Ave, at 86th St; mains $9-20, bagel with cream cheese $5; ⊙8:30am-6pm Tue-Sun; 👶; S 1 to 86th St)

Peacefood Cafe

VEGAN $$

16 🍴 Map p182, C5

Bright, airy Peacefood keeps vegans purring with its popular fried seitan panini (served on homemade focaccia and topped with cashew, arugula, tomatoes and pesto), as well as pizzas, roasted vegetable plates and an excellent quinoa salad. Extras include daily raw specials, organic coffees and delectable bakery selections. (☏212-362-2266; www.peacefoodcafe.com; 460 Amsterdam Ave, at 82nd St; paninis $12-13, mains $10-17; ⊙10am-10pm; 🚭; S 1 to 79th St)

Salumeria Rosi Parmacotto

ITALIAN $$

17 🍴 Map p182, C6

Slip into this intimate, carnivorous nook for graze-friendly cheeses, salumi, slow-roasted pork loin, sausages, cured hams and every other piece of the pig you care to imagine. The tasty, Tuscan-inspired offerings continue with homemade lasagna, savory leek tart, escarole-anchovy salad and hand-rolled ricotta and goat cheese gnocchi. (☏212-877-4801; www.salumeriarosi.com; 284 Amsterdam Ave, at 73rd St; mains $12-17; ⊙11am-11pm; S 1/2/3 to 72nd St)

Fairway

SELF-CATERING $

18 🍴 Map p182, B6

Like a museum of good eats, this epic grocery spills its produce into sidewalk bins, luring the gluttonous inside. Follow them and give in to a gleeful range of cheeses, charcuterie, bread loaves and bagels, fruits, vegetables, and ready-to-eat meals. Stairs near the checkout lead up to an organic market and cafe. (www.fairwaymarket.com/store-upper-west-side; 2127 Broadway, at 75th St; ⊙6am-1am; S 1/2/3 to 72nd St)

Gray's Papaya

HOT DOGS $

19 🍴 Map p182, C7

It doesn't get more New York than bellying up to this classic stand-up joint in the wake of a beer bender. The lights are bright, the color palette is 1970s and the hot dogs are unpretentiously good. Granted, the papaya drink is more 'drink' than papaya, but you can't go wrong with Gray's famous, (and long-running) 'Recession Special' – $4.95 for two grilled dogs and a beverage. Deal. (☏212-799-0243; 2090 Broadway, at 72nd St, entrance on Amsterdam Ave; hot dog $2; ⊙24hr; S A/B/C, 1/2/3 to 72nd St)

Belvedere Castle (p184) overlooks rowers in Central Park

Hummus Place
MIDDLE EASTERN $

20  Map p182, C6

Hummus Place is nothing special in the way of ambiance – about eight tables tucked just below street level, fronting a cramped, open kitchen – but it's got amazing hummus platters. They're served warm and with various toppings, from whole chickpeas to fava-bean stew with chopped egg. You'll also find tasty salads, couscous and stuffed grape leaves. Great value. (www.hummusplace.com; 305 Amsterdam Ave, btwn 74th & 75th Sts; hummus from $8; ⏲lunch & dinner; ✈; Ⓢ1/2/3 to 72nd St)

Burke & Wills
MODERN AUSTRALIAN $$

21 Map p182, C5

New in 2013, this ruggedly attractive bistro and bar brings a touch of the outback to the Upper West Side. The menu leans toward Modern Australian pub grub: juicy kangaroo burgers with triple-fried chips, grilled prawns, kale cobb salad, merguez sausage sliders, and roasted cod with cauliflower, dates and pomegranate. (☎646-823-9251; 226 W 79th St, btwn Broadway & Amsterdam Ave; mains $17-28; ⏲4pm-2am Mon-Fri, from noon Sat & Sun; Ⓢ1 to 79th St)

Drinking

Barcibo Enoteca
WINE BAR

22 Map p182, C7

Just north of Lincoln Center, casual-chic Barcibo is ideal for sipping, with a long list of vintages from all over Italy, including 40 different varieties sold by the glass. There is a short menu of small plates and light meals. The staff are knowledgeable; ask for recommendations. (www.barciboenoteca.com; 2020 Broadway, cnr 69th St; ☺4:30pm-12:30am Mon-Fri, from 3:30pm Sat & Sun; ⑤1/2/3 to 72nd St)

Dead Poet
BAR

23 Map p182, C5

Skinny, mahogany-paneled Dead Poet pub has been a neighborhood favorite for over a decade, with a mix of locals and students nursing pints of Guinness. Appropriately, cocktails are named after long-gone scribes, including a Jack Kerouac margarita ($12) and a Pablo Neruda spiced rum sangria ($9). Funny, because we always pegged Neruda as a pisco sour kind of guy. (www.thedeadpoet.com; 450 Amsterdam Ave, btwn 81st & 82nd Sts; ☺noon-4am; ⑤1 to 79th St)

Ding Dong Lounge
BAR

24 Map p182, C1

It's hard to be too bad-ass in the Upper West, but this former crack den turned punk bar makes a wholesome attempt by supplying graffiti-covered bathrooms to go with its exposed-brick walls. Curiously, it also features an array of cuckoo clocks. It's popular with Columbia students and guests from nearby hostels for its can-of-beer-and-a-shot combo (only $7). (www.dingdonglounge.com; 929 Columbus Ave, btwn 105th & 106th Sts; ☺4pm-4am; ⑤B, C, 1 to 103rd St)

Prohibition
BAR

25 Map p182, C5

Buzzing Prohibition features a live band almost every night up front, but decibel levels are low enough that your ears won't bleed; the quieter back area is band free. Sexy red walls and refreshing drinks (passion fruit mojitos, agave nectar margaritas) add a little flair, while the bite-sized burgers make for a satisfying snack. (☎212-579-3100; www.prohibition.net; 503 Columbus Ave, near W 84th St; ☺5pm-4am; ⑤B, C, 1 to 86th St)

Manhattan Cricket Club
COCKTAIL LOUNGE

Above Mod Oz bistro Burke & Wills (see 21 ⊗ Map p182, C5,) Manhattan Cricket Club channels the elegant Anglo-Australian cricket clubs of the early 1900s. Sepia-toned photos of batsmen and bowlers in action adorn the gold brocaded walls, while a mahogany-lined wall of books, Chesterfield sofas and an elaborate tin ceiling all create a suitable setting for quaffing seamless libations. (226 W 79th St, btwn Amsterdam Ave & Broadway; ☺7pm-2am Tue-Sat; ⑤1 to 79th St)

Entertainment

Metropolitan Opera House

OPERA

26 ⭐ Map p182, C8

New York's premier opera company, the Metropolitan Opera is the place to see classics such as *Carmen, Madame Butterfly* and *Macbeth,* not to mention Wagner's *Ring Cycle.* The Opera also hosts premieres and revivals of more contemporary works, such as Peter Sellars' *Nixon in China,* which played here in 2011. The season runs from September to April. (www.metopera.org; Lincoln Center, 64th St, at Columbus Ave; **S**1 to 66th St-Lincoln Center)

Film Society of Lincoln Center

CINEMA

27 ⭐ Map p182, C7

One of New York's cinematic gems, the Film Society provides an invaluable platform for a wide gamut of documentary, feature, independent, foreign and avant-garde art pictures. Films screen in one of two facilities at Lincoln Center: the new Elinor Bunin Munroe Film Center, a more intimate, experimental venue, or the Walter Reade Theater, with wonderfully wide, screening room-style seats. (📞212-875-5456; www.filmlinc.com; **S**1 to 66th St-Lincoln Center)

New York Philharmonic

CLASSICAL MUSIC

28 ⭐ Map p182, C8

The oldest professional orchestra in the US (dating back to 1842) holds its season every year at Avery Fisher Hall. Directed by Alan Gilbert, the son of two Philharmonic musicians, the orchestra plays a mix of classics (Tchaikovsky, Mahler, Haydn) and some contemporary works, as well as concerts geared toward children. (www.nyphil.org; Avery Fisher Hall, Lincoln Center, cnr Columbus Ave & 65th St; ♿; **S**1 to 66 St-Lincoln Center)

Local Life
Lincoln Center

This vast cultural complex is ground zero for high art in Manhattan. In addition to the venues and companies listed, the **Vivian Beaumont Theater** (Map p182, C8; 📞212-721-6500; www.lincolncenter.org; Lincoln Center, 65th St btwn Broadway & Amsterdam; **S**1 to 66th St-Lincoln Center) and the **Mitzi E Newhouse Theater** (Map p182, C8; Lincoln Center, 65th St btwn Broadway & Amsterdam Ave) showcase works of drama and musical theater. Both of these have programming information listed on Lincoln Center's main website at www.new.lincolncenter.org.

New York City Ballet
DANCE

29 ⭐ Map p182, C8

This prestigious company was first directed by renowned Russian-born choreographer George Balanchine back in the 1940s. Today, the company has 90 dancers and is the largest ballet organization in the US, performing 23 weeks a year at Lincoln Center's David H Koch Theater. During the holidays, the troop is best known for its annual production of *The Nutcracker*. (☎212-496-0600; www.nycballet.com; David H Koch Theater, Lincoln Center, Columbus Ave, at 62nd St; ♿; S1 to 66th St-Lincoln Center)

American Ballet Theatre
DANCE

This seven-decade-old traveling company presents a classic selection of ballets in the Metropolitan Opera House at the Lincoln Center (see 1 ◉ Map p182, C8) every spring (generally in May). Tickets are by subscription only. The Orchestra, Parterre and Grand Tier sections offer the best views. Avoid the top tier or all you'll see are the dancers' heads. Box seats towards the rear have highly obscured views. (☎212-477-3030; www.abt.org; Lincoln Center, 64th St, at Columbus Ave; S1 to 66th St-Lincoln Center)

Beacon Theatre
LIVE MUSIC

30 ⭐ Map p182, C6

Dating back to 1929, the Beacon is a perfect in-between-size venue, with 2600 seats (not a terrible one in the house) and a constant flow of popular acts, from Nick Cave to the Allman Brothers. A $15 million restoration in 2009 has left the gilded interiors – a mix of Greek, Roman, Renaissance and Rococo design elements – sparkling. (www.beacontheatre.com; 2124 Broadway, btwn 74th & 75th Sts; S1/2/3 to 72nd St)

Cleopatra's Needle
CLUB

31 ⭐ Map p182, B3

Named after an Egyptian obelisk that resides in Central Park, this venue is small and narrow like its namesake. There's no cover, but there is a $10 minimum spend. Come early and celebrate happy hour (3:30pm to 6 or 7pm), when select cocktails are half-price. Just be prepared to stay late: Cleopatra's is famous for all-night jam sessions that hit their peak around 4am. (www.cleopatrasneedleny.com; 2485 Broadway, btwn 92nd & 93rd Sts; ◷4pm-late; S1/2/3 to 96th St)

Merkin Concert Hall
CLASSICAL MUSIC

32 ⭐ Map p182, C7

Just north of Lincoln Center, this 450-seat hall, part of the Kaufman Center, is one of the city's more intimate venues for classical music, as well as jazz, world music and pop. The hall hosts Tuesday matinees (a deal at $18) that highlight emerging classical solo artists. Every January, it is home to the New York Guitar Festival. (www.kaufman-center.org/mch; 129 W 67th St, btwn Amsterdam Ave & Broadway; S1 to 66th St-Lincoln Center)

Wollman Skating Rink (p185), Central Park

Smoke
JAZZ

33 Map p182, B1

Swank yet laid-back, Smoke offers good stage views from plush sofas, with acts including old-timers and local faves like George Coleman and Wynton Marsalis. Most nights there's a $10 cover, plus a $20 to $30 food and drink minimum. Purchase tickets online for weekend shows. (www.smoke-jazz.com; 2751 Broadway, btwn 105th & 106th Sts; 5:30pm-3am Mon-Fri, 11am-3am Sat & Sun; S 1 to 103rd St)

Shopping

Greenflea
MARKET

34 Map p182, C6

Friendly, well-stocked Greenflea is just the ticket for a lazy Upper West Side Sunday morning. Expect a bit of everything here, from vintage and contemporary furnishings, to antique maps, custom eyewear, hand-woven scarves, even handmade jewelry. The market is also open on occasional Saturdays in warm months; call ahead to check. (212-239-3025; www.green-fleamarkets.com; Columbus Ave, btwn 76th & 77th Sts; 10am-5:30pm Sun; S B, C to 81st St-Museum of Natural History, 1 to 79th St)

Understand

New York City on Page & Screen

New York City, more than any other place in the world, has been the setting of countless works of literature, television and film. From critical commentary on class and race to the lighter foibles of falling in love, New York's stories are not just entertainment; they are carefully placed tiles in the city's diverse mosaic of tales. In the lists below, you'll find some of our favorite movies and books that take place in – and are inspired by – this most wild and whimsical city.

Books

The Amazing Adventures of Kavalier & Clay (Michael Chabon, 2000) Beloved Pulitzer-winning novel that touches upon Brooklyn, escapism and the nuclear family.

A Tree Grows in Brooklyn (Betty Smith, 1943) An Irish-American family living in the Williamsburg tenements at the beginning of the 20th century.

Down These Mean Streets (Piri Thomas, 1967) Memoirs of tough times growing up in Spanish Harlem.

Invisible Man (Ralph Ellison, 1952) Poignant prose exploring the situation of African Americans in the early 20th century.

The Age of Innocence (Edith Wharton, 1920) Tales and trials of NYC's social elite in the late 1800s.

Films

Annie Hall (1977) Oscar-winning romantic comedy by the king of New York neuroses, Woody Allen.

Manhattan (1979) Allen's at it again with tales of twisted love set among NYC's concrete landscape.

Taxi Driver (1976) Scorsese's tale of a troubled taxi driver and Vietnam vet.

West Side Story (1961) A modern-day Romeo and Juliet set on the gang-ridden streets of New York.

Precious (2009) An unflinching tale of an obese, abused Harlem teenager determined to rise above her circumstances.

Time for Children
TOYS

35 🔒 Map p182, C5

Prepare to coo: tiny Time stocks criminally cute clothes for babies and toddlers, not to mention colorful books, plush toys, block sets, handmade cards and other treasures for the under-6 set. Best of all, Time donates 100% of its profits to the Children's Aid Society of New York. (✆212-580-8202; www.atimeforchildren.org; 506 Amsterdam Ave, btwn 84th & 85th Sts; ⏰10am-7pm Mon-Sat, 11am-6pm Sun; 👶; Ⓢ1 to 86th St)

Harry's Shoes
SHOES

36 🔒 Map p182, B5

Around since the 1930s, Harry's is an undisputed classic. It's staffed by gentlemen who measure your foot in an old-school metal contraption and then wait on you patiently, making sure the shoe fits. If your feet are killing you from all the walking, you'll find sturdy, comfortable brands like Merrel, Dansko and Birkenstock. (www.harrys-shoes.com; 2299 Broadway, at 83rd St; ⏰10am-6:45pm Tue, Wed, Fri & Sat, to 7:45pm Mon & Thu, 11am-6pm Sun; Ⓢ1 to 86th St)

Westsider Books
BOOKS

37 🔒 Map p182, B5

A great little shop packed to the gills with rare and used books, including a good selection of fiction and illustrated tomes. There are first editions and a smattering of vintage vinyl. (www.westsiderbooks.com; 2246 Broadway, btwn 80th & 81st Sts; ⏰10am-10pm; Ⓢ1 to 79th St)

Westsider Records
MUSIC

38 🔒 Map p182, B6

Stocked with over 30,000 LPs, Westsider has your ears covered when it comes to anything from funk, jazz and classical, to silver-screen soundtracks, spoken word and other curiosities. A good place to lose all track of time. (✆212-874-1588; www.westsiderbooks.com/recordstore.html; 233 W 72nd St, btwn Broadway & West End Ave; ⏰11am-7pm Mon-Thu, to 9pm Fri & Sat, noon-6pm Sun; Ⓢ1/2/3 to 72nd St)

Century 21
DEPARTMENT STORE

39 🔒 Map p182, C7

Exceedingly popular with fashionable locals and foreign travelers, the Century 21 chain is a bounty of season-old brand name and designer brands sold at steeply discounted prices. Featuring everything from Missoni to Marc Jacobs, prices may sometimes seem high, but compared to retail, they're a steal. (www.c21stores.com; 1972 Broadway, btwn 66th & 67th Sts; ⏰10am-10pm Mon-Sat, 11am-8pm Sun; Ⓢ1 to 66th St-Lincoln Center)

Local Life
Harlem

This is the neighborhood where Cab Calloway crooned. Where Ralph Ellison penned his epic novel on truth and intolerance, *Invisible Man*. Where acclaimed artist Romare Bearden pieced together his first collages. It's a place that is soaked in history – and then some. And it remains one of the country's most fabled centers of black American life.

Getting There

Harlem is 5 miles north of Midtown.

S Take the A/D one stop from Columbus Circle. The 2/3 takes 15 minutes to reach Harlem from Times Sq.

🚌 The M10 follows the west side of Central Park up into Harlem.

❶ College Campus Caffeine

Rev your engine with a cuppa joe alongside Columbia University students at **Community Food & Juice** (www.communityrestaurant.com; 2893 Broadway btwn 112th & 113th Sts; sandwiches $11-15, mains $14-29; ⊙8am-3:30pm & 5-9:30pm Mon-Fri, from 9am Sat & Sun; 🖉🛗; Ⓢ1 to 110th St).

❷ Come to Jesus

The **Cathedral Church of St John the Divine** (🖉tours 212-932-7347; www.stjohndivine.org; 1047 Amsterdam Ave at W 112th St; suggested donation $10, highlights tour $6, vertical tour $15; ⊙7:30am-6pm; Ⓢ B, C, 1 to 110th St-Cathedral Pkwy), with its Byzantine-style facade, is the largest place of worship in the United States.

❸ Rows of Cornrows

The semi-enclosed **Malcolm Shabazz Harlem Market** (🖉212-987-8131; 52 W 116th btwn Malcolm X Blvd & Fifth Ave; ⊙10am-7pm; Ⓢ2/3 to 116th St) does a brisk trade in just about everything: textiles, essential oils, leather goods, weaves – you name it.

❹ Art & Community

The small **Studio Museum in Harlem** (🖉212-864-4500; www.studiomuseum.org; 144 W 125th St at Adam Clayton Powell Jr Blvd, Harlem; suggested donation $7, free Sun; ⊙noon-9pm Thu & Fri, 10am-6pm Sat, noon-6pm Sun; Ⓢ2/3 to 125th St) has been exhibiting the works of African American artists for more than four decades. It's also an important point of connection for Harlem cultural figures of all stripes.

❺ Strivers' Row

On the blocks of 138th and 139th Sts, **Strivers' Row** (W 138th & W 139th Sts btwn Frederick Douglass & Adam Clayton Powell Jr Blvds; Ⓢ B, C to 135th St) is lined with 1890s townhouses. The area earned its nickname in the 1920s when aspiring African Americans first moved here.

❻ Sunday Gospel

Sunday gospel services are done best at the **Abyssinian Baptist Church** (www.abyssinian.org; 132 W 138th St btwn Adam Clayton Powell Jr & Malcolm X Blvds; Ⓢ2/3 to 135th St) – they even have a designated 'tourist' section.

❼ Cock-A-Doodle-Do

Dine at **Red Rooster** (www.redroosterharlem.com; 310 Malcolm X Blvd btwn 125th & 126th Sts, Harlem; mains $17-36; ⊙11:30am-10:30pm Mon-Fri, 10am-11pm Sat & Sun; Ⓢ2/3 to 125th St), where upscale comfort food meets global influences.

❽ Cheers & Jeers

End at the **Apollo Theater** (🖉212-531-5300, tours 212-531-5337; www.apollotheater.org; 253 W 125th St at Frederick Douglass Blvd; tours weekdays/weekends $16/18; Ⓢ A/C, B/D to 125th St), Harlem's leading space for concerts and political rallies – the ever-popular Wednesday 'Amateur Night' draws notorious crowds.

Local Life
South Brooklyn

Getting There

Prospect Park and South Brooklyn are about 6 miles south-east of Times Sq.

S The 2/3, 4/5, B/D and N/Q/R stop at Atlantic Av-Barclays Ctr. The 2/3 also stops at Grand Army Plaza.

To really know New York City is to explore its other boroughs, and no one will blame you for starting here. A city unto itself (it's three times larger than Manhattan), Brooklyn is a sprawling checkerboard of distinct neighborhoods where hipsters engage in their ironic pursuits. If you can, check out the following walk over the weekend to maximize your experience.

❶ The Other Central Park

Start in **Prospect Park** (☏718-965-8951; www.prospectpark.org; Grand Army Plaza; ⏰5am-1am; ⟋2/3 to Grand Army Plaza, F to 15th St-Prospect Park). It's Brooklyn's less-crowded answer to Central Park, designed by the same architects.

❷ Grand Army Plaza

Crowning **Grand Army Plaza** (Prospect Park, Prospect Park West & Flatbush Ave; ⏰6am-midnight; 👶; ⟋2/3 to Grand Army Plaza, B, Q to 7th Ave) is a handsome, 19th-century ceremonial arch. If you're swinging by on a Saturday, check out the greenmarket.

❸ Unique Finds

The Saturday **Brooklyn Flea** (www.brooklynflea.com; 176 Lafayette Ave, btwn Clermont & Vanderbilt Aves, Fort Greene; ⏰10am-5pm Sat Apr-Nov; 👶; ⟋G to Clinton-Washington Aves) hosts some 150 vendors peddling everything from antiques and vintage clothes to lip-smacking snacks.

❹ BAM!

America's oldest performing arts center, the **Brooklyn Academy of Music** (BAM; ☏718-636-4100; www.bam.org; 30 Lafayette Ave, at Ashland Pl, Fort Greene; ⟋2/3, 4/5, B, Q to Atlantic Ave) supplies NYC with edgier works of modern dance, music and theater. Free performances are known to boil up on weekends.

❺ Rock Climbing

Get high at **Brooklyn Boulders** (www.brooklynboulders.com; 575 Degraw St, at Third Ave, Boerum Hill; day pass $25; ⏰8am-midnight; ⟋R to Union St), BK's biggest indoor climbing area.

❻ Homegrown Art

In a converted factory, interdisciplinary arts center **Invisible Dog** (www.theinvisibledog.org; 51 Bergen St; ⟋F, G to Bergen St) embodies Brooklyn's creativity. Frequent exhibitions are held on the ground floor.

❼ Dinner: Big Spender

Reserve a table at **Dover** (☏347-987-3545; www.doverbrooklyn.com; 412 Court St, btwn 1st & 2nd Pl; mains $28-40; ⏰5:30-10:30pm; ⟋F, G to Carroll St), one of Brooklyn's newest dining hotspots. The seven-course tasting menu has foodies frothing.

❽ Dinner: Smaller Wallet

Cash-only **Lucali** (☏718-858-4086; 575 Henry St, at Carroll St, Carroll Gardens; pizza $24, calzone $10, toppings $3; ⏰6-10pm, closed Tues; 👶; ⟋F, G to Carroll St) dishes out superlative pizzas. It's justifiably popular, so arrive at 6pm, give them your cell number, and plan on dining a few hours later.

❾ Crafty Suds

Finish the evening at **61 Local** (www.61local.com; 61 Bergen St, btwn Smith St & Boerum Pl, Cobble Hill; snacks $2-5, sandwiches $5-10; ⏰7am-late Mon-Fri, from 9am Sat & Sun; 📶; ⟋F, G to Bergen), a brick-and-wood hall with large communal tables and clued-in craft beers.

Q Local Life
Williamsburg

Williamsburg is essentially a college town without a college – it's New York's of-the-moment Bohemian magnet, drawing slouchy, baby-faced artists, musicians, writers and graphic designers. Once a bastion of Latino working-class life, it's become a prominent dining and nightlife center – and although it's not full of traditional attractions, the neighborhood nonetheless packs a satisfying punch.

Getting There

Williamburg is less than 5 miles from Times Sq.

S Hop on the L train – Williamsburg is one stop outside of Manhattan. Not bad, eh?

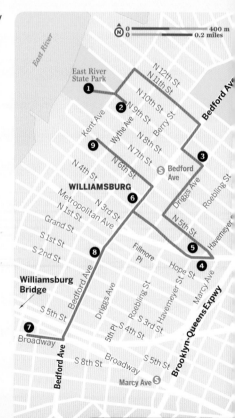

❶ Seeing Green

The seven-acre **East River State Park** (www.nysparks.org/parks/155; Kent Ave, btwn 8th & 9th Sts; ☉9am–dusk; 👶; §L to Bedford Ave) is the latest hot spot for outdoor parties and free summer concerts. During the summer, the Brooklyn Flea sets up shop here too.

❷ Music Mecca

Sprawling record store **Rough Trade** (☎718-388-4111; www.roughtradenyc.com; 64 N 9th St, btwn Kent & Wythe; ☉9am–11pm Mon-Sat, 10am-9pm Sun; §L to Bedford Ave) features in-store DJs, art exhibitions, coffee and tea from Brooklyn purveyor Five Leaves, as well as live bands throughout the week.

❸ Hipster Threads

The large **Buffalo Exchange** (504 Driggs Ave, at 9th St, Williamsburg; ☉11am-8pm Mon-Sat, noon-7pm Sun; §L to Bedford Ave) is the go-to spot for Brooklynites on a budget. Warning: you'll waste hours searching for vintage treasure.

❹ Bodega Ephemera

Housed in a former bodega, the curious **City Reliquary** (☎718-782-4842; www.cityreliquary.org; 370 Metropolitan Ave, near Havemeyer St; by donation; ☉noon-6pm Thu-Sun; §L to Lorimer Ave) is filled with sundry New Yorkiana, from shop signs and vintage postcards to subway tokens and paint chips off the L train.

❺ Drink with the Devil

If it's after 5pm weekdays or post-noon on weekends, pause for obscure brews at **Spuyten Duyvil** (www.spuyten-duyvilnyc.com; 359 Metropolitan Ave, btwn Havemayer & Roebling, Williamsburg; ☉from 5pm Mon-Fri, from noon Sat & Sun; §L to Lorimer St, G to Metropolitan Ave).

❻ Scan the Shelves

Williamsburg's favorite bookshop, **Spoonbill & Sugartown** (www.spoon-billbooks.com; 218 Bedford Ave, at 5th St, Williamsburg; ☉10am-10pm; §L to Bedford Ave) is a wonderland of coffee-table tomes, cultural journals, rare titles and locally made works.

❼ Dine Local

Raise your fork at buzzing **Marlow & Sons** (☎718-384-1441; www.marlowandsons.com; 81 Broadway, btwn Berry St & Wythe Ave; mains lunch $13-16, dinner $17-27; ☉8am-midnight; §J/M/Z to Marcy Ave, L to Bedford Ave), a dimly lit, wood-lined classic serving tip-top cocktails and locavore specialties.

❽ More Brooklyn Booze

Nostalgic **Maison Premiere** (www.maisonpremiere.com; 298 Bedford Ave, btwn 1st & Grand Sts, Williamsburg; ☉4pm-2am Sun-Wed, to 4am Thu-Sat; §L to Bedford Ave) is famed for its laboratory's worth of punch and poison. Bottoms up!

❾ Indie HQ

The perennially popular **Music Hall of Williamsburg** (www.musichallofwilliamsburg.com; 66 N 6th St, btwn Wythe & Kent Aves, Williamsburg; show $15-35; §L to Bedford Ave) is *the* place to see indie bands in Brooklyn.

The Best of
New York City

New York City's Best Walks

New York City's Best...

New York Public Library (p138)
SIEGFRIED LAYDA/GETTY IMAGES ©

Best Walks
Village Vibe

🏃 The Walk

Of all the neighborhoods in New York City, the West Village is easily the most walkable, its cobbled corners straying from the signature gridiron that unfurls across the rest of the island. An afternoon stroll is not to be missed; hidden landmarks and quaint cafes abound.

Start Commerce St; **S** 1 to Christopher St–Sheridan Sq, 1 to Houston St

Finish Washington Sq Park; **S** A/C/E, B/D/F/M to W 4th St

Length 1 mile; one hour

🍴 Take a Break

There are perhaps more cafes per acreage in the West Village than anywhere else in the world. Pause at any point during your stroll to slurp a latte streetside and enjoy the colorful crew of passing pedestrians: students, hipsters, moneyed professionals and celebrities hiding behind oversized sunglasses.

Washington Square (p92)

❶ Cherry Lane Theater

Start your walkabout at the **Cherry Lane Theater** (p107). Established in 1924, the small theater is the city's longest continuously running off-Broadway establishment and was the center of the city's creative performance art moment during the 1940s.

❷ The Friends Apartment

Turn left and you'll see **90 Bedford St** on the corner of Grove St. You might recognize the apartment block as the fictitious home of the cast of *Friends* (sadly Central Perk was just a figment of the writers' imaginations).

❸ Carrie Bradshaw's Stoop

For another iconic TV landmark, wander up Bleecker and make a right, stopping at **66 Perry St**, which was used as the apartment of the city's it girl, Carrie Bradshaw, in *Sex and the City* (though in the show, her address was on the Upper East Side).

❹ Christopher Park

Follow West 4th St until you reach **Christopher Park**, where two white, life-sized statues of same-sex couples (*Gay Liberation*, 1992) stand guard. On the north side of the green space is the legendary Stonewall Inn, where a clutch of fed-up drag queens and their supporters rioted for their civil rights in 1969, signaling the start of what would become the gay revolution.

❺ Jefferson Market Library

Head toward Sixth Ave to find the **Jefferson Market Library** straddling a triangular plot of land at the intersection of several roads. The unmissable 'Ruskinian Gothic' spire was once a fire lookout tower. In the 1870s, it was used as a courthouse and today it houses a branch of the public library.

❻ Café Wha?

Take in the flurry of passers-by on Sixth Ave, then swing by **Café Wha?**, the notorious institution where many young musicians and comedians – like Bob Dylan and Richard Pryor – got their start.

❼ Washington Square Park

Further down MacDougal St is **Washington Square Park** (p92), the Village's unofficial town square, which plays host to loitering students, buskers and a regular crowd of protestors chanting about various global and municipal injustices.

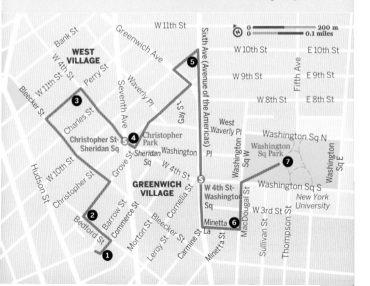

Best Walks
Iconic Architecture

🏃 The Walk

Ah, the skyscraper – mankind's phallic homage to human progress. New York City has plenty of 'em in every shape and size. And while staring into the city's infinite abyss of twinkling lights from atop a skyscraper ranks high on everyone's to-do list, we often prefer those quintessential New York moments down on the street when the crown of a soaring spire winks hello amid honking taxis in the early evening.

Start St Patrick's Cathedral; **S** B/D/F/M to Rockefeller Center

Finish Empire State Building; **S** N/Q/R to Herald Square

Length 2 miles; two to three hours

❌ Take a Break

Tucked within the peaks of stone and glass, Koreatown is Midtown's biggest surprise. But if you're looking for the latest iteration of Korean fusion, make a beeline to 52nd St for **Danji** (p141), one of the brightest stars in the city's galaxy of Michelin stars.

ALAN COPSON/GETTY IMAGES ©

View of Empire State Building (p130) from Rockefeller Center (p136)

❶ St Patrick's Cathedral

The neo-Gothic **St Patrick's Cathedral** (p139) was built at a cost of nearly $2 million during the Civil War and is the largest Catholic cathedral in America.

❷ Rockefeller Center

Rockefeller Center (p136) is a magnificent complex of art deco skyscrapers and sculptures. Enter between 49th and 50th Sts into the main plaza with its golden statue of Prometheus, then head up to the 70th floor of the GE Building just behind for an unforgettable view at the Top of the Rock observation deck.

❸ Bank of America Tower

The 366m **Bank of America Tower** (p137) is New York City's third-tallest building and – perhaps surprisingly – one of the most ecofriendly.

❹ New York Public Library

At the corner of 42nd St and Fifth Ave stands the stately **New York Public Library** (p138), guarded by a pair of regal lions called Patience and Fortitude. Step inside to peek at the spectacular Rose Main Reading Room.

❺ Grand Central Terminal

New York's beaux arts diva is **Grand Central Terminal** (p136). Star gaze at the Main Concourse ceiling and share sweet nothings at the Whispering Gallery.

❻ Chrysler Building

Although William Van Alen's 1930 masterpiece, the **Chrysler Building** (p136), is best appreciated from afar, it's worth slipping into the sumptuous art deco lobby, lavished with exotic inlaid wood, marble and purportedly the world's largest ceiling mural.

❼ Empire State Building

End your Midtown meander at the **Empire State Building** (p130), which provides a beautiful bird's-eye view of Manhattan and beyond.

It's especially magical at sunset from the open-air observation deck on the 86th floor.

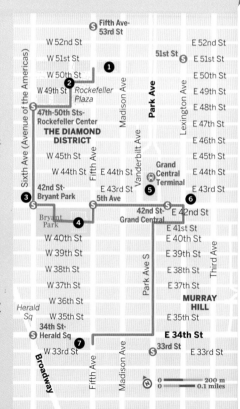

Best Walks
East Village Nostalgia

🏃 The Walk

Gentrification may be taming the beast, but few neighborhoods exude that old-school NYC cool like the East Village. For decades an epicenter of counterculture, its gritty streets sizzle with tales of drugs, drag and rocking punks. Countless cultural icons got their break here, from Patti Smith and the Ramones, to Blondie and Madonna. Times may have changed, but clues to the Village's halcyon days live on.

Start CBGB; **S** to 6 to Bleecker St or F to 2nd Ave

Finish Tompkins Sq Park; **S** 6 to Astor Pl

Length 1.5 miles; 1½ hours

❌ Take a Break

The streets below 14th St and east of First Ave are packed with excellent snack-food spots, offering styles and flavors from around the world. It's a mixed bag, indeed, and perhaps one of the most emblematic of the city today.

LONELY PLANET/LONELY PLANET IMAGES ©

31

CBGB

❶ CBGB

Start at the former **CBGB** (315 Bowery), a famous music venue that opened in 1973 and launched punk rock via the Ramones. Now a John Varvatos boutique, the fading wall posters and wild graffiti remain untouched.

❷ Joey Ramone Place

The corner to the north marks the block-long **Joey Ramone Place**, named in honor of the Ramones' singer, who succumbed to cancer in 2001.

❸ Cooper Union

Head north on the Bowery to Astor Pl. Turn right and head east through the square to **Cooper Union**, where in 1860 presidential hopeful Abraham Lincoln rocked a skeptical New York crowd with a rousing anti-slavery speech that ensured his candidacy.

❹ St Marks Place

Continue east on **St Marks Place** (p68), a block full of tattoo parlors and cheap eateries that haven't changed much since the 1980s. At number 4 stands **Trash & Vaudeville**, a landmark goth-and-punk shop.

❺ Fillmore East

Head south down Second Ave to the site of the long-defunct **Fillmore East** (105 Second Ave), a 2000-seat live-music venue run by promoter Bill Graham from 1968 to 1971. In the '80s the space was transformed into the Saint – the legendary 5000-sq-ft dance club that kicked off a joyous, drug-laden, gay disco culture.

❻ Physical Graffiti Cover

Head a block east to First Ave, turn left, rejoin St Marks Place and turn right. The row of tenements is the site of Led Zeppelin's **Physical Graffiti cover** (96-98 St Marks Pl), where Mick and Keith sat in 1981 in the Stones' hilarious video for 'Waiting on a Friend.'

❼ Tompkins Square Park

End your stroll at the infamous **Tompkins Square Park** (p69), where drag queens started the Wigstock summer festival at the bandshell where Jimi Hendrix played in the 1960s.

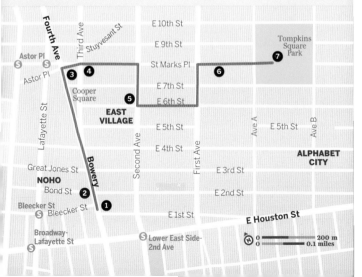

Best
Museums

New York City is America's culture capital, a cerebral wonderland bursting with museums and galleries that showcase an incredible spectrum of exhibits. You'll find everything from blockbuster attractions famed for their cache of priceless treasures to tiny, super-specialized showrooms exploring a single – and oftentimes offbeat – subject. Get set for some serious enlightenment.

Metropolitan Museum of Art.
Chuck Close painting courtesy of
Pace Gallery.

Planning Your Visit

Most museums close at least one day a week, usually Monday, and sometimes Sunday and/or Tuesday. Many stay open late one or more nights a week – often a Thursday or Friday. You can save time at the most popular museums by purchasing tickets in advance online.

Galleries

Chelsea is home to the highest concentration of art galleries in the entire city – and the cluster continues to grow with each passing season. Most lie in the 20s, on the blocks between Tenth and Eleventh Aves. For a complete guide and map, pick up Art Info's *Gallery Guide,* available for free at most galleries, or visit chelseagallerymap.com. Wine-and-cheese openings for new shows are typically held on Thursday evenings, while most art houses tend to shutter their doors on Sundays and Mondays.

For Free

Many museums offer free or reduced admission once a month – check the museum websites to find out when. Although most of the city's gallery openings occur on Thursday, you'll find gratis events throughout the week.

Best Art Museums

MoMA NYC's darling museum space has brilliantly curated galleries featuring no shortage of iconic modern works. (p132)

Metropolitan Museum of Art Museum heavyweight of the Americas, the Met comes with its own Egyptian temple and the country's most famous canvas of George Washington. (p158)

Guggenheim Museum The exhibits can be uneven, but the architecture is the real star at this Frank Lloyd Wright creation. (p162)

Frick Collection A Gilded Age mansion sparkling with Vermeers, El Grecos, Goyas, and a courtyard fountain. (p165)

Fuentiduena Chapel, Cloisters Museum & Gardens

New Museum A cutting-edge, world-class temple to contemporary art in all its forms. (p68)

Best New York Museums

Lower East Side Tenement Museum An evocative insight into life as an immigrant during the 19th and early 20th centuries. (p69)

Merchant's House Museum Step back in time at this perfectly preserved Federal home from well over a century ago; a revealing glimpse into a long-gone New York. (p52)

Museum of the City of New York Details of the city's past abound in this refurbished Georgian mansion. (p167)

New York City Fire Museum Situated in an old firehouse, this museum recounts the story of New York's firemen and includes a haunting tribute to those who perished in 9/11. (p53)

Best Lesser-Known Treasures

Morgan Library & Museum Rare manuscripts, books, drawings and paintings in a lavish steel magnate's mansion. (p138)

Neue Galerie Fans of Klimt and Schiele should not miss this intimate treasure, housed in a former Rockefeller mansion. (p166)

Worth a Trip

Overlooking the Hudson River, the **Cloisters Museum & Gardens** (www.metmuseum.org/cloisters; Fort Tryon Park; suggested donation adult/child $25/free; ⏲10am-5pm; ⓢA to 190th St) is a curious mish-mash of European monasteries. Built in the 1930s to house the Metropolitan Museum of Art's medieval treasures, it also contains the beguiling 16th-century tapestry *The Hunt of the Unicorn*.

Best
Fine Dining

Tasting trends in New York City come and go, but there's one thing that will forever remain certain: fine dining never goes out of style. Sure, the culture of haute eats may have changed, but locals and visitors alike will never tire of dressing up to chow down. Defining the current scene is 'new American' cuisine and inventive new fusions, from Mexican-meets-Korean to Israeli-meets-Scottish.

WALTER BIBIKOW/GETTY IMAGES ©

Reservations

Popular restaurants abide by one of two rules: either they take reservations and you need to plan in advance (weeks or months early for the real treasures) or they only seat patrons on a first-come basis, in which case you should arrive when it opens. Last-minute cancellations do occur, so try your luck calling that hotspot restaurant around 4pm. Lunch is another option – many of the city's dinner hotspots have midday prix fixe service.

Celebrity Chefs

In NYC, restaurateurs are often just as famous as their fare. It's not just buzz though – these taste masters really know their trade. Big-ticket names abound: Mario Batali has painted the town red with his spaghetti sauces, while Michael Chernow's empire continues to expand with his meatballs.

New American Eats

A gourmet spin on traditional comfort food, the 'New American' movement seeks to fuse repast standards with market-fresh produce and seasonal ingredients. Many of the city's most critically acclaimed chow houses offer souped-up versions of family recipes – a tribute to Gotham's citizenry of immigrants.

☑ **Top Tips**

▶ New Yorkers are famous for offering their opinion, so why not capitalize on their taste-bud experiences and click through scores of websites catering to the discerning diner. Some of our favorite blog-style rags include **Eater** (www.ny.eater.com), **New York Magazine** (www.nymag.com) and **Serious Eats** (www.newyork. seriouseats.com).

Best Celebrity-Chef Restaurants

Le Bernardin Triple Michelin-star earner and New York's holy grail of fine dining is the domain of French meister Eric Ripert. (p141)

Red Rooster Marcus Samuelsson gives southern comfort food creative twists at his Harlem hotspot. (p197)

Dutch From juicy oysters to delicate homemade pies, Andrew Carmellini gives surf and turf the comfort touch. (p55)

Best Gourmet Groceries

Eataly Gorgeous gourmet grocery saluting the bustling markets of Italy. (p124)

Zabar's The Upper West Side's kosher contribution to upscale market eats. (p186)

Dean & DeLuca Luxe SoHo grocer bursting with pantry fillers and gourmet baked treats. (p49)

Best Buzzworthy Bites

Betony Whimsy and soul feed the menus at this swank Midtown hotspot. (p141)

PETER PTSCHELINZEW/GETTY IMAGES ©

Fresh produce at Eataly (p124)

Saxon + Parole Revamped comfort grub gets galloping in NoHo. (p55)

Danji Wildly inventive 'Korean tapas' crafted by a young-gun pro. (p141)

Worth a Trip

There are scores of Brooklyn restaurants that lure stalwart Manhattanites out for a foodie pilgrimage. Try **Battersby** (☎718-852-8321; 255 Smith St, btwn Douglass & Degraw Sts; mains $16-34, tasting menu $75-95; ⏱5:30-11pm; ⓢF, G to Bergen St) for dinner, or hipster haunt **Roberta's** (www.robertaspizza.com; 261 Moore St, near Bogart St, Bushwick; pizzas $9-17, mains $13-28; ⏱11am-midnight; 🖋; ⓢL to Morgan Ave) for locavore pizza.

Best
Local Eats

From inspired iterations of world cuisine to quintessentially local nibbles, New York City's dining scene is infinite, all-consuming and a proud testament to the kaleidoscope of citizens that call the city home. So go ahead, take a bite out of the Big Apple – we promise you won't be sorry.

To Market, to Market

Don't let the concrete streets and buildings fool you – New York City has a thriving greens scene. At the top of your list should be the Chelsea Market (p92), packed with gourmet goodies of all kinds – both shops (where you can assemble picnics) and food stands (where you can eat on-site). Also worth a look is the Union Square Greenmarket (p124), open four days weekly throughout the year. Check Grow NYC (www.grownyc.org/greenmarket) for a list of NYC's other 50-plus markets.

Food Trucks & Carts

Skip the bagel- and hot-dog-vending food carts. These days, there's a new mobile crew in town dishing up high-end treats and unique fusion fare. The trucks ply various routes, stopping in designated zones throughout the city – namely around Union Sq, Midtown and the Financial District – so if you're looking for a particular grub wagon, it's best to follow them on Twitter. Among our favorites are **Cinnamon Snail Vegan Lunch Truck** (www.twitter.com/VeganLunchTruck), **Kimchi Taco** (www.twitter.com/kimchitruck), **Red Hook Lobster Pound** (twitter.com/lobstertruckny), **Calexico Cart** (www.twitter.com/calexiconyc) and the fabulously named **Big Gay Ice Cream** (www.twitter.com/biggayicecream).

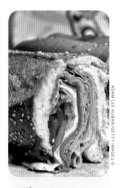

ADAM LEE KUBAN/GETTY IMAGES ©

☑ Top Tips

▶ Reserve a table at a number of restaurants around the city using **Open Table** (www.opentable.com).

Best for Old-School NYC

Katz's Delicatessen Classic pastrami on rye is the name of the game at this New York stalwart and tourist haven. (p73)

Zabar's New York Jewish charm fills the knish-tinged air on the Upper West Side. (p186)

William Greenberg Desserts Sweet treats a la New York yenta await: *hamantaschen* (you'll see) and the best black-and-white cookies around. (p170)

Spices at Chelsea Market (p92)

Best Vegetarian

Hangawi Delicate Korean flavors define this soothing, Zen-like oasis, set snugly in the canyons of Midtown. (p141)

Candle Cafe Affluent vegans sip, sup and gossip at this Upper East Side favorite. (p170)

Angelica Kitchen Ridiculously fresh produce gets creative at this East Village classic. (p74)

Peacefood Cafe A vegan oasis in the Upper West Side, famed for its fried seitan panini. (p188)

Best Quick Bites

Chelsea Market From tacos and pastries to gourmet ice cream, Manhattan's best-loved gourmet market is a foodie's Promised Land. (p92)

Ess-a-Bagel Jaw-busting bagels meet NYC attitude at Manhattan's top old-school bagel peddler. (p118)

Shake Shack American classics meet quality produce at Danny Meyer's citywide burger empire. (p120)

Gray's Papaya New York's wieners are perfect to grab on the go for a fast feed between sights. (p188)

Joe's Pizza The pie at this Greenwich Village institution has a city-wide fan base. (p100)

El Margon An eclectic cast of regulars pile into this retro classic for Midtown's juiciest Cuban sandwiches. (p144)

 Worth a Trip

Multicultural Queens spans all kitchens of the world, from Flushing's Chinese noodle houses – try **Hunan Kitchen of Grand Sichuan** (www.thegrandsichuan. com; 42-47 Main St, Flushing; mains $9.50-23; ⏰11am-12:30am; **S** 7 to Flushing-Main St) – to Astoria's Greek eats: try **Taverna Kyclades** (☏718-545-8666; www. tavernakyclades.com; 33-07 Ditmars Blvd, at 33rd St, Astoria; mains $11.50-35; ⏰noon-11pm Mon-Sat, to 10pm Sun; **S** N/Q to Astoria-Ditmars Blvd).

Best
Drinking

Considering that 'Manhattan' is thought to be a derivation of the Munsee word *manahactanienk* ('place of general inebriation'), it shouldn't be surprising that New York truly lives up to its nickname 'the city that never sleeps.' In fact, some 20 years after the city was founded, over a quarter of New Amsterdam's buildings were taverns. Sometimes it feels like things have barely changed.

Prohibition Chic

Here in the land where the term 'cocktail' was born, mixed drinks are still stirred with the utmost gravitas. Often, it's a case of history in a glass, New York's obsession with rediscovered recipes and Prohibition-era style showing no signs of abating.

Craft Beer

NYC's craft beer culture is increasingly dynamic, with an ever-expanding booty of breweries, bars and shops showcasing local artisan brews. Top local sud makers include Brooklyn Brewery, Sixpoint and SingleCut Beersmiths.

Coffee Culture

A boom in specialty coffee roasters is transforming New York's once-dismal caffeine culture. More locals are clueing-in on single-origin beans and different brewing techniques, with numerous roasters now offering cupping classes for curious drinkers. Many are transplants from A-list coffee cities, among them Portland's Stumptown, the Bay Area's Bluebottle, and Sydney's Toby's Estate. The antipodean influence is especially notable, with a growing number of top-notch cafes and roasters claiming Aussie roots.

Best Cocktails

Dead Rabbit Meticulously researched cocktails, punches and pop-inns in a cozy Financial District den. (p40)

Weather Up The place barkeeps go for a well-crafted drink in Tribeca. (p41)

Little Branch Travel back to the Prohibition Era – barkeeps, dressed in slacks and suspenders, mix carefully blended cocktails in the basement. (p101)

Maison Premiere A chemistry-lab-style bar full of syrups and essences that costume-clad barkeeps mix up and shake around. (p201)

Spuyten Duyvil (p201)

Best Wine Selection

Gramercy Tavern
Extraordinary top-shelf and lower-priced surprises in a bar/fine-dining hybrid. (p118)

Barcibo Enoteca Italian wine HQ a stone's throw from the Lincoln Center. (p190)

Best for Beer

Keg No 229 A veritable who's who of boutique American brews. (p42)

Birreria Unfiltered, unpasteurized Manhattan ales on a Flatiron rooftop. (p122)

Proletariat Tiny East Village bar serving up extremely uncommon brews. (p78)

Spuyten Duyvil Unique, high-quality crafts in hipster haven Williamsburg. (p201)

Best for Spirits

Brandy Library Blue-blooded cognacs, brandies and more for Tribeca connoisseurs. (p41)

Rum House Unique, coveted rums and a pianist to boot in Midtown. (p144)

Mayahuel An East Village temple to mescal and tequila. (p78)

Dead Rabbit NYC's finest collection of Irish whiskeys, in the Financial District. (p40)

Best for Coffee

Stumptown Coffee Roasters Hipster baristas serving Portland's favorite Joe. (p145)

Little Collins Australia's famous cafe culture comes to Midtown East. (p145)

Toby's Estate Another antipodean star serving strong, complex brews in the Flatiron District. (p122)

Abraço Expertly made espresso defines this closet-sized East Village cafe. (p76)

Kaffe 1668 Coffee-sippers of every ilk swing by for smooth house blends in Tribeca. (p40)

Via Quadronno This Upper East Side haven for 'ladies who lunch' touts brilliant sandwiches, but its coffee is worthy of an encore. (p170)

Best **Entertainment**

Hollywood may hold court when it comes to the motion picture, but it's NYC that reigns supreme over the pantheon of other arts. Actors, musicians, dancers and artists flock to the bright lights of the Big Apple like moths to a flame. It's like the old saying goes: if you can make it here, you can make it anywhere.

GRANT FAINT/GETTY IMAGES ©

Comedy

A good laugh is easy to find in the Big Apple, where comedians sharpen their stand-up chops hoping to get scouted by a producer or agent. The best spots for some chuckles are downtown around Chelsea and Greenwich Village.

Dance

Dance fans are spoiled for choice in this town, home to both the New York City Ballet (p192) and the American Ballet Theatre (p192), plus modern dance venue the Joyce Theater (p108). There are two major dance seasons: first in spring (March to May), then in late fall (October to December).

Live Music

NYC is the country's capital of live music and just about every taste is catered for – check out **New York Magazine** (www.nymag.com) and the **Village Voice** (www.villagevoice.com) for listings.

Theater

From the legendary hit factories of Broadway to the scruffy black-box theaters that dot downtown blocks, NYC boasts the full gamut of theater experiences. The term 'off-Broadway' is not a geographical one – it simply refers to theaters that are smaller in size, with less glitzy production budgets.

☑ Top Tips

▶ Cheaper, classical concerts can be scouted at various churches (oh the acoustics!) and smaller recital halls.

Best Broadway Shows

Book of Mormon Uproariously brilliant Broadway musical appreciated citywide for its wit, charm and pitch-perfect performances. (p148)

Kinky Boots A fun, sweet, feel-good tale of an old English shoe factory saved by a drag queen. Great costumes. (p148)

Chicago Fosse hands swirl and the girls from the cell block make dirty deals, cabaret-style. (p149)

Lincoln Center (p184)

Best for Theater (non-Broadway)

Playwrights Horizons
The place to catch what could be the next big thing to hit the stages of New York. (p150)

Signature Theatre
A playwright-focused center that showcases the work of its writers-in-residence. (p148)

Flea Theater One of New York's top off-off-Broadway companies performs a regular rotation of theater. (p43)

Lincoln Center The mothership of the performing arts on the Upper West Side. (p184)

Brooklyn Academy of Music A hallowed theater hosting cutting-edge works in Brooklyn. (p199)

Best for Laughs

Upright Citizens' Brigade Theatre Improv at its finest by many who go on to star in *Saturday Night Live*. (p105)

Comedy Cellar Celebrity joke-tellers regularly plow through this basement club. (p106)

Best for Film

Angelika Film Center Foreign and independent films galore with a side of quirky charms (subway rumbles and occasionally bad sound). (p107)

Film Society of Lincoln Center One of New York's cinematic gems, providing an invaluable platform for a wide gamut of moving pictures. (p191)

Museum of Modern Art Midtown's modern art museum also screens everything from Hollywood classics to experimental works. (p132)

Best for Jazz

Village Vanguard Major jazz haven for over 50 years – the heart and soul of the Village scene. (p106)

Jazz at Lincoln Center Top-notch talent in three state-of-the-art venues, including the panoramic Dizzy's Club Coca-Cola. (p147)

Blue Note Famous worldwide for its rotating cast of visiting musicians. (p106)

Birdland Named in honor of the great Charlie 'Bird' Parker, this Midtown classic still pulls jazz greats to the stage. (p150)

Best
Nightlife &
Clubbing

Trendy all-night lounges tucked behind the walls of a crumby Chinese restaurant, stadium-size discotheques that clang to the thump of DJ-rubbed beats and after-after-after-parties on the roof as the sun rises. An alternate universe lurks between the cracks of everyday life and it welcomes savvy visitors just as much as the locals in the know.

DIVERSE IMAGES/GETTY IMAGES ©

Clubbing 101

New Yorkers are always looking for the next big thing, and thus the city's club scene changes faster than a New York minute. Promoters drag revelers around the city for weekly events held at all of the finest addresses, and when there's nothing on, it's time to hit the dance floor stalwarts. When clubbing it never hurts to plan ahead; having your name on a guest list can relieve unnecessary frustration and disappointment. If you're an uninitiated partier, dress the part. If you're fed the 'private party' line, try to bluff – chances are high that you've been bounced.

Also, don't forget a wad of cash as many nightspots (even the swankiest ones) often refuse credit cards, and in-house ATMs scam a fortune in fees.

Best Clubs

Cielo An icon of the Meatpacking District, with Euro DJ talent and attitude-free dance fans. (p105)

Le Bain Sharp party people, skyline views and a plunge-pool studded dancefloor atop the Standard Hotel. (p102)

Top of the Standard If you got into Le Bain, try your luck next door at this more selective spot, a schmooze fest of *Vogue* photographers and real-deal fashionistas swaying to DJ-spun sounds. (p102)

☑ **Top Tip**

While the NYC club scene may be fickle, there's no shortage of websites confirming what's hot and what's not.

▶ **New York Magazine** (www.nymag.com/nightlife) offers brilliantly curated nightlife options by the people who know best.

▶ **Urbandaddy** (www.urbandaddy.com) delivers up-to-the-minute info and a handy 'hot right now' list.

▶ **Time Out** (www.timeout.com/newyork/clubs-nightlife) serves up articles and listings of where to get your groove on.

Best
Festivals

It seems as though there's always some sort of celebration going on in NYC. National holidays, religious observances, arts festivals and just plain ol' weekends prompt parades, parties or street fairs.

JOE DRIVAS/GETTY IMAGES ©

Mercedes Benz Fashion Week (www.mbfashionweek.com) The February fashion shows are not open to the public, yet provide a general vicarious thrill.

St Patrick's Day Parade (☏718-793-1600; www.nycstpatricksparade.org) Crowds line Fifth Ave on March 17 for this parade of bagpipe blowers, sparkly floats and clusters of Irish-lovin' politicians.

Tribeca Film Festival (☏212-941-2400; www.tribecafilm.com; ⊙late Apr & early May) Robert De Niro's downtown film festival is an undisputed star of the indie movie circuit.

NYC Pride (☏212-807-7433; www.nycpride.org; ⊙Jun) Gay Pride culminates in a major march down Fifth Ave on the last Sunday of June.

HBO Bryant Park Summer Film Festival (www.bryantpark.org) From June to August, Midtown's Bryant Park hosts weekly outdoor screenings of classic Hollywood films.

Independence Day America's Independence Day – July 4 – is celebrated with fireworks and fanfare.

Shakespeare in the Park (www.shakespeareinthepark.org) Pays tribute to the Bard, with free performances in Central Park. You'll have to wait hours in line to score tickets or win them in the online lottery.

Open House New York (www.ohny.org) The country's largest architecture and design event unfurls at the start of October, with architect-led tours and other events.

Thanksgiving Day Parade (www.macys.com) Massive helium-filled cartoons soar overhead, and high-school marching bands rattle their snares.

New York City Marathon (www.nycmarathon.org) Held in the first week of November, this 26-mile run draws thousands of athletes and just as many excited spectators.

Rockefeller Center Christmas Tree Lighting (www.rockefellercenter.com) The flick of a switch ignites the massive Christmas tree in Rockefeller Center, bedecked with over 25,000 lights.

New Year's Eve (www.timessquarenyc.org/nye/) Times Sq is the ultimate place to ring in the New Year.

Best
With Kids

New York City has loads of activities for young ones, including imaginative playgrounds and leafy parks where kids can run free, plus lots of kid-friendly attractions. While the Central Park Zoo, American Museum of Natural History and New York City Fire Museum are good places to start, the list of highs continue, from carousel rides and puppet shows, to market feasting and tram rides across the East River.

Dining with Kids

Restaurants in the most touristy corners of the city are ready at a moment's notice to bust out the highchairs and kiddy menus. In general, however, dining venues are small – eating at popular joints sans reservation can often be more of a hassle with the little ones in tow. Early dinners can alleviate some of the stress, as most locals tend to take to their tables between 7:30pm and 9:30pm. In good weather, we recommend grabbing a blanket and food from one of the city's excellent grocers, and heading to Central Park or one of the many other green spaces for a picnic in the grass.

For Parents, Not For Parents

If you're hitting the Big Apple with kids, you can check for upcoming events online at **Time Out New York Kids** (www.timeoutnewyorkkids.com) and **Mommy Poppins** (www.mommypoppins.com). For an insight into New York aimed directly at kids, pick up a copy of Lonely Planet's *Not for Parents: New York*. Perfect for children aged eight and up, it opens up a world of intriguing stories and fascinating facts about New York people, places, history and culture.

BARRY WINIKER/GETTY IMAGES ©

Best Museums

American Museum of Natural History Dinosaurs, butterflies, a planetarium and IMAX films. My, oh my! (p184)

Metropolitan Museum of Art A fun trip back in time for the young ones – make sure to stop at the Egyptian Wing. (p158)

New York City Fire Museum Old-fashioned firefighting carriages, curious old-school uniforms, and amiable staff make this a winner for wide-eyed little ones. (p53)

Best Shopping

FAO Schwartz Santa's workshop has crash-landed in the heart of Midtown. (p153)

Yoyamart Memorable gifts for kids, but a much more interesting

Brooklyn Bridge Park (p29)

shopping experience for their parents. (p111)

Dinosaur Hill A petite, old-school toy shop packed with whimsical gifts, from shadow puppets and calligraphy sets to natural-fibre outfits for munchkins. (p81)

Books of Wonder Storybooks, teen novels, NYC-themed gifts and in-house storytime make this rainy-day perfection. (p125)

Best Parks & Playgrounds

Central Park Row a boat, visit the zoo and say hello to the giant Alice in Wonderland statue, then hit Heckscher playground, the biggest and best of Central Park's 21 playgrounds. (p178)

The High Line NYC's celebrated elevated green space has food vendors, water features (which kids can splash through) and great views, plus warm-weather family events, from story time to science and craft projects. (p86)

Hudson River Park Get indecisive over mini-golf near Moore St (Tribeca), a fun playground near West St (West Village), a carousel off W 22nd St, watery fun at W 23rd & 11th Ave, and a science-themed play space near W 44th St. (p36)

Prospect Park Brooklyn's 585-acre Prospect Park has abundant amusement for kids, including a zoo, hands-on playthings at Lefferts Historic House and a new

ice-skating rink – that becomes a water park in summer. (p199)

Brooklyn Bridge Park Come summer, hit the squeal-inducing water park on Pier 6 (bring swimsuits, all will get wet). Watered out, head further north for the grassy hills of Pier 1 and Jane's Carousel. (p29)

Best Carousels

Bryant Park Steps from Times Sq and the New York Public Library, find Le Carrousel in Bryant Park, an old-time charmer revolving to the tune of French cabaret music. (p139)

Central Park At the level of 64th St in the heart of Central Park awaits a 1908 carousel with painted horses. (p178)

Best
Shopping

You can blame the likes of Holly Golightly and Carrie Bradshaw for making it darned impossible not to associate New York City with diamonds for breakfast or designer labels for dinner – and the locals are all too happy to oblige. NYC isn't the world's fashion or technology capital, but private capital reigns supreme: there's no better place to shop till you drop.

SILVIA OTTE/GETTY IMAGES ©

Sample Sales

While clothing sales happen year-round – usually when seasons change and old stock must be moved out – sample sales are held frequently, mostly in the huge warehouses in the Fashion District of Midtown or in SoHo. While the original sample sale was a way for designers to get rid of one-of-a-kind prototypes that weren't quite up to snuff, most sample sales these days are for high-end labels to get rid of overstock at wonderfully deep discounts.

Flea Markets & Vintage Adventures

As much as New Yorkers gravitate towards all that's shiny and new, it can be infinitely fun to rifle through closets of unwanted wares and threads. The most popular flea market is the Brooklyn Flea (p199), housed in all sorts of spaces throughout the year. The East Village is the city's de facto neighborhood for secondhand, hipster-pulling stores. For antiques and assorted ephemera from the past – records, artwork, books, home furnishings, toys – don't miss the sprawling Antiques Garage Flea Market (p110) held on weekends in Chelsea.

Best Department Stores

Barneys Perfectly curated fashion labels lure serious New York fashionistas. (p152)

Bergdorf Goodman Exclusive labels, lunching ladies, and brilliant Christmas window installations. (p152)

Bloomingdale's A veritable museum to the world of shopping. (p152)

Saks Fifth Ave A shoe department so big it has its own zip code. (p153)

Century 21 A giant wonderland of cut-price fashion, kicks and more. (p43)

Best Fashion Boutiques

Rag & Bone Beautiful tailoring and vintage inspiration define this

Barneys (p152)

homegrown unisex favorite. (p60)

Steven Alan Unique edits of men's and women's threads and accessories from NYC and beyond. (p44)

John Varvatos Rockstar chic feeds this high-end menswear label. (p82)

Personnel of New York A petite boutique selling cognoscenti men's and women's labels from the East and West coasts, and beyond. (p109)

Best for Unique Souvenirs & Gifts

MoMA Design & Book Store Take home a piece of the Museum of Modern Art at its famous store, curated as beautifully as the museum itself. (p152)

Philip Williams Posters Over half a million original posters of all shapes and sizes hankering to be hung. (p44)

Obscura Antiques A curious haven for the historic and the macabre, from antique posion bottles to taxidermy critters. (p81)

MiN New York Hard-to-find perfumes and grooming products in an apothecary-like setting. (p49)

Shinola A super-cool boutique stocking design-savvy, American-made objects, from customized bags to watches. (p43)

Kiosk A quirky collection of doodads from all over the globe. (p61)

Best Bookshops

McNally Jackson Everyone's favorite indie bookshop has a slew of tomes and hosts regular speaker series. (p49)

Strand Book Store New York's best-loved bookstore heaves with over 18 miles of books. (p109)

Printed Matter Limited-edition magazine and monographs – it's a veritable art gallery unto itself. (p110)

Drama Book Shop Playscripts, musicals and regular events in the shadow of glittering Broadway. (p154)

Best
For Free

From free concerts, theater and film screenings, to pay-what-you-wish nights at legendary museums, there's no shortage of ways to kick open the NYC treasure chest without spending a dime. Sometimes the best things in life *are* actually free!

Staten Island Ferry Hop on the free ferry bound for Staten Island for postcard-perfect views of Manhattan's southern edge. (p32)

Chelsea Galleries Over 300 galleries are open to the public along Manhattan's West 20s. (p88)

New Museum Ethereal tooth-white boxes house a serious stash of contemporary art that's free for visitors on Thursday evenings after 7pm. (p68)

Central Park New York's giant backyard is yours for the taking, with acre after acre of tree-lined bliss. Go for a jog, relax on the lawn or throw bread crumbs at the ducks in the pond. (p178)

The High Line The city's proudest achievement in urban renewal in the last decade, this catwalk of parkland is great for a stroll and some skyline ogling. (p86)

New York Public Library The grand, beaux arts gem (aka the Stephen A Schwarzman Building) merits a visit for its sumptuous architecture, superlative collections and free exhibitions. (p138)

MoMA The glorious Museum of Modern Art is free from 4pm to 8pm on Fridays – be prepared for massive crowds and long lines. (p132)

National September 11 Memorial The largest man-made waterfalls in North America are a spectacular tribute to the victims of terrorism. (p26)

Neue Galerie The gracious Neue is gratis from 6pm to 8pm on the first Friday of the month. It's well worth visiting this somewhat under-the-radar beauty on the Upper East Side. (p166)

Studio Museum in Harlem Up in the heart of the city's African American roots, this museum is free to browse on Sundays. (p197)

National Museum of the American Indian Beautiful textiles, objects and art are a vivid testament to native American cultures at this free gem in Lower Manhattan. (p32)

WOSTOCK/GETTY IMAGES ©

Best
LGBT

With one of the largest disposable incomes of any demographic, queer New Yorkers seem to run the city, from the fashion runways and major music labels, to Wall Street downtown. And now that same-sex couples can say 'I Do', it's never been more 'in' to be 'out'.

Weekdays are the New Weekend

In NYC, any night of the week is fair game to paint the town rouge – especially for the gay community. Wednesdays and Thursdays roar with a steady stream of parties and locals love raging on Sundays (especially in summer).

On the Pulse

There are tons of websites dedicated to the city's LGBT scene. Check out what's happening around town by clicking onto **Next Magazine** (www.next magazine.com) or **Get Out!** (getoutmag.com).

Beware the Haters

Much to the shock of most New Yorkers, 2013 saw a spike in gay hate crimes in the city, from verbal assaults to the fatal shooting of a young man in Greenwich Village. While NYC remains one of the world's gayest cities, caution is always recommended, especially when leaving bars and clubs at night.

Best for Classic NYC Gay

Marie's Crisis A onetime hooker hangout turned showtune piano bar in the West Village. (p108)

Julius Bar As seen in the movie *Boys in the Band*, Julius is the oldest gay in the Village. (p104)

Best for Dancing Queens

XL Nightclub A sprawling danceteria of hot, glistening muscle in where-it's-at Hell's Kitchen. (p147)

Industry As night deepens, this Hell's Kitchen hit turns from buzzing bar and lounge into a thumping club. (p145)

Best for Weeknights

Therapy Late-night music and drag give school nights a little razzle dazzle at this Hell's Kitchen staple. (p146)

Boxers NYC From post-work to late-night, this classic sports bar sees dudes tackling the tighter ends on and off the field. (p123)

Eastern Block Iron Curtain chic meets a sweaty sea of boys exchanging glances and downing drinks. (p78)

Best
Architecture

New York's architectural history is a layer cake of ideas and styles. Colonial farmhouses and graceful Federal-style buildings are found alongside ornate beaux arts palaces from the early 1900s. There are the revivals (Greek, Gothic, Romanesque and Renaissance) and the unadorned forms of the International Style. For the architecture buff, it's a bonanza.

RAINER GROSSKOPF/GETTY IMAGES ©

City of Skyscrapers

By the time New York settled into the 20th century, elevators and steel-frame engineering had allowed the city to grow up – literally. This period saw a building boom of skyscrapers, starting with Cass Gilbert's neo-Gothic 57-story Woolworth Building (1913). To this day it remains one of the 50 tallest buildings in the United States.

Others soon followed. In 1930, the Chrysler Building, the 77-story art deco masterpiece designed by William Van Alen, became the world's tallest structure. The following year, the record was broken again by the Empire State Building, a clean-lined art deco monolith crafted from Indiana limestone. Its spire was meant to be used as a mooring mast for dirigibles (airships) – an idea that made for good publicity, but which proved to be impractical and unfeasible.

A Starchitect's Canvas

New York City's heterogenous landscape lends itself well to the dabbling sketching pencils of some of the world's leading architectural personalities, or 'starchitects' as they've come to be known. You'll find Frank O Gehry's rippling structures, SANAA's white-box exteriors and Renzo Piano's signature facade tucked between the city's glass towers and low-rise bricked behemoths.

Best Skyscrapers

Empire State Building Like a martini, a good steak and jazz, this Depression-era skyscraper never ever gets old. (p130)

Chrysler Building Manhattan's most elegant skyscraper boasts steel ornamentation inspired by the automobile, including gargoyles that are shaped like retro hood ornaments. (p136)

Flatiron Building This is New York's original flavor of skyscraper with 20 triangular-shaped floors tucked behind ornate brick. (p115)

One World Trade Center This blue, tapered monolith is now the tallest building in America and the Western Hemisphere. (p27)

Brooklyn Bridge (p28)

Best Places of Worship

St Patrick's Cathedral A neo-Gothic wonder and the largest Catholic cathedral in America. (p139)

Grace Church Rescued from disrepair, it's now one of the daintiest structures in the city, complete with spires and ornate carvings. (p94)

Trinity Church Stunning stained glass accents what was once the tallest structure in New York. Don't miss the on-site cemetery. (p35)

Temple Emanu-el This imposing Romanesque synagogue on the Upper East Side has ceilings that are painted in gold. (p167)

Best Beaux Arts Beauties

Grand Central Terminal Crowned by America's greatest monumental sculpture, The Glory of Commerce, this romantic ode to train travel also features a ballroom-like concourse capped by a celestial vaulted ceiling. (p136)

New York Public Library A vision in Vermont marble, this Midtown marvel takes civic architecture to elegant heights. (p138)

Best of the Rest

Whitney Museum of American Art Modernism doesn't get more brutal than this: Marcel Breuer's inverted staircase structure looks like the very well-designed lair of an action movie villain. (p165)

New Museum SANAA's stacked-cube structure has a translucent aluminum exterior that is all kinds of sexy. (p68)

Guggenheim Museum Frank Lloyd Wright's inverted ziggurat structure is as quintessentially New York as Lady Liberty, yellow taxis and the deco-fabulous Chrysler Building. (p162)

Brooklyn Bridge Featured in countless films, TV shows and music videos, this Neo-Gothic wonder is one of the world's most handsome connectors. (p28)

Best
Sports & Activities

Although hailing cabs in New York City can feel like a blood sport and waiting on subway platforms in summer heat is steamier than a sauna, New Yorkers still love to stay active in their spare time. And considering how limited the green spaces are in New York, it's surprising for some visitors just how active the locals can be.

ALESSANDRO RIZZI/GETTY IMAGES ©

Running & Bicycling

The 1.6-mile path surrounding the Jacqueline Kennedy Onassis Reservoir is for runners and walkers only. Also try the paths along the Hudson River in Lower Manhattan or FDR Dr and the East River in the UES. NYC has added more than 250 miles of bike lanes in the last five years, but the uninitiated should stick to the less hectic trails in the parks and along the rivers.

Indoor Sports & Activities

Yoga and Pilates studios dot the city. If you're looking to score some gym action, try your luck getting a complimentary pass from one of the franchised studios.

Best Spectator Sports

New York Yankees
(☎718-293-6000, tickets 877-469-9849; www.yankees.com; Yankee Stadium, E 161st St at River Ave, the Bronx; tickets $20-300; Ⓢ B/D, 4 to 161st St-Yankee Stadium) Even if you're not into baseball, trek out to Queens to experience the rabid fandom.

New York Mets (☎718-507-8499; www.mets.com; Citi Field, 123-01 Roosevelt Ave, Flushing; tickets $19-130; Ⓢ 7 to Mets-Willets Pt) NYC's other loved baseball team.

New York Knicks (www.nyknicks.com; Madison Sq Garden, Seventh Ave btwn 31st & 33rd Sts, Midtown West; tickets from $109; Ⓢ A/C/E, 1/2/3 to 34th St-Penn Station) The basketball team calls Madison Sq Gardens home.

☑ Top Tips

▶ Most teams sell tickets via **Ticketmaster** (☎800-448-7849, 800-745-3000; www.ticketmaster.com). The other major outlet is **StubHub** (☎866-788-2482; www.stubhub.com).

New Jersey Devils
(☎973-757-6200, tickets 800-745-3000; www.newjerseydevils.com; Prudential Center, 165 Mulberry St, Newark, NJ; ▣NJ Transit or PATH to Newark Penn station) Hockey games in New Jersey.

New York Giants (☎201-935-8222; www.giants.com; Meadowlands Stadium, Meadowlands Sports Complex, East Rutherford, NJ; ▣351 from Port Authority, ▣NJ Transit from Penn Station to Meadowlands) One of the NFL's oldest teams; now in New Jersey.

Best
Parks

New York's parks, gardens and squares are its collective backyards. The larger parks are ideal for strolling or simply soaking up the sunshine, with plenty of seating as well as kiosks and nearby cafes. Smaller squares offer serendipitous moments of encounter, wonder and surprise.

Outdoor Activities

New Yorkers have perfected the art of turning their green spaces into places of recreation and encounter. During the summer months you'll find outdoor film screenings, Shakespeare performed in Central Park and concerts at Battery Park's Hudson River Park, not to mention Lincoln Center Dance Nights.

Beyond Manhattan

If you're looking for sprawling acres of green space beyond Central Park, it's best to head to Brooklyn. The borough's newest park is the 85-acre Brooklyn Bridge Park (p29), which has revitalized a once-barren stretch of shoreline, turning a series of abandoned piers into public park land. Nearing completion, it will ultimately become the largest new park in Brooklyn since Calvert Vaux and Frederick Olmsted designed the 585-acre Prospect Park in the 19th century.

Best Parks

Central Park The city's most famous park has more than 800 acres of rolling meadows and boulder-topped hillocks. (p178)

The High Line A thin stripe of green that unfurls up the western slice of downtown. (p86)

Gramercy Park New York exclusivity at its finest: it's cut off from the public by wrought-iron fences, but it's oh-so wonderful to peek in. (p116)

Madison Square Park A refurbished green oasis that showcases large-scale sculptures, wields popular burgers from its Shake Shack and relieves visitors with its public restroom facility. (p116)

Riverside Park A 100-block park running alongside the Hudson on Manhattan's west side – an ideal spot for a bike ride. (p186)

Bryant Park A welcome respite from the restless motion of Midtown, Bryant Park offers film screenings in summer and ice-skating in winter. (p139)

Best
Tours

While the streets of New York lend themselves well to unguided discovery, it's often worth joining a tour to gain greater insight into the city's rich history and lesser-known anecdotes.

CAVAN IMAGES/GETTY IMAGES ©

Sidetour (www.sidetour. com; tours $50-60) Offers off-the-beaten path experiences for those who want to delve deep into NYC, from jazz jams and ethnic food walks, to renegade art tours through the Met or the galleries of Chelsea.

Big Apple Greeter Program (☎212-669-8159; www.bigapplegreeter. org; admission free) Set up an intimate stroll in the neighborhood of your choice, led by a local volunteer who just can't wait to show off his or her city to you. Reserve four weeks in advance.

Bike the Big Apple (☎877-865-0078; www. bikethebigapple.com; tours incl bike & helmet around $95) Offers a variety of tours including a six-hour Ethnic Apple Tour that covers a bit of Queens, northern Brooklyn and the Lower East Side of Manhattan.

Foods of New York (☎212-913-9964; www.foods ofny.com; tours $52-65) The official foodie tour of NYC & Company offers various three-hour tours that help you eat your way through the city. Prepare thyself for a moving feast of fresh Italian pasta, sushi, global cheeses and real New York pizza.

On Location Tours (☎212-683-2027; www. screentours.com; tours around $45) Offers various tours covering TV shows and both small and silver screen locations, letting you live out your entertainment-obsessed fantasies.

Gray Line (☎212-397-2620; www.newyorksightseeing.com; tours $44-60) The most ubiquitous tour in the city, Gray Line is responsible for bombarding the streets with the red double-decker buses that locals love to hate. Really, though, for a comprehensive tour of the big sights, it's a great way to go.

Strayboots (☎877-787-2929; www.strayboots.com; tours from $12) Self-guided hybrid tours that fuse interesting urban info and a scavenger hunt element to help New York neophytes find their way around the neighborhood of their choice. Go at your own pace as you text in your answers to central command to receive your next clue.

Municipal Art Society (☎212-935-3960; www.mas. org; 111 W 57th St; tours adult/child $20/15; ⑤F to 57th St) Scheduled tours focusing on architecture and history, including a walking tour of Grand Central Terminal.

Survival Guide

Survival Guide

Before You Go

When to Go

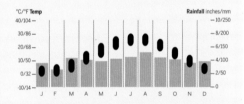

°C/°F Temp
40/104 —
30/86 —
20/68 —
10/50 —
0/32 —
-10/14 —

J F M A M J J A S O N D

Rainfall inches/mm
— 10/250
— 8/200
— 6/150
— 4/100
— 2/50
— 0

➡ **Winter (Dec–Feb)**
Snowfalls and sub-zero temperatures. The holiday season keeps things light despite the shivers.

➡ **Spring (Mar–May)**
Eager cafes drag their patio furniture out at the first hint of warm weather.

➡ **Summer (Jun–Aug)**
Oppressively hot in height of summer. Locals flock to their Hamptons share on weekends.

➡ **Fall (Sep–Nov)** Brilliant bursts of red and gold illuminate the city's parks.

Book Your Stay

➡ The average room rate is well over $300. But don't let that scare you, there are great deals to be had – almost all of which can be found through savvy online snooping. Unlike many destinations, New York City doesn't have a 'high season.' Sure, there are busier times of the year when it comes to tourist traffic, but with over 54 million visitor per annum, the Big Apple never loses sleep over filling up beds. As such, room rates fluctuate based on availability; in fact, most hotels have a booking algorithm in place that spits out a price quote relative to the number of rooms already booked on the same night. The busier the evening, the higher the price.

➡ If you're looking to find the best room rates, flexibility is key – weekdays are often cheaper and you'll generally find that accommodations in winter months have smaller price tags. If you are visiting over a weekend, try the business hotels in the Financial District, which tend to empty out when the work week ends.

➡ If you don't have your heart set on a particular property, check out discount juggernauts like **Expedia** (www.expedia. com), **Orbitz** (www.orbitz. com) and **Priceline** (www. priceline.com).

➡ If you do have an inkling of where you'd like to stay, it's best to start at your desired hotel's website as it'll often include deals and package rates.

➡ Also worth checking out are the slew of members-only websites, such as **Jetsetter** (www. jetsetter.com), that offer discounted rates and 'flash sales' for their devotees.

➡ These days, finding a place to sleep is hardly restricted to the traditional spectrum of lodging. Websites like **Airbnb** (www. airbnb.com) are providing a truly unique – and not to mention economical – alternative to the wallet-busting glitz and glam by offering locals the opportunity to rent out their apartments while

they're out of town or lease a space (be it a bedroom or pull-out couch) in their home.

Useful Websites
➡ **Lonely Planet** (www. lonelyplanet.com) Lots of accommodation reviews and online booking.

➡ **Playbill** (www.playbill. com) It may seem counter-intuitive to join the Playbill Club, but members get select rates on a variety of Manhattan hotels.

➡ **Kayak** (www.kayak. com) Simple all-purpose search engine.

Best Budget
➡ **Cosmopolitan Hotel** (www.cosmohotel.com) Cosmo is a hero if you'd rather save your bills for chic eateries and boutiques. It's clean and comfy but there's not too much to brag about.

➡ **Pod Hotel** (www.thepod hotel.com) With two Midtown locations, this affordable hot spot has a range of room types, most barely big enough for the bed but all pimped with cool, mod cons.

➡ **East Village Bed & Coffee** (www.bedandcof-fee.com) Owner Anne has turned her family

home into a quirky, arty, offbeat B&B with colorful, themed private rooms (one shared bathroom per floor) and great amenities.

➡ **Sugar Hill Harlem** (www.sugarhillharleminn.com) An airy townhouse has been restored to its turn-of-the-century splendor, with suites named after African American jazz greats.

Best Midrange
➡ **Ace Hotel New York City** (www.acehotel.com/ newyork) A hit with social-media types and cashed-up creatives, the Ace's standard and deluxe rooms are best described as upscale bachelor pads.

➡ **Nu Hotel** (www.nuhotel brooklyn.com) The 93 rooms in this Brooklyn hotel are of the stripped-down variety, featuring lots of crisp whiteness (sheets, walls, duvets) and furnishings made from recycled teak.

➡ **Yotel** (www.yotelnewyork. com) Part futuristic spaceport, part Austin Powers set, Yotel bases its slick, compact rooms (called 'cabins') on airplane classes, with DJ-spun tunes in the Club

Lounge and NYC's largest outdoor hotel terrace.

➡ **Country Inn the City** (www.countryinnthecity.com) Just like staying with your big-city friend – if, that is, your big-city friend happens to own a landmark 1891 limestone townhouse on a picturesque tree-lined block.

➡ **Hôtel Americano** (www.hotel-americano.com) It's like sleeping in a bento box, but the food's been replaced by a carefully curated selection of minimalist furniture.

➡ **Inn on 23rd St** (www.innon23rd.com) Housed in a lone 19th-century, five-story townhouse on busy 23rd St, this 14-room B&B is a Chelsea gem. The rooms are big and welcoming, with fanciful fabrics on big brass or poster beds.

Best Top End
➡ **Gramercy Park Hotel** (www.gramercyparkhotel.com) The rooms – overlooking nearby Gramercy Park – have customized oak furnishings, 400-count Italian linens, and big, feather-stuffed mattresses on sprawling beds.

➡ **Andaz Fifth Avenue** (http://andaz.hyatt.com) Uber-chic yet youthful and relaxed, the Andaz ditches

stuffy reception desks for hip, mobile staff who check you in on tablets in the art-laced lobby.

➡ **Crosby Street Hotel** (www.firmdalehotels.com) A boutique favorite in SoHo, the ever-fashionable Crosby Street offers a see-and-be-seen bar and one-of-a-kind rooms ranging from the starkly black and white to the floral and whimsical.

➡ **Greenwich Hotel** (www.greenwichhotelny.com) From the plush drawing room (complete with crackling fire), to the lantern-lit pool inside a reconstructed Japanese farmhouse, nothing about Robert De Niro's Greenwich Hotel is generic.

➡ **Langham Place** (http://newyork.langhamplacehotels.com) Rooms at the luxurious, skyscraping Langham Place are more akin to suites. Understatedly chic, all feature neutral hues, handsome wood paneling, Duxiana mattresses and Nespresso machines.

➡ **Chatwal New York** (www.thechatwalny.com) A restored art deco jewel in the heart of the Theater District, the Chatwal is as atmospheric as it is historic.

Arriving in New York City

☑ **Top Tip** For the best way to get to your accommodations, see p17.

John F Kennedy International Airport
John F Kennedy International Airport (JFK), 15 miles from Midtown in southeastern Queens, has eight terminals, serves nearly 50 million passengers annually and hosts flights coming and going from all corners of the globe.

➡ **Taxi** A yellow taxi from Manhattan to the airport will use the meter. Prices depend on traffic (often about $60) and it can take 45 to 60 minutes. From JFK, taxis charge a flat rate of $52 to any destination in Manhattan (not including tolls or tip).

➡ **Vans & car service** Shared vans cost around $20 to $25 per person, depending on the destination. If traveling to the airport from NYC, car services have set fares from $45.

➡ **Private vehicle** If you're driving from the airport, either go around . Brooklyn's south tip via the Belt Parkway to US 278 (the Brooklyn-Queens Expressway or BQE), or via US678 (Van Wyck Expressway) to US 495 (Long Island Expressway or LIE), which heads into Manhattan via the Queens-Midtown Tunnel.

➡ **Express bus** The NYC Airporter runs to Grand Central Station, Penn Station or the Port Authority Bus Terminal from JFK. The one-way fare is $16.

➡ **Subway** The AirTrain ($5, payable before you exit) links JFK to the subway. Take the AirTrain to Howard Beach–JFK Airport station for the A line through Brooklyn and into Manhattan, or opt for Sutphin Blvd–Archer Ave (Jamaica Station) for the E, J or Z line to Queens and Manhattan.

➡ **Long Island Rail Road (LIRR)** Take the AirTrain to Jamaica Station, from where LIRR trains depart frequently to Penn Station in Manhattan or to Atlantic Terminal in Brooklyn. One-way fares to either Penn Station or Atlantic Terminal cost $7.50 ($9 at peak times).

LaGuardia Airport

Used mainly for domestic flights, LaGuardia is smaller than JFK but only eight miles from midtown Manhattan; it sees about 26 million passengers per year.

➡ **Taxi** A taxi to/from Manhattan costs about $42 for the approximately half-hour ride.

➡ **Car service** A car service from LaGuardia costs around $35.

➡ **Express bus** The NYC Airporter costs $13.

➡ **Private vehicle** The most common driving route from the airport is along Grand Central Expressway to the BQE (US 278), then to the Queens-Midtown Tunnel via the LIE (US 495). Downtown-bound drivers can stay on the BQE and cross (free) via the Williamsburg Bridge.

➡ **Subway/bus** It's less convenient to use public transportation to get from LaGuardia into the city. The best subway link is the 74th St–Broadway station (7 line, or the E, F, M and R lines at the connecting Jackson Hts-Roosevelt Ave station) in Queens, where you can pick up the new Q70 Express Bus to the airport (about 10 minutes to the airport).

Newark Liberty International Airport

Don't write off New Jersey when looking for air fares to New York. The same distance from Midtown as JFK, Newark's airport, 16 miles from Midtown, brings many New Yorkers out for flights (there's some 36 million passengers annually).

➡ **Car service/taxi** A car service runs about $45 to $60 for the 45-minute ride to Midtown – a taxi is roughly the same. You only have to pay the $13 toll to go through the Lincoln Tunnel (at 42nd St) or Holland Tunnel (at Canal St) coming into Manhattan from Jersey; there's no charge going back through to NJ.

➡ **Subway/train** NJ Transit runs rail services (with an AirTrain connection) between Newark airport (EWR) and New York's Penn Station for $12.50 each way. The trip takes 25 minutes and runs every 20 or 30 minutes from 4:20am to about 1:40am. Hold onto your ticket, which you must show upon exiting at the airport.

→ **Express bus** The Newark Airport Express has a bus service between the airport and Port Authority Bus Terminal, Bryant Park and Grand Central Terminal in Midtown ($16 one way). The 45-minute ride goes every 15 minutes from 6:45am to 11:15pm (and every half hour from 4:45am to 6:45am and 11:15pm to 1:15am).

Getting Around

Subway

☑ **Best for...** making a beeline across town – up or down – regardless of the above-ground traffic situation.

→ The New York subway's 660-mile system, run by the **Metropolitan Transportation Authority** (MTA; ☎ 718-330-1234; www.mta.info), is iconic, cheap ($2.50 per ride), round-the-clock and easily the fastest and most reliable way to get around the

city. It's also safer and (a bit) cleaner than it used to be (and now has overly cheerful automated announcements on some lines).

→ New York's classic subway tokens now belong to the ages: today all buses and subways use the yellow-and-blue MetroCard, which you can purchase or add value to at one of several easy-to-use automated machines at any station. You can use cash or an ATM or credit card. Just select 'Get new card' and follow the prompts. Tip: if you're not from the US, when the machine asks for your zip code, enter 99999.

→ The card itself costs $1. You then select one of two types of MetroCard. The 'pay-per-ride' is $2.50 per ride, though the MTA tacks on a 5% bonus on MetroCards over $5. (Buy a $20 card, and you'll receive $21 worth of credit.) If you plan to use the subway quite a bit, you can also buy an 'unlimited ride' card ($30 for a seven-day pass).

→ It's a good idea to grab a free map, available from any attendant. When in

doubt, ask someone who looks like they know what they're doing. They may not, but subway confusion (and consternation) is the great unifier in this diverse city. And if you're new to the underground, never wear headphones when you're riding, as you might miss an important announcement about track changes or skipped stops.

Taxi

☑ **Best for...** getting to and from the airports with luggage in tow, or zigzagging across Manhattan.

→ The Taxi & Limousine Commision has set fares for rides (which can be paid with credit or debit card). It's $2.50 for the initial charge (first one-fifth of a mile), 50¢ for each additional one-fifth mile as well as per every 60 seconds of being stopped in traffic. There's also a $1 peak surcharge (weekdays 4pm to 8pm) and a 50¢ night surcharge (8pm to 6am), plus a NY State surcharge of 50¢ per ride.

→ Tips are expected to be 10% to 15%, but give less if you feel in any way mistreated – and be sure to ask for a receipt and

Subwary Cheat Sheet

➡ **Numbers, letters, colors** Subway train lines have a color and a letter or number. Trains with the same color run on the same tracks, often following roughly the same path through Manhattan before branching out into the other boroughs.

➡ **Express & local lines** Each color-coded line is shared by local trains and express trains; the latter make only select stops in Manhattan (indicated by a white circle on subway maps). If you're covering a greater distance, you're better off transferring to the express train (usually just across the platform from the local) to save time.

➡ **Getting in the right station** Some stations have separate entrances for downtown or uptown lines (read the sign carefully). If you swipe in at the wrong one, you'll either need to ride the subway to a station where you can transfer for free, or just lose the $2.50 and re-enter the station (usually across the street). Also look for the green and red lamps above the stairs at each station entrance; green means that it's always open, while red means that particular entrance will be closed at certain hours, usually late at night.

➡ **Lost weekend** All the rules switch on weekends, when some lines combine with others and some get suspended, some stations get passed and others get reached. Locals and tourists alike stand on platforms confused, sometimes irate. Check the www.mta.info website for weekend schedules. Sometimes posted signs aren't visible until after you reach the platform.

use it to note the driver's license number.

➡ The TLC keeps a Passenger's Bill of Rights, which gives you the right to tell the driver which route you'd like to take, or ask your driver to stop smoking or turn off an annoying radio station. Also, the driver does not have the right to refuse you a ride based on where you are going. Tip: Get in first, then say where you're going.

➡ In 2014, new rules went into effect regarding availability. If the light on the roof is lit, it's available. It's particularly difficult to score a taxi in the rain, at rush hour and around 4pm, when many drivers end their shifts.

➡ Private car services are a common taxi alternative in the outer boroughs. Fares vary depending on the neighborhood and length of ride, and must be determined

beforehand, as they have no meters.

Walking

☑ **Best for...** exploring quaint neighborhoods like the West Village, the East Village, Chinatown and SoHo.

➡ Screw the subway, cabs and buses, and go green. New York, down deep, can't be seen until you've taken the time to hit the sidewalks: the whole thing, like Nancy Sinatra's

Citi Bike

Hundreds of miles of designated bike lanes were added throughout the city by former Mayor Bloomberg's very pro-cycling City Hall. And even more potentially momentous, the Bloomberg administration launched **Citi Bike** (www.citibikenyc. com; 24hr/7 days $11/27), its long awaited bikesharing program – the largest in the country – in 2013.

Hundreds of kiosks in Manhattan and parts of Brooklyn house the iconic bright blue and very sturdy bicycles available for rides of 30-minutes or less. However, unless you're an experienced urban cyclist, pedaling through the streets can be a risky activity, as bike lanes are often blocked by trucks, taxis and double-parked cars. Helmets are obviously recommended but not obligatory.

➡ **New York Water Taxi** (☏ 212-742-1969; www. nywatertaxi.com; hop-on-hop-off service 1-day $26) has a fleet of zippy yellow boats that provide hop-on, hop-off service around Manhattan and Brooklyn.

➡ **Staten Island Ferry** Another bigger, brighter ferry (this one's orange) is the commuter-oriented Staten Island Ferry (p32), which makes free constant journeys across New York Harbor.

boots, is made for pedestrian transport.

➡ Broadway runs the length of Manhattan, about 13.5 miles. Crossing the East River on the pedestrian planks of the Brooklyn Bridge is a New York classic. Central Park trails can get you to wooded pockets where you can't even see or hear the city.

Bus

☑ **Best for...** taking in the city's atmosphere as you travel across town.

➡ Buses are operated by the MTA, the same folks that run the subway. They share an identical ticketing system.

➡ The standard local bus fare is $2.50 ($6 for express buses), payable with MetroCard or exact change (no dollar bills or pennies).

➡ Crosstown buses are numbered according to the street they traverse.

Boat

☑ **Best for...** visiting the Statue of Liberty and snapping photos of the skyline.

➡ **East River Ferry** (www. eastriverferry.com) runs year-round commuter service connecting a variety of locations in Manhattan, Queens and Brooklyn.

Essential Information

Business Hours

Nonstandard hours are listed in specific reviews through the neighborhood chapters in the Explore section of this guide. Standard business hours are as follows:

➡ **Banks** 9am to 6pm Monday to Friday, some also 9am to noon on Saturday.

➡ **Businesses** 9am to 5pm Monday to Friday.

➡ **Restaurants** Breakfast 6am to 11am, lunch 11am

to 3pm and dinner 5pm to 11pm. The popular Sunday brunch (often served on Saturdays too) lasts from 10am until 2pm and sometimes later.

➔ **Bars** 5pm to 4am.

➔ **Clubs** 10pm to 4am.

➔ **Shops** 10am to around 7pm Monday to Friday, 11am to around 8pm Saturdays. Sundays can be variable – some stores stay closed while others keep weekday hours. Stores tend to stay open later in the neighborhoods that are located downtown.

Discount Cards

The following discount cards offer a variety of passes and perks to some of the city's must-sees. Check the websites for more details.

➔ **Downtown Culture Pass** (www.downtownculturepass.org)

➔ **New York CityPASS** (www.citypass.com/new-york)

➔ **Explorer Pass** (www.nyexplorerpass.com)

➔ **The New York Pass** (www.newyorkpass.com)

Electricity

The US electric current is 110V to 115V, 60Hz AC. Outlets are made for flat two-prong plugs (which often have a third, rounded prong for grounding).

If your appliance is made for another electrical system (eg 220V), you'll need a step-down converter, which can be bought at hardware stores and drugstores for around $25 to $60. Most electronic devices (laptops, camera-battery chargers etc) are built for dual-voltage use, however, and will only need a plug adapter.

120V/60Hz

120V/60Hz

Emergency

➔ **Police, Fire & Ambulance** (🕿911)

➔ **Poison control** (🕿800-222-1222)

Money

☑ **Top Tip** US dollars are the only accepted currency in NYC. While debit and credit cards are widely accepted, it's wise to have a combination of cash and cards on hand.

ATMs

➔ Automatic teller machines are on practically every corner. You can either use your card at banks – usually in a 24-hour-access lobby, filled with up to a

Money-Saving Tips

➡ Browse our list of free attractions (p226).

➡ Check museum websites to see when they offer free admission.

➡ Save on theater tickets by buying tickets at the TKTS booth at Times Square (p129) or in Lower Manhattan (p42).

➡ Stock up on picnic fodder at the many fun gourmet markets.

dozen monitors at major branches – or you can opt for the lone wolves, which sit in delis, restaurants, bars and grocery stores, charging fierce service fees that go as high as $5.

➡ Most New York banks are linked by the New York Cash Exchange (NYCE) system and you can use local bankcards interchangeably at ATMs – for an extra fee if you're banking outside your system.

Credit Cards

➡ Major credit cards are accepted at most hotels, restaurants and shops throughout New York City. In fact, you'll find it difficult to perform certain transactions, such as purchasing tickets to performances and renting a car, without one.

➡ Stack your deck with a Visa, MasterCard or American Express, as these are the cards of choice. Places that accept Visa and MasterCard also accept debit cards, but first check with your bank to confirm that your debit card will be accepted in other states or countries.

➡ If your cards are lost or stolen, contact the company immediately.

Changing Money

➡ Banks and moneychangers, found all over New York City (including all three major airports), will give you US currency based on the current exchange rate.

Public Holidays

This is a list of major NYC holidays and special events. These holidays may force the closure of many businesses or attract crowds, making dining and accommodations reservations difficult.

➡ **New Year's Day** January 1

➡ **Martin Luther King Day** Third Monday in January

➡ **Presidents' Day** Third Monday in February

➡ **Easter** March/April

➡ **Memorial Day** Late May

➡ **Gay Pride** Last Sunday in June

➡ **Independence Day** July 4

➡ **Labor Day** Early September

➡ **Rosh Hashanah & Yom Kippur** Mid-September to mid-October

➡ **Halloween** October 31

➡ **Thanksgiving** Fourth Thursday in November

➡ **Christmas Day** December 25

➡ **New Year's Eve** December 31

Safe Travel

Crime rates in NYC are still at their lowest in years. There are a few neighborhoods remaining where you might feel apprehensive, no matter what time of night (and they are mainly in the outer boroughs). Subway stations are generally safe, too, though in some low-income neighborhoods, especially in the outer boroughs, they can be dicey. There's no reason to be paranoid, but it's better to be safe than sorry, so use common sense. Don't walk around alone at night in unfamiliar, sparsely populated areas. Carry your daily walking-around money somewhere inside your clothing or in a front pocket rather than in a handbag or a back pocket, and be aware of pickpockets, particularly in mobbed areas, such as Times Square or Penn Station at rush hour.

Telephone

Cell Phones

Most US cell phones besides the iPhone operate on CDMA, not European standard GSM – make sure you check compatibility with your phone service provider. North Americans should have no problem, but it is best to check with your service provider about roaming charges.

If you require a cell phone, you'll find many store fronts – most run by Verizon, T-Mobile or AT&T – where you can buy a cheap phone and load it up with prepaid minutes, thus avoiding a long-term contract.

Phone Codes

No matter where you're calling within New York City, even if it's just across the street in the same area code, you must always dial 1 + the area code first.

➜ **Manhattan** 212, 646

➜ **Outer boroughs** 347, 718, 929

➜ **All boroughs** (usually cell phones) 917

International and Domestic Calls

Phone numbers within the USA consist of a three-digit area code followed by a seven-digit local number. If you're calling long distance, dial 1 + the three-digit area code + the seven-digit number. To make an international call from NYC, call 011+ country code + area code + number. When calling Canada, there is no need to use the 011.

Useful Numbers

➜ **Local directory** 411

➜ **Municipal offices and information** 311

➜ **National directory information** 1-212-555-1212

➜ **Operator** 0

➜ **Toll-free number information** 800-555-1212

Toilets

☑ **Top Tip** The NY Restroom website (www.nyrestroom.com) is a handy resource for scouting out a loo.

Considering the number of pedestrians, there's a noticeable lack of public restrooms around the city. You'll find restrooms in Grand Central Terminal, Penn Station and Port Authority Bus Terminal, and in parks, including Madison Sq Park, Battery Park, Tompkins Sq Park, Washington Sq Park and Columbus Park in Chinatown, plus several places scattered around Central Park. The good bet, though, is to pop into a Starbucks (there's one about every three blocks), a department store (Macy's, Century 21, Bloomingdales) or a neighborhood park.

Dos & Don'ts

➡ Hail a cab only if the roof light is on.

➡ You needn't obey 'walk' signs – simply cross the street when there isn't oncoming traffic.

➡ When negotiating pedestrian traffic on the sidewalk, think of yourself as a vehicle – don't stop short, follow the speed of the crowd around you and pull off to the side if you need to take out your map or umbrella. Most New Yorkers are respectful of personal space, but they will bump into you – and not apologize – if you get in the way.

➡ When boarding the subway, wait until the passengers disembark, then be aggressive enough when you hop on so that the doors don't close in front of you.

➡ In New York you wait 'on line' instead of 'in line.'

➡ Oh, and it's How-sten Street, not Hew-sten.

Tourist Information

➡ In this web-based world, you'll find infinite online sources to get up-to-the-minute information about New York.

➡ In person, try one of the five official bureaus (the Midtown office is the shining star) of **NYC & Company** (☎212-484-1222; www.nycgo.com), listed below.

➡ **Midtown** (Map p134, D2; ☎212-484-1222; www.nycgo.com; 810 Seventh Ave btwn 52nd & 53rd Sts; ⊙8:30am-6pm Mon-Fri, 9am-5pm Sat & Sun; **S**B/D, E to 7th Ave)

➡ **Times Square** (Map p134, D3; ☎212-484-1222; Seventh Ave btwn 46th & 47th Sts, Times Square; ⊙9am-7pm; **S**1/2/3, 7, N/Q/R to Times Sq)

➡ **Macy's Herald Square** (Map p134, D5; 151 W 34th St; ⊙9am-9:30pm Mon-Fri, 10am-9:30pm Sat, 11am-8:30pm Sun)

➡ **Lower Manhattan** (Map p30, C4; ☎212-484-1222; City Hall Park at Broadway; ⊙9am-6pm Mon-Fri, 10am-5pm Sat & Sun; **S**R/W to to City Hall)

➡ **Chinatown** (Map p50, D7; ☎212-484-1222; cnr Canal, Walker & Baxter Sts; ⊙10am-6pm; **S**J/M/Z, N/Q/R/W, 6 to Canal St)

➡ The **Brooklyn Tourism & Visitors Center** (☎718-802-3846; www.visitbrooklyn. org; 209 Joralemon St btwn Court St & Brooklyn Bridge Blvd; ⊙10am-6pm Mon-Fri; **S**2/3, 4/5 to Borough Hall) has all sorts of info on Manhattan's rival borough.

Travelers with Disabilities

Federal laws guarantee that all government offices and facilities are accessible to the disabled. For information on specific places, you can contact the mayor's **Office for People with Disabilities** (☎212-639-9675; ⊙9am-5pm Mon-Fri), which will send you a free copy of its *Access New York* guide if you call and request it.

Another excellent resource is the **Society for Accessible Travel & Hospitality** (SATH; ☎212-447-7284; www.sath.org; 347 Fifth Ave at 34th St, New York, USA, Suite 605; ☺9am-5pm; ⊠M34 to 5th Ave, M1 to 34th St, ⑤6 to 33rd St), which gives advice on how to travel with a wheelchair, kidney disease, sight impairment or deafness.

For detailed information on subway and bus wheelchair accessibility, call the **Accessibility Line** (☎511; http://web.mta.info/accessibility) for a list of subway stations with elevators or escalators. Also visit www.nycgo.com/accessibility.

Visas

The USA Visa Waiver Program (VWP) allows nationals from 37 countries to enter the US without a visa for up to 90 days, provided they are carrying a machine-readable passport. For the updated list of countries included in the program and current requirements, see the **US Department of State** (http://travel.state.gov/visa) website.

Citizens of VWP countries need to register with the **US Department of Homeland Security** (http://esta.cbp.dhs.gov) three days before their visit. There is a $14 fee for registration application; when approved, the registration is valid for two years or until your passport expires, whichever comes first.

You must obtain a via from a US embassy or consulate in your home country if you:

➡ do not currently hold a passport from a VWP country

➡ are from a VWP country, but don't have a machine-readable passport

➡ are from a VWP country, but currently hold a passport issued between October 26, 2005, and October 25, 2006, that does not have a digital photo on the information page or an integrated chip from the data page. (After October 25, 2006, the integrated chip is required on all machine-readable passports.)

➡ are planning to stay longer than 90 days

➡ are planning to work or study in the US.

Behind the Scenes

Send Us Your Feedback

We love to hear from travelers – your comments help make our books better. We read every word, and we guarantee that your feedback goes straight to the authors. Visit **lonelyplanet.com/contact** to submit your updates and suggestions.

Note: We may edit, reproduce and incorporate your comments in Lonely Planet products such as guidebooks, websites and digital products, so let us know if you don't want your comments reproduced or your name acknowledged. For a copy of our privacy policy visit lonelyplanet.com/privacy.

Cristian's Thanks

As always, an immeasurable thank-you to generous, on-the-ball Kathy Stromsland and her wonderful family. Many thanks also to Regis St Louis, Julian Yeo, Lane Wilson, Anthony Leung, Michael Chernow, Lucinda East, Massimiliano Gioni, Gabriel Einsohn, Rick Herron, Mark McCray, Sarah Shirley, Matt Wood, Mary Ann Gardner, Lambros Hajisava, Les Hayden, Brock Waldron, Jose Francisco Chavez and Sean Muldoon for the tips, insight and support.

Acknowledgments

Cover photograph: Brooklyn Bridge, Walter Chen

This Book

This 5th edition of Lonely Planet's *Pocket New York* was researched and written by Cristian Bonetto. This guidebook was produced by the following:

Destination Editor Dora Whitaker **Product Editor** Alison Ridgway **Senior Cartographer** Alison Lyall **Book Designer** Jessica Rose **Assisting Editors** Samantha Forge, Paul

Harding **Cover Researcher** Naomi Parker **Thanks to** Richard Carden, Claire Naylor, Karyn Noble, Katie O'Connell, Roger Thomas, Eric Waters, Tony Wheeler, Amanda Williamson

Index

See also separate subindexes for:

- ⊗ **Eating p250**
- ⊙ **Drinking p251**
- ⊕ **Entertainment p252**
- ⊙ **Shopping p252**

Our Writer

Cristian Bonetto

Planet-roaming Cristian has played both visitor and local in New York City, a place he has been obsessed with since his *Sesame Street* diaper days. From mainstream Midtown to the far-flung corners of outer Queens, the one-time TV and theater scribe has explored countless corners of the city, his musings appearing in newspapers, magazines and online publications around the world.

Published by Lonely Planet Publications Pty Ltd
ABN 36 005 607 983
5th edition – October 2014
ISBN 978 1 74220 887 9
© Lonely Planet 2014   Photographs © as indicated 2014
10 9 8 7 6 5 4 3 2
Printed in China

Although the authors and Lonely Planet have taken all reasonable care in preparing this book, we make no warranty about the accuracy or completeness of its content and, to the maximum extent permitted, disclaim all liability arising from its use.